MEDITATION

For Fidgety Skeptics

MEDITATION

For Fidgety Skeptics

A 10% HAPPIER HOW-TO BOOK

Dan Harris
and Jeff Warren

with Carlyle Adler

yellow
kite

First published in Great Britain in 2018 by Yellow Kite
An imprint of Hodder & Stoughton
An Hachette UK company

First published in the United States of America in 2017
by Spiegel & Grau, an imprint of Random House,
a division of Penguin Random House LLC, New York

This paperback edition published in 2020

1

A CIP catalogue record for this title is available from the British Library

Paperback ISBN 978 1 473 69139 1
eBook ISBN 978 1 473 69140 7

Printed and bound in Great Britain by Clays Ltd, Elcograf S.p.A.

Hodder & Stoughton policy is to use papers that are natural, renewable
and recyclable products and made from wood grown in sustainable forests.
The logging and manufacturing processes are expected to conform to the
environmental regulations of the country of origin.

Yellow Kite
Hodder & Stoughton Ltd
Carmelite House
50 Victoria Embankment
London EC4Y 0DZ

www.yellowkitebooks.co.uk

'The untrained mind is stupid.'
—AJAHN CHAH, meditation master

CONTENTS

HOW TO USE THIS BOOK

Perhaps unsurprisingly, given that this is a book about meditation, you will find plenty of meditations in these pages. In each one, Jeff Warren, our resident maestro, lays out the basic instructions and holds forth (often in a very amusing way) on his overall philosophy about the practice. When you encounter a meditation, we do not expect you to drop what you're doing and hurl yourself into the lotus position. Instead, we recommend that you read it through, and then come back whenever you are ready to give it a try.

All the meditations in this book are also available for free on the 10% Happier app. When you see this symbol 🧘, that's to remind you that you have the option of toggling over to the app and having Jeff walk you through the meditation in question. My advice is to experiment with both guided and unguided meditations and see what works. For what it's worth, I switch back and forth in my personal practice.

Go to **tenpercent.com/access** to download the app and unlock the content. (If you already have the app, use the same URL to get the meditations.) You'll also be able to watch videos of many of the adventures and misadventures described in the book.

The Case for Meditation

If you had told me as recently as a few years ago that I would someday become a traveling evangelist for meditation, I would have coughed my beer up through my nose.

In 2004, I had a panic attack while delivering the news, live, on ABC's *Good Morning America*. Being a masochist, I asked our research department to tell me exactly how many people were watching. They came back with the vastly reassuring number of 5.019 million. (If you are in the mood for a nice dose of schadenfreude, you can readily find the whole clip on YouTube. Just search for "panic attack on live TV," and it will pop right up. Which is awesome for me.)

In the wake of my nationally televised freak-out, I learned something even more embarrassing: the entire episode had been caused by some phenomenally stupid behavior in my personal life. After spending years covering war zones for ABC News as an ambitious and idealistic young reporter, I had developed an undiagnosed depression. For months I was having trouble getting out of bed in the morning, and felt as if I had a permanent, low-grade fever. Out of desperation, I began self-medicating with recreational drugs, including cocaine and ecstasy. My drug use was short-lived and intermittent. If you've ever seen the movie *The Wolf of Wall Street*, in which the characters are pounding Quaaludes every five minutes—it was nothing like that. However, my consumption was enough, according to the doctor I consulted after the panic attack, to artificially raise the level of adrenaline in my brain, exacerbating my baseline anxiety and priming me to have my very public meltdown.

Through a strange and circuitous series of events, the panic attack ultimately led me to embrace a practice I had always dismissed as ridiculous. For most of my life, to the extent that I'd ever even considered meditation, I ranked it right alongside aura readings, Enya, and the unironic use of the word "namaste." Further, I figured my racing, type-A mind was way too busy to ever be able to commune with the cosmos. And anyway, if I got too happy, it would probably render me completely ineffective at my hypercompetitive job.

Two things changed my mind.

The first was the science.

In recent years, there has been an explosion of research into meditation, which has been shown to:

- Reduce blood pressure
- Boost recovery after the release of the stress hormone cortisol
- Improve immune system functioning and response
- Slow age-related atrophy of the brain
- Mitigate the symptoms of depression and anxiety

Studies also show meditation can reduce violence in prisons, boost productivity in the workplace, and improve both behavior and grades for school children.

Things really get interesting when you look at the neuroscience. In recent years, neuroscientists have been peering into the heads of meditators, and they've found that the practice can rewire key parts of the brain involved with self-awareness, compassion, and resiliency. One study from the *Harvard Gazette* found that just eight weeks of meditation resulted in measurable decreases in gray matter density in the area of the brain associated with stress.

The science is still in its early stages and the findings are preliminary. I worry that it has provoked a certain amount of irrational exuberance in the media. ("Meditation can cure halitosis and enable you to dunk on a regulation hoop!") However, when you aggregate the most rigorous studies, they strongly suggest that daily meditation can deliver a long list of health benefits.

The research has catalyzed a fascinating public health revolution, with the ancient practice of meditation catching on among corporate executives, athletes, U.S. marines, and entertainers, including the rapper 50 Cent. That man got shot nine times; I believe he deserves some peace of mind.

The second thing I learned that changed my mind about meditation is that it does not necessarily entail a lot of the weird stuff I feared it might.

Contrary to popular belief, meditation does not involve folding yourself into a pretzel, joining a group, or wearing special outfits. The word "meditation" is a little bit like the word "sports"; there are hundreds of varieties. The type of meditation we'll be teaching here is called "mindfulness meditation," which is derived from Buddhism but does not require adopting a belief system or declaring oneself to be a Buddhist. (In defense of Buddhism, by the way, it is often practiced not as a faith but as a set of tools to help people lead more fulfilled lives in a universe characterized by impermanence and entropy. One of my favorite quotes on the matter is "Buddhism is not something to believe in, but rather something to *do*.")

In any event, what we're teaching here is simple, secular exercise for your brain. To give you a sense of exactly how simple it is, here are the three-step instructions for beginning meditation. You don't actually have to do this right now; I'll bring in a ringer soon.

1. Sit comfortably. It's best to have your spine reasonably straight, which may help prevent an involuntary nap. If you want to sit cross-legged on the floor, go for it. If not, just sit in a chair, as I do. You can close your eyes or, if you prefer, you can leave them open and adjust your gaze to a neutral point on the ground.

2. Bring your full attention to the feeling of your breath coming in and out. Pick a spot where it's most prominent: your chest, your belly, or your nostrils. You're not thinking about your breath, you're just *feeling* the raw data of the physical sensations. To help maintain focus, you can make a quiet mental note on the in-breath and out-breath, like *in* and *out*.

3. The third step is the key. As soon as you try to do this, your mind is almost certainly going to mutiny. You'll start having all sorts of random thoughts, such as: *What's for lunch? Do I need a haircut? What was Casper the Friendly Ghost before he died? Who was the Susan after whom they named the lazy Susan, and how did she feel about it?* No big deal. This is totally normal. The whole game is simply to notice when you are distracted, and begin again. And again. And again.

Every time you catch yourself wandering and escort your attention back to the breath, it is like a biceps curl for the brain. It is also a radical act: you're breaking a lifetime's habit of walking around in a fog of rumination and projection, and you are actually focusing on what's happening right now.

I have heard from countless people who assume that they

could never meditate because they can't stop thinking. I cannot say this frequently enough: the goal is not to clear your mind but to *focus* your mind—for a few nanoseconds at a time—and whenever you become distracted, just start again. Getting lost and starting over is not failing at meditation, it is succeeding.

I think this pernicious clear-the-mind misconception stems in part from the fact that meditation has been the victim of the worst marketing campaign for anything ever. The traditional art depicting meditation, while often beautiful, can be badly misleading. It usually shows practitioners with beatific looks on their faces. Examples abound in Buddhist temples, in airport spas, and in this picture of a man in a loincloth I found on the Internet.

Based on my own practice, this image better captures the experience of meditation:

Meditation can be difficult, especially at the beginning. It's like going to the gym. If you work out and you're not panting or sweating, you're probably cheating. Likewise, if you start meditating and find yourself in a thought-free field of bliss, either you have rocketed to enlightenment or you have died.

The practice does get easier the longer you keep at it, but even after doing it for years, I get lost all the time. Here's a random sample of my mental chatter during a typical meditation session:

In

Out

Man, I am feeling antsy. What's the Yiddish term my grandmother used to use for that? Shpilkes. *Right.*

Words that always make me giggle: "ointment," "pianist."

Wait, what? Come on, man. Back to the breath.

In

Out

Likes: baked goods.

Dislikes: fedoras, dream sequences, that part in techno songs where the French accordion kicks in.

Dude. Come. On.

In

Out

In

Alternative jobs: papal nuncio, interpretive dancer, working double time on the seduction line . . .

You get the idea.

So why put yourself through this?

Meditation forces you into a direct collision with a fundamental fact of life that is not often pointed out to us: we all have a voice in our heads.

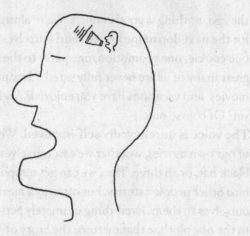

(The reason the above looks amateurish and slightly creepy is that I drew it, but bear with me.)

When I talk about the voice in your head, I'm not referring to schizophrenia or anything like that; I'm talking about your internal narrator. It's sometimes called your "ego." The Buddha had a cool name for it: "the monkey mind."

Here are some key attributes of the voice in my head. I suspect they will sound familiar.

- **It's often fixated on the past and future, at the expense of whatever is happening right now.** The voice loves to plan, plot, and scheme. It's always making lists or rehearsing arguments or drafting tweets. One moment it has you fantasizing about some halcyon past or Elysian future. Another moment you're ruing old mistakes or catastrophizing about some not-yet-arrived events. As Mark Twain is reputed to have said, "Some of the worst things in my life never even happened."
- **The voice is insatiable.** The default mental condition for too many human beings is dissatisfaction. Under the sway of

the ego, nothing is good enough. We're always on the hunt for the next dopamine hit. We hurl ourselves headlong from one cookie, one promotion, one party to the next, and yet a great many of us are never fully sated. How many meals, movies, and vacations have you enjoyed? And are you done yet? Of course not.

· **The voice is unrelievedly self-involved.** We are all the stars of our own movies, whether we cast ourselves as hero, victim, black hat, or all three. True, we can get temporarily sucked into other people's stories, but often as a means of comparing ourselves to them. Everything ultimately gets subordinated to the one plotline that matters: the Story of Me.

In short, the voice in my head—and perhaps also yours—can be an asshole.

To be fair, our internal narrator is not all bad. It is capable of brilliance, humor, and compassion. It is also extremely useful when designing irrigation systems and composing piano sonatas. Nevertheless, when I bother to listen, most of what I hear inside is rather obnoxious. I am not alone in this. I have a friend, a fellow meditator, who jokes that when he considers the voice in his head, he feels like he's been kidnapped by the most boring person alive, who says the same baloney over and over, most of it negative, nearly all of it self-referential.

When you are unaware of this ceaseless inner talkfest, it can control and deceive you. The ego's terrible suggestions often come to the party dressed up as common sense:

You should eat that entire sleeve of Oreos; you've had a hard day.
Go ahead, you have every right to make the wisecrack that will ruin the next forty-eight hours of your marriage.
You don't need to meditate. You'll never be able to do it anyway.

One of the things that most powerfully drew me to meditation was the realization—many years after the fact, sadly—that the voice in my head was responsible for the most mortifying moment of my life: my on-air panic attack. It was because of my ego that I went off to war zones without considering the psychological consequences, was insufficiently self-aware to recognize my subsequent depression, and then blindly self-medicated.

I began my meditation practice slowly, with just five to ten minutes a day, which is what I recommend everyone aim for at the start. (And, frankly, if you only find time for one minute a day, you can count that as a win. Much more on this soon.) For me, the first sign that meditation was not a waste of time came within weeks, when I started to overhear my wife, Bianca, at cocktail parties telling friends that I had become less of a jerk.

Internally, I pretty quickly began to notice three primary benefits, in ascending order of importance:

1. Calm

The act of stepping out of my daily busyness for a few minutes and simply breathing often injected a dose of sanity into my hectic day. It served to interrupt, if only briefly, the current of mindlessness that often carried me along. The issue of calmness is a bit tricky, though. Many people are drawn to meditation because they want to relax, but they end up disappointed because the ever-declaiming ego keeps butting in or because itches and knee pain arise. While meditation can often be calming, it's best not to go into it expecting to feel a certain way. And, importantly, even if an individual meditation session isn't mellow, I've found that the net effect of having a daily practice is that, overall, my emotional weather is significantly balmier.

2. Focus

We live in an era defined by what's been called "omni-connectivity." Many of us are beset by emails, texts, status updates, and push notifications. It can leave us feeling frayed and frazzled. In my job, I actually have other people's voices piped directly into my head, and I have to get the facts straight, on short notice, in front of large audiences. I found that the daily exercise of trying to focus on one thing at a time—my breath—and then getting lost and starting again (and again, and again) helped me stay on task during the course of my day. Studies show the more you meditate, the better you are at activating the regions of the brain associated with attention and deactivating the regions associated with mind-wandering.

3. Mindfulness

This rather anodyne-sounding word has become quite buzzy of late. There are now countless books and articles on mindful eating, mindful parenting, mindful sex, mindful dishwashing, mindful yarn-bombing, mindful conjugation of verbs in Esperanto, and on and on. The media fuss has, at times, turned this down-to-earth, universally accessible concept into an impossibly precious thing, and provoked a not-entirely-unjustified backlash. And yet, if you can get past the breathless headlines and press releases, mindfulness is an enormously useful skill.

It is a rich, ancient term with lots of meanings, but here's my personal definition:

Mindfulness is the ability to see what's happening in your head at any given moment, so that you don't get carried away by it.

As an example, imagine you're driving down the road and someone cuts you off. How does that moment go for you, usually? If you're like me, you may feel a big blast of anger, which is normal. But then you might automatically act on that anger, honking, and cursing, and so on. There's no buffer between the stimulus and your reflexive reaction.

With mindfulness on board—the self-awareness generated by a deliberate, daily reckoning with the voice in your head—that moment might go a little differently. After getting cut off, you'll probably still have that upsurge of anger, but this time you may have room for a saner thought-track: *Oh, my chest is buzzing, my ears are turning red, I'm experiencing a starburst of self-righteous thoughts. . . . I'm working myself up into a homicidal rage.* Now that you've developed this mindful early warning system, however, you actually have a choice in the matter. You don't have to take the bait, succumb to your anger, and chase the other driver down the road, hurling expletives, with your kids in the backseat fearing you've lost your mind.

It's a little bit like the picture-in-picture function on your television. All of a sudden, the story that has been taking up the whole screen can be seen with some perspective.

Another way to think about this concept is to visualize the mind as a waterfall.

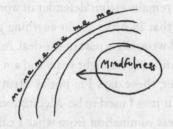

(I drew this one, too. Deal with it.)

The water represents your nonstop stream of consciousness, which consists mostly of "me, me, me" thoughts. Mindfulness is the area behind the waterfall, which allows you to step out of the cascade and view your urges, impulses, and desires without getting caught up in it all.

I am not making this up. Our species is classified as *Homo sapiens sapiens:* the one who thinks and knows he or she thinks. However, that second *sapiens* often falls by the wayside because nobody bothers to point out to us that we have this natural capacity to view the contents of our consciousness with some nonjudgmental remove. Mindfulness is your birthright. The ego's writ only extends so far; you have the ability to resist its misrule, to break out of the prison of neurotic self-obsession.

I hasten to add that the idea is not that you should be rendered into a lifeless blob, passively letting people cut you off or walk all over you. What mindfulness has allowed me to do is respond wisely to things, instead of reacting impulsively.

Respond, not react: this is a game changer. Most meditation clichés—invocations of a "sacred space," injunctions to "be here now"—make me want to put a pencil through my eye (although I have learned, through meditation, to let that urge pass too). However, this venerable cliché—"respond, not react"—is genuinely transformational. If I weren't so allergic to pain, I might get it tattooed on my chest.

To be sure, I remain a stout defender of worrying. It seems obvious to me that in order to do anything great, a certain amount of hand-wringing is part of the deal. As of this writing, I have been meditating for eight years and am still plenty ambitious. However, these days I'm not as sweaty, agitated, and unpleasant about it as I used to be. Meditation has helped me to sort my useless rumination from what I call "constructive anguish."

The less enchanted you are by the voice in your head, the more you can make room for entirely new kinds of thoughts and feelings to emerge. Switching out of egoic autopilot may help you clear away space for concern about other people, or to better connect with what is right in front of you. In my case, it has enabled me to take even more delight in my work, my wife, and our toddler son, Alexander, who suffuses me with warmth whether he's offering me a chicken nugget or wiping macerated muffin on my sleeve. I am less in thrall to my desires and aversions, which has given me a wider perspective and, at times, a taste of a deep, ineffable unclenching. In sum, meditation empowers you to tap into what lies beneath or beyond the ego. Call it creativity. Call it your innate wisdom. Some people call it your heart. *Ew.*

While meditation is an amazing inner technology, it is not a one-way ticket to flawlessness. Which is why I called my first book *10% Happier*. It buys me a lot of leeway to continue to mess up. If my wife were writing this book, she could marshal plenty of evidence behind her "90% still a moron" thesis. Similarly, my younger brother, Matt, who has always enjoyed puncturing my pretense, argues that the real title for my first book should have been *From Deeply Flawed to Merely Flawed*.

Perfection may not be on offer, but something profound and empowering is, indeed, available: the fact that our minds are trainable. We spend so much time working on our stock portfolios, our cars, and our interior design, but almost no time working on the one filter through which we experience it all, our minds.

Many of us assume that happiness can be measured solely by the quality of our work life, our love life, or our childhood. These are vitally important, of course, but what the science is showing us is that happiness is not just something that happens to you; it is a *skill*. That is a huge headline, which has fueled both my personal practice and my career as a meditation proponent.

At the outset of my unlikely evangelical side hustle, I assumed that if I simply explained all of the foregoing—the scientific research, the blazingly obvious utility of mindfulness, the aspirational figures who are now on the meditation bandwagon—everyone would just start meditating. That's how it worked with me. As a journalist, when I took a hard look at the studies, I began practicing every day.

I certainly do not mean to imply that I am an avatar of discipline. One night last year, I ate so many cookies that I puked. True story. It was not my unique willpower that made my adoption of meditation relatively seamless, it was pain. I have endured episodic depression and anxiety—along with the odd serving of panic and substance abuse—since I was a little boy. Anyone who's lived under the low cloud ceiling of despair will understand my eagerness to embrace a potential antidote. When it became clear to me that meditation could help stave off or alleviate what Churchill called "the black dog," by helping me achieve some distance from my sometimes bleak and repetitive patterns of thought, establishing the habit became a non-issue.

I now realize my somewhat idiosyncratic adoption of daily meditation led me to underestimate the myths, misconceptions, and self-deceptions that can keep people from meditating—and to drive a message that was both artless and a little cavalier. In essence, my argument to anyone who asked me how to get started was: just suck it up and do it. Turns out, changing human behavior is not that simple. Not by a long shot.

Studies suggest millions of Americans are meditating. I suspect there are tens of millions more who are eager—but somehow unable—to start their own practice. As a friend of mine involved in corporate well-being at Google has said, "We have medicine that works, and most people don't do it." Even my own wife—who, if she's reading this, is beautiful and perfect in every other way—does not meditate. She's a scientist; she unquestionably groks the potential health benefits. She lives with me; she deeply appreciates how the practice has made me less annoying. And yet she can't overcome inertia and make herself do it with any consistency. I wonder sometimes whether I've hurt my cause by regularly asking her, "What's it like to be married to your spiritual leader?"

Whereas I was once obsessed with simply demystifying meditation as a way to popularize the practice, I am now fixated on finding specific ways of helping people get over the hump and actually do the thing. My first move was to cofound a company that teaches meditation through an app, called 10% Happier: Meditation for Fidgety Skeptics. Our strategy has been to recruit the world's best teachers, strip away the pan flute music, and inject a little humor into the teaching of meditation.

Building this business has given me a front-row seat at the rich pageant of human neuroses that stand in the way of committing to a short, daily habit that is manifestly beneficial. As part of our marketing research, during which we conduct extensive interviews with customers and ex-customers, my team and I started to develop a list of the primary obstacles to meditation, such as finding the time, fearing you might lose your edge, or believing the practice somehow entails magically clearing your mind. We called them "the secret fears" (although technically they were not all fears). I got so interested in helping people overcome these "fears" that I decided to write this book, which is designed to systematically taxonomize and tackle the most common stumbling blocks and also teach you to meditate. But since I am not a meditation teacher, I needed to enlist someone who actually knows what he's talking about.

So I reached out to a man I like to call the Meditation Mac-Gyver.

The first time I heard the name Jeff Warren was when I happened upon an article he penned for the *New York Times* website about how he went on a crazy thirty-day solo silent meditation retreat. (Before you dismiss him as a nutjob, realize that this is exactly the kind of thing you want your meditation teacher to be doing, just as you want your fitness coach to have done triathlons and the like.)

The piece was written with style and humor. In the following passage Jeff talks about a moment, several days in, when all the boredom and doubt that one normally encounters at the beginning of a retreat began to dissipate:

Then one afternoon . . . I realized that, actually, things were fine. Better than fine. I felt as though I had atomic vision. My attention was zingy; electric. I noticed everything—bap, bap,

bap—flickers of intention before each movement, a vibrating topography of tensions and fluctuations under my belly skin, even my own keenly observant self. Such a good noticer. I noticed my ambition, my self-satisfaction, my disappointment that there was no one around to brag to about my progress ("You wouldn't believe how hard I can look at that tree").

After reading the article, I mounted a campaign of what could fairly be called digital stalking. I learned that Jeff had happened upon the practice in much the same way I had: through journalism. While writing a book about the science of consciousness (which was entitled *The Head Trip* and was published to great reviews), he became intrigued by meditation. He discovered that it helped in his lifelong struggle with the hyperkinetic voice in his head, which often left him feeling "trapped behind a spinning barrier of rumination." My kind of guy. He became an avid student, although he only reluctantly took on the role of teacher. When he initially founded his meditation group in Toronto, which he called the Consciousness Explorers Club (CEC), he was simply looking for contemplative compatriots. But so many people started showing up and asking him questions that his own teacher advised him to pay it forward. My online sleuthing took me to the group's website, where I subscribed to the monthly email newsletter, in which Jeff talked about all of the CEC's cool activities: meditation, fun community service projects, epic dance parties. For the first time in my life, I actually kinda wanted to move to Canada.

Here was this person who was young (meaning my age—which I will always consider young), a fantastic writer, and obviously way further along than I was on the meditative path. I made it my business to force him to be my friend.

I tracked him down via email and made him promise to alert

me whenever he next came to New York City. Not long there-after, we met for brunch at a French spot near my apartment. In person, Jeff did not disappoint. He said he was a little hung-over from a big night out with friends, but I saw no evidence of diminished capacity. We bonded over our mutual love of the practice. As nerdy as I had become about meditation by this time, Jeff thoroughly outdid me; he seemed to have read about and/or tried nearly every contemplative tradition under the sun. He spoke with infectious ardor about the potential of meditation to mold the mind, his tastefully tattooed forearms gesticulating magisterially as he made his points. He did, at times, lapse into a sort of mystical poesy that I didn't fully un-derstand, but I didn't care.

We took a rambling postprandial walk around upper Man-hattan, talking about meditation, writing, and relationships. He mentioned that he'd been dating a whip-smart reporter named Sarah for over a year, and that they were currently dis-cussing whether to get more serious. Reflecting back on my own issues, as someone who had waited until relatively late in life to get married, I told him that sometimes you won't know how good a relationship can be until you get out of your own way and commit. By the end of our afternoon together, I was thoroughly invigorated. I had collected innumerable medita-tion tips as well as a long list of recommended reading. My man-crush was sealed.

Two years later—during which time we stayed connected via email and shared meals when we were in the same city—I re-cruited Jeff for a special project for the 10% Happier app. Until this point, most of the video content we produced was pretty basic: me and a teacher, sitting on chairs in a studio, talking about the practice. My team and I decided to up our game by taking the show on the road. We wanted to do a modern version of what monks had been doing for millennia, a "wandering retreat." We hatched a plan to bring Jeff to New York City, wire up a car with cameras, fill it with camping gear, and drive off, with no itinerary, for three days.

During our long, chatty car rides, I got to know Jeff even better. On many levels, we have a lot in common. We both come from loving families (Jeff's parents, an engineer and a public health nurse, raised him and his two younger siblings in Montreal and Toronto), are mildly obsessed with indie rock, and spend way too much time thinking about meditation. On many other levels, however, we are polar opposites. Jeff, for example, was thrilled that we were going camping—an activity I have loathed ever since my parents, recovering hippies, forced me into the mountains with them practically every summer of my childhood. More significantly, when it came to major life choices, Jeff and I had traveled very different paths. After college, Jeff bounced around Europe and North and Central America, sometimes following women he was dating. He was in search of both adventure and meaning. He did landscaping, mixed cement, wrote movie reviews, worked on software for children, and later became a radio reporter. Even now, in his mid-forties and firmly established as a meditation teacher, he lived in a big rental house in downtown Toronto with artsy roommates. In stark contrast to Jeff's bohemian bent, I was decidedly more careerist. I had started in television news at age twenty-two and had been working my way up the ladder ever since. It wasn't that Jeff lacked ambition; he was profoundly committed to building the CEC, pursuing his writing, and deepening his meditation practice. It's just that his measures of success were less bougie than mine.

It was on this trip that I started calling Jeff "Meditation MacGyver," because anytime an issue arose—a traffic jam, a disagreement about where to pitch our tents, or someone (me) getting cranky—Jeff would always pipe up with "I've got a practice for that!" He just loves getting under the hood and helping people figure out how their minds work.

While I was incredibly impressed with Jeff's performance on this trip, I did notice one slight tic: an occasional penchant for embarking on excitable verbal jags about esoteric meditation topics. What was charming and intoxicating over dinner could be suboptimal when filming a course for rank-and-file meditators. For example, he actually uttered the following sentence: "You can just shift into a kind of feeling of your own being, of your own headlessness. That just immediately diminishes the figure of content you were suffering about. You know?"

Uh, no, Jeff, I don't.

Regardless, the reaction to Jeff from app users was overwhelmingly positive. One person affectionately described him as a cross between the Buddha and Jeff Spicoli. Most people, though, had the same question: "Is he single?"

Before you get too excited: no, he isn't. He's still with Sarah. Also, check out this goofy picture I found of him:

This shot was taken during his brief stint as bassist for that nineties band Toad the Wet Sprocket. (All right, he was never in Toad the Wet Sprocket. But still, the hair.)

Beyond the fact that he can take a joke, the true source of Jeff's appeal—and a big part of why I recruited him as my co-author for this book—is something much deeper: he is one of us. "I'm like the anti-Buddha," he says.

One of my biggest beefs with the meditation world is that too many teachers present themselves as paragons of imperturbability. Making matters worse, many of them talk in creamy voices that are supremely soporific, and also deeply off-putting to hard-charging, skeptical people like me.

Jeff talks like a normal person. Moreover, he is a normal—and openly flawed—person. "I've never been calm, naturally placid, what you might imagine a meditation teacher to look like. I'm super-ADD," he says. "I get dysregulated really easily. Or I'll be overthinking stuff too much, because I can still get in my head a lot."

That ADD line is not a throwaway. Jeff has struggled with attention deficit disorder since he was a child. For him, it doesn't manifest the way you might think. Instead of being unable to focus, he often gets hyperfocused—before his attention is inevitably hijacked by something new. As he's explained it to me, he considers ADD to be both his greatest strength and his greatest liability. On the one hand, it allows him to lock in and be extremely engaged and open with people. It's part of what makes him such a popular teacher. But in many other areas of his life, ADD had been "a disaster." For years it made it hard for him to finish writing projects or stay interested in jobs and relationships. That provoked a pattern of endless strategizing and disappointment, which left him "in agony."

Meditation, he says, calmed and grounded him. And it taught him that you can't run from your baggage; you need to see it clearly, so that it doesn't yank you around. "Meditation," says Jeff, "is about bringing into awareness some habit that was previously unconscious. Insofar as it's unconscious, you have no perspective around it. It totally governs you; it owns you. You're being hurtled along automatically by it. As soon as you can start to notice that happening and see it, then it becomes less and less of a problem. So I'm at the point in my life, having practiced enough, that I can now see where most of my neurotic struggles are. And, because I can see them, I can admit to them, and they end up being less of a problem."

This is the beauty of meditation. The superpower. The judo move. What you see clearly cannot drive you. Ignorance is not bliss.

Meditation really can change your life. That is why both Jeff and I feel so strongly about helping people overcome the many stumbling blocks so they can actually start practicing. "If I had one thing on my agenda," says Jeff, "it would be to make people feel better about the fact that everyone's got their own neurotic stuff. Also, I don't require anyone to join my cult, although I do encourage it."

So, yeah, I recruited a wiseass Canadian with ADD to join me on this mission to help people meditate. Our initial thought was that we wanted to do some sort of road trip, since our wandering retreat had worked so well. The idea was to travel around, meet people struggling with various "secret fears," and give them a hand. In one of our many brainstorming meetings with members of the 10% Happier team, someone casually mentioned we should get a rock star bus and go across the country. Everyone laughed at how ridiculous the notion was. So we did it.

We ended up renting this sexy rig:

THE 10% HAPPIER
MEDITATION TOUR
MEDITATION FOR FIDGETY SKEPTICS

(I assure you, the absurdity was not lost on us.)

The bus rental company, Rock Safaris, promptly provided us with two key data points: (1) every experienced road warrior knows there is one hard-and-fast rule, which is that there is no making number two on the bus (you're supposed to hold it until you get to a rest stop), and (2) the most recent occupants of this particular vehicle were the members of the legendary band Parliament Funkadelic. I was pretty sure we were going to be the most boring people ever to ride on this bus.

We spent months planning the trip. There were nearly a dozen key players involved (many of whom you will soon meet). We held weekly planning calls. Where should we go? Whom should we see? Can we make it from New Orleans to El Paso in one go? (No.) Where is the world's largest ball of yarn? (Not on our route.)

We aimed to find interesting and diverse groups of people who wanted to practice but weren't actually doing it. We mapped a cross-country itinerary. We got a crash course in the rules that govern how long bus drivers can legally be behind the wheel. We had the brilliant idea to order a customized "meditation booth," where we could offer free lessons to the passing masses. The entire endeavor was a logistical nightmare.

The primary goal of the trip was to create a thorough classification of all the different kinds of jacked-up meditators out there, but we set ourselves two firm rules. First, be realistic. We wanted to be as pragmatic as possible about what it takes to establish a meditation practice. The fact is, habit formation is hard. What works for you may not work for others. And what may do the trick for you at one time may no longer cut it at some later date. So the essence of our approach is: Here are some tactics that seem to work. Try them, experiment. And if you fall off the wagon, we can troubleshoot that, too.

The second rule: no proselytizing. Although this book is shamelessly pro-meditation, we are not interested in strong-arming people who aren't into it. On our road trip we would speak only with people who actually wanted to meditate. Living with a wife who is a non-meditator, I have learned the hard way that proselytizing is a shortcut to getting the stink-eye or, worse, a smack in the head. I try to remain mindful of a great *New Yorker* cartoon that shows two women having lunch. One of them says to the other, "I've been gluten free for a week, and I'm already annoying."

After eleven days and eighteen states, I feel confident in saying we fulfilled our mission. We met cops, military cadets, politicians, celebrities, social workers, and formerly incarcerated youth. We covered more than three thousand miles. We ate deliciously fattening food. And we didn't kill each other. (Although we came close.)

The resulting book, which you hold in your hands, is designed not only to provide practical advice for surmounting the obstacles to meditation but also to teach you, in a simple and accessible manner, how to practice. One of the unique things Jeff offers in these pages is different meditations for different kinds of situations and challenges and temperaments. Neither of us believes there is a one-size-fits-all meditative solution.

Nor, as I've said before, do we believe that meditation is a miracle cure for everything that ails you. We make no grandiose promises. If you're looking for instant enlightenment, a third-eye optician, or a cup of fresh-brewed kombucha, you have come to the wrong place. What we do hope to provide is a well-reasoned route toward increased sanity through mindfulness. Chicken soup for the skeptic.

The best way to understand both the benefits and the challenges of meditation is to see how the practice plays out in an individual mind. Which is why Jeff and I offer ourselves up as guinea pigs, allowing you to see the inside story, so to speak. As we traveled across the country, ostensibly with the goal of helping other people, some of our deepest foibles were exposed. While meditation is not a cure-all, it is an adventure—and sometimes a bumpy one at that.

Especially bumpy, in this case, for me. During the course of our meditation tour, I ended up learning some hard, even humiliating lessons about my own hang-ups and insecurities. Indeed, as you are about to see, on the very first day, it was powerfully revealed to me that I was very often failing to practice what I preach—that, in fact, I had been a towering hypocrite.

2

"I Can't Do This"

TV newsrooms are like the embodiment of "the monkey mind," characterized by bright lights, bottomless vanity, and the collective attention span of a syphilitic squirrel.

I've spent my entire adult life in this milieu, one that is decidedly uncongenial to meditation. My on-air colleagues and I are conditioned to avoid dead air at all costs, so we are constantly scanning the conversational landscape for the opportunity to make the next quip. We monitor the ratings, read our Twitter replies, and tend to develop the kind of self-consciousness that comes from always being watched and evaluated. All of which, I figured, made my workplace the perfect crucible in which to kick off our road trip.

It was five o'clock on Sunday morning and I was walking onto the set where we record the weekend editions of *Good Morning America*. I had a camera crew in tow from the 10% Happier app that would be documenting the entire expedition. On this inaugural morning, the plan was to film some behind-the-scenes footage of me preparing for the show, after which we would convene my fellow anchors and see if they could stay quiet long enough to meditate.

As I sat down at my computer, nested in a pod of workstations off to the side of the set, my co-host, Paula Faris, sauntered over and made herself at home on my desk. She had noticed the crew and decided she did not want to waste a prime opportunity to mock me.

"Has Dan told you what our idea for his follow-up book should be? The sequel? Can we say it on camera?" she asked, glint in her eye, clearly intent on revealing her idea no matter what. "*10% Happier . . . but Still a Douchebag.*"

Every weekend morning since 2010 I've been getting up at 3:45 to anchor this show. When the alarm goes off at that ungodly hour, the first thought that often pops into my head is: *Why the hell am I doing this?* But then I realize I'm going to a job I adore with people I love. Paula—who alternately refers to herself as my "work wife" or "the little sister Dan never wanted"—is a big part of the draw. On paper, we are diametric opposites. She grew up in a conservative Christian family in the Midwest; I was raised in ultraliberal Massachusetts by a pair of secular scientists. Paula and her husband take their three kids to church on Sundays; Bianca and I are devout agnostics. But these differences have formed the foundation of a real friendship. On workdays, Paula and I jointly craft the questions we ask of the political analysts who appear on the show, our differing backgrounds ensuring, we believe, increased fairness. On our off days, we text about child rearing, theology, and the latest office gossip. People often come up to me—strangers at airports, staffers in the newsroom, even members of senior management—and ask, "Do you guys really like each other as much as it seems on TV?" The answer is yes.

That Sunday, after we wrapped up the show, Paula and I retired, along with the rest of the on-air team, to a conference room on the thirteenth floor of our office building for a meditation tutorial.

Jeff was already there when we arrived, looking sharp—in a first-day-of-school kind of way—wearing a blue button-down shirt, a new pair of black sneakers, and striped socks. (He later told me that a stylist friend of his had taken pity on his out-moded wardrobe and hooked him up with better clothes for this road trip.) The 10% Happier crew had set up all the cameras and lights and were ready to roll.

Rob and Ron loped in. Ron Claiborne is the news reader on weekend *GMA,* meaning he comes on near the top of the show to deliver the morning's headlines. A Yalie with an allergy to bullshit and pretense of any variety, he's been with ABC News for thirty years and is beloved for his journalistic experience and wry humor. (Shortly after my first book came out, he held up his own, homemade version on the air, called *11% Happier.* "If you're only going to buy one book," he told the audience, "do the math.") Today he was wearing a suit coat and tie with cargo pants and sneakers. In other words, the sartorial version of a mullet.

Rob Marciano is our meteorologist. If I looked like him, I'd probably be insufferable. He's tall and impossibly handsome, although he doesn't seem to know it. He is goofy and warm. He manages to dress impeccably—generally a tailored suit, silver tie clip, and white pocket square—and yet not look like a fop.

Finally, Sara Haines came bounding in, late and breathless, after running from the subway station. Until recently, Sara had been our spirited, irrepressible pop news anchor (basically *GMA* branding for "entertainment reporter"), but she had recently left for a job as co-host of *The View,* ABC's weekday morning chat show, where she was a rising star. Even though it was her day off, she had agreed to join our meditation confab.

All four of my co-hosts were what I would call "meditation curious." Everyone but Ron had tried it. All of them, given their stressful jobs and busy lives, were intrigued by the advertised benefits—or at least they pretended to be, after having been forced to listen to me yammer about the practice for years—but none of them had managed to establish an abiding habit.

As soon as the discussion got going, we very quickly bumped into one of the biggest obstacles facing aspiring meditators: the "I can't do this" myth.

This myth takes many forms, one of which is a feeling of being completely at sea about how to even begin. Check out the tsunami of logistical questions from my colleagues:

Rob: "Are we meditating today? Because I didn't dress for that."

Ron: "I don't have to lay on the floor?"

Paula: "Are we gonna sit with our legs crossed?"

Rob (about the breathing): "Nose, mouth, doesn't matter?"

Sara: "How do you know when you're done?"

Jeff sat there, taking in the rapid-fire queries from these professional talkers with a combination of amusement and bemusement.

Surely, however, my co-hosts are not alone in their confusion. What follows are answers to the most common early questions.

FAQ: *Meditation Basics*

So Jeff, where do you recommend that people meditate?

It's good to have a quiet place with minimal distractions, but it doesn't have to be perfect. Natural settings can also be nice places to meditate.

Look at you with your own font, Fancypants. Does meditation require special clothes?

Not really. Loose pants are better for circulation.

Do your eyes need to be closed when you meditate?

Up to you. Many people meditate with their eyes closed. Others like to have the eyes half open, staring at the floor three feet in front of them with a soft gaze. Both are fine. See what feels most natural and agreeable for you.

What's your view on how people should sit?

Sit in a way that allows you to be still, comfortable, and alert. This can happen in many ways: on a chair, on a floor cushion, even lying down or standing up. But don't fool yourself—if lying down makes you fall asleep, then you are not being alert. If standing up makes you tense, then you are not being comfortable. Most people sit on a straight-backed chair or on a cushion. For this, your spine should be vertical, and your knees should be below the pelvis. If your knees are crossed and bent upward above your pelvis—like the way people for some reason imagine you are supposed to sit in meditation—then this will create tension in the lower back and you'll spend your entire meditation cursing Dan's name. Better to sit in a decent chair with back support, or to sit at the edge of a chair with your back straight. As for the hands, either place them gently on the knees or fold them in your lap.

Can you move at all?

Stillness is the ideal; the stiller you get, the cleaner and clearer the signal from the sensation you are paying attention to (like the breath), and ultimately the more absorbed and settled you'll be able to get. That said, if you need to move, that's totally fine—just try to bring your awareness to that movement and make it part of the meditation, instead of moving unconsciously.

What if you're in physical pain?

It's normal for your ankle (or back, or knee) to start hurting after a while, or for you to have an unusually persistent face itch, at which point all that may be going on in your meditation is you obsessing about your pain. There are a couple of strategies here. One: gently move your leg. That really is fine. Two: investigate the discomfort. There is much to say here about how valuable this kind of investigation can be, about how we can learn to tease apart our actual pain from our much larger resistance to the pain, which is where the majority of our tension and discomfort actually lives. We will explore these fascinating—and rather life-changing—dynamics in a later chapter.

How do you know when you're done with a meditation session?

Use a timer. That way you can hit start and then do your best to forget about it (otherwise you may keep peeking, wondering, *Is it time yet, is it time yet?*).

Speaking of timing, how long and how often should people meditate?

Finding the time to meditate is probably the biggest roadblock to establishing a meditation habit; we'll have more to say on the subject as the book progresses. It's important to set realistic goals. We recommend you shoot for five to ten minutes a day, with the important qualification that if this is not possible, one minute of meditation absolutely counts.

As a general rule, the more often you meditate, the easier it gets and the deeper and more enduring the benefits. Consistency matters more than length. Meditating every day or two—even for a minute—will help you get a meditation habit off the ground. Once it becomes part of your everyday routine, you can experiment with length to see what works best for you.

All the meditations in the book can be done in under ten minutes. We include suggested times. Longer sits are always worth exploring.

Is it helpful to listen to ambient music while you meditate?

It's not ideal, because then your attention is split between the thing you are meditating on and the background music. That said, two caveats. One, everyone is a bit different. You may find that music is actually a helpful aide to concentration and doesn't distract from your practice. Two, music itself can be the *object* of meditation. You can zoom in on the auditory qualities. Just keep in mind that music casts a spell and can easily cause you to lose mindfulness.

What about other kinds of meditation, like using a mantra?

In this book, we teach mindfulness meditation, which does not involve a mantra. But there are many other ways to meditate. It's really a matter of personal preference. In mantra practice, most famously taught in a school called Transcendental Meditation (TM), you lightly pay attention to a short repeated phrase in your head. For many people, this is a powerful way to get still and concentrated.

So in mindfulness all we do is . . . pay attention to our breath?

That's the first move. The core practice. But there are a few others. Let me put it in context.

Most traditions teach a logical progression of techniques, each building off the previous one. That's what we're going to do here, with three basic steps.

Step one: We focus and calm the mind by concentrating on the breath. In meditation-speak, we call the thing we focus on the meditation "object." If you don't like the breath, I'll offer some other options. This will be our "home base" meditation. Concentration is key, because you can't get far in meditation if your mind is skittering all over the place like a frenzied chipmunk on a sheet of linoleum. (Although some skittering is inevitable.)

Step two: Once our mind has stabilized a bit, we'll widen our attention to include our thoughts, urges, and emotions. When you can see your mental patterns clearly, they don't have as much power over you. It's a hugely useful skill.

Step three: We'll explore a few specialized meditations: on movement, on sound, on compassion, and others.

Since Dan likes to make crappy drawings, here are a few of my own.

If simple concentration is home base . . .

concentration
(breath, body, sound)
HOME BASE

. . . then we'll build outward and use our more stable and balanced awareness to see our unique patterns of thinking and feeling and reacting.

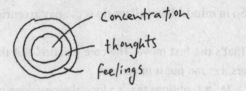

Finally, throughout the book, I'll drop in those specialized, satellite techniques, which can be used as needed:

But, as I said, we start with concentration. It is *the* foundational skill.

Many people have negative associations with concentration. It sounds hard. Unfun. Like when our teachers would holler at us, "Pay attention!"

The irony here is that the *fruit* of concentration is actually one of the most fun parts of meditation. It feels *good*. Concentration is being in the zone, it's unifying attention into a single stream of activity. It quiets things down inside, which for many of us comes as a huge relief. It's only when we get a break from our endless mental churn of opinions, obsessions, and exuberances that we realize how completely exhausting our so-called normal state is. The mind is constantly finding and making problems. As it settles, there are fewer problems. It's that easy.

• • •

Back in the room with my *GMA* colleagues, once Jeff had answered the basic questions, he got down to the actual meditation.

He had us close our eyes, straighten our spines, and relax our faces. His tone, as always, was both warm and matter-of-fact. I love the way Jeff guides meditation. He sounds like a regular guy—no weird affectations or hushed, singsong delivery.

Below is a version of the basic instructions Jeff delivered to my co-hosts. You don't actually have to meditate right now if you don't want to. I usually find it annoying when authors ask me to do things on their timetable, not mine. That said, the way Jeff teaches meditation is anything but annoying; I find his style fascinating and often very funny. As you read, you can try to connect to some of the qualities of mind he describes. And whenever you do decide to try the full-on, eyes-closed version of meditation, you can consult the cheat sheet summaries Jeff provides at the end of each section. Also, as mentioned earlier, both short and long versions of all the book's guided meditations are available for free, in audio form, on the 10% Happier app.

CONCENTRATION 101

5 to 10 minutes; longer is worth exploring

Start by taking a couple of deep breaths. On the inhale, stretch up the spine, find some alertness and composure. On the exhale, settle and soften the body.

We start with our attitude. Can you sit in a way that's relaxed and open? This is the quality of equanimity. It's a kind of easygoingness in the way we hold ourselves. I think of it as the Fonzie effect. You're just sitting cool inside your skin. You're making a commitment to not get uptight about the fact that (1) this meditation thing may feel weird at first and (2) there are almost definitely going to be unwanted distractions and sounds and thoughts and feelings. It's all fine. You're letting all this stuff be there right from the start. This maturity and affability are the essence of the meditative attitude.

Bring your attention to the breath. You don't want to control or interfere with it. Just breathe normally. What does it *feel* like? Get nerdily curious about it.

The instruction is to notice some part of the sensation of breathing. It might be the feeling of air at the nostrils, or the feeling of the breath moving into the chest or belly, or even the continuous flow of all these together—whatever jumps out most at you. The idea is to pay attention to your breathing without trying to control it in any way.

If you can bring an attitude of enjoyment to it, all the better. You want to become a connoisseur of breathing, enjoying it the way you'd enjoy the flavors of a good meal. The

more you try to connect to the subtle *enjoyment* of the
sensation—its softness, its smoothness, the end of each
breath, the space in between—the more concentrated you
will become. It's okay if you have to fake the interest a bit
at first. If you like, take a moment now to notice the feeling
of your breath in an easygoing way.

To help, you have the option of doing something called
"noting." This means you silently say to yourself (i.e., note)
in when you breathe in, and *out* when you breathe out. Or
you can count breaths—one to ten, then start from one
again. Up to you. Lots of people find noting helps them stay
on track. It's the skillful use of thinking to *hack* thinking.
You take over the thinking bandwidth for your own meditative purposes.

If you don't like working with the breath, no problem.
Choose another sensation: maybe the feeling in your hands,
or the feeling of contact with the chair or cushion. You can
even use sound if you prefer—continuous background
sounds work best, like the distant drone of traffic, or the
hum of a ceiling fan or radiator. Many objects can work.
Choose one and then stay on it as best you can. Try not to
jump around looking for a "better" sensation. Any sensation
can get weirdly fulfilling with time.

See if you can let the simplicity of the activity come as a
relief. No hundred-item to-do lists—nothing you need to
do here except breathe (or feel, or listen). One breath at a
time. How *delicately* can you feel the sensation? Not grabbing at it, or anticipating the next breath while this one is
still happening. Just this breath. Stillness helps—the stiller
and more relaxed you are, the clearer the signal. Be curious.
This is an exploration.

And . . . know that it is totally normal for distractions to come up. No doubt they are already there: your own commentary and criticisms, aches and pains, unwanted sounds warbling in from the external world. In fact, let's tune in to what I imagine is happening in Dan's mind right now.

Jeff's meditation is too long. What were we thinking? I'm losing my rugged good looks. Bianca always looks perfect—why is that? Maybe I am aging more quickly. What's that smell? Gas leak!

This is what minds do. They like to run with stuff. It's actually quite entertaining. The trick with this meditation is to good-naturedly let all that material be the background. You don't have to stop it, or chase it, or start analyzing it, even though the urge to do so can be quite mighty. Just let it all play itself out while you stay with the breath.

If you do find that a stealthy thought has come up from below and carried you off to some other planet, then do one of those cartoon double takes and try to notice what happened. This is the mindfulness part. *Where has my mind been? Oh, it was planning/blanking/fantasizing.* Now you know. The move now is to try to let the distraction go, in a leisurely and non-uptight way. Return to the breath.

This is a big moment, and an important one. It's not unusual to start judging yourself here—to think about how bad you are as a meditator and to go off on some catastrophizing tangent about how you are uniquely doomed, et cetera. Instead, try the opposite: take a moment to generate a brief sense of satisfaction at having noticed your distraction. Can you notice the subtle electric clarity of your mindfulness? Yup: you are here, snapping back into awareness. You can do this right now as you read this—notice your own mindful awareness. *Snap.* Takes a split second. The appreciation of "waking up" is one of the rewards that dramatically accelerates our capacity to stay mindful. This is the other training we are engaged in here: the training of letting go of distractions, of taking pleasure in being mindful, of beginning again.

So: back to your object of concentration. The breath, the sensation, the sound. How *into* the breath can you get? Can you breathe like Stevie Wonder plays piano? That dude is *into it.* Breathe normally, but also like it's the softest and most interesting thing going. Like you never noticed before how satisfying it is to breathe.

When you're ready, open your eyes.

Once you're done with any meditation, it is not a bad idea to take a few minutes to relax with your eyes closed or even lie down. This seems to help lock in the benefits. Plus, jumping directly into action mode after sitting can be a bit jarring.

CHEAT SHEET

1. Breathe normally, and try to tune in to the subtle sensations. If it helps, note *in* as you breathe in and *out* as you breathe out. If you don't like the breath, choose another body sensation, or some regular external sound.

2. Try to enjoy both the feeling and the simplicity of the activity.

3. If your mind wanders, no problem. Just notice what has hijacked you, and then return to the breath with a sense of mindful satisfaction.

PRO TIPS: *Little tricks and tips that may make breath meditation easier:*

- Count the breaths from one to ten, and then start over. Breathe in, *one,* then out. Breathe in, *two,* then out. Et cetera.
- Some people like to recite a little phrase to help them stay with what's going on. "Just this breath" is a good one. It reminds us not to start anticipating the next breath, or to think about the last one, or to imagine in any of the innumerable ways the mind imagines that anything else is supposed to be happening other than exactly what *is* happening—which is noticing exactly this breath. "Just this breath." Repeating this helps soothe and simplify our experience, reminding us again and again not to overcomplicate things.
- Get *forensically* curious about the breath. Can you notice the exact moment the breath ends? The exact moment it begins? Can you notice the mysterious little space between breaths? Be like a private investigator of breathing.
- For particularly busy minds, some teachers recommend the use of "touch points." So: breathe in, feel your rear/hands/whatever, breathe out, feel your rear/hands/whatever, and so on. The idea is to keep your mind occupied by filling up every possible "down" moment with a new noticing.
- Recruit an image. Sometimes I imagine the in-breath as a gentle wave moving up the beach, *pshhhh,* and on the out-breath the wave recedes, *sssssshh.* Back and forth. This rhythm can be very entrancing, so make sure to stay mindful. Find an image that works for you. This can be especially helpful if the breath starts to get subtle and hard to notice. It is possible this vague image may gradually replace the sensation of breathing and become the new object of focus. If this starts to happen, just go with it.
- Give guided audio meditations a shot. Some people wrongly assume that guided audio meditations are a form of cheating—or

training wheels. I disagree. Anyone who has ever meditated will know that even the simplest instructions are quickly forgotten. Having someone in your ear can be really helpful. My advice is to experiment with both audio and solo meditations and see what works.

As Jeff was delivering the basic instructions to my *GMA* colleagues, there was an amusing micro-drama unfolding. Out of the hush, we kept hearing Paula's voice, interrupting with questions. I've never seen anyone turn a guided meditation into a call-and-response before, but it was kind of amazing.

"I feel like I'm slouching. Is that okay now, because I'm relaxing?"

"You can shift, can't you?"

Then she got to the biggie, the mother of all "I can't do this" concerns: mind-wandering.

"When I'm feeling a distraction—like I can feel my stomach hanging over, or I just heard Ron's stomach growl—what do I do with all of those distractions?"

Paula was under the sway of one of the central misconceptions that stop people from meditating: the idea that if you get distracted, you're "doing it wrong." Here's how Paula summed it up in our post-meditation debrief: "I've always thought it was clearing your brain of everything."

The dreaded clear-your-head myth is responsible for untold numbers of aborted meditation careers. I hear people espousing this faulty belief all the time. "I know I should meditate," they tell me, "but I can't stop thinking!" People tend to assume they are distinctively distractible—that they exhibit a sui generis kind of lunacy that prevents them, and only them, from ever meditating. I call this the "fallacy of uniqueness." And Paula is the perfect mascot.

"I mean, I literally have switched positions twenty-five times since we've been talking," she told us. "I cannot sit still."

"I have a similar thing, as a kind of agitated, hyperactive person," Jeff said. "I'll just sit, and I'll just feel all the energy swirling around like a deranged chipmunk."

"So I have a chipmunk inside of me?" asked Paula.

"Yes, you've got a chipmunk inside of you."

The truth is, we all have chipmunks; we are all nuts.

You really can't hear this enough: *Meditation does not require you to stop thinking.* If you go into meditation with the expectation that you will suspend all thought, you are going to have a rough go of it. Meditation is unlike anything else you do in life, in that here, "failing"—that is, noticing you've gotten distracted and starting again—is succeeding.

When you wake up from distraction, that is the magic moment, the victory. And it is a victory of real consequence. You are achieving the first big insight of meditation: it's a zoo inside your skull. Why is this important? Because the more you see all this clamor, the less likely you are to be controlled by it. You are no longer trapped inside your thoughts; you're momentarily stepping outside them, watching with a combination of horror and amusement and curiosity. The fact that humans can do this is astounding and probably should be taught in grade school, because, as Jeff likes to argue, it points to an inner geography that is a lot more fundamental than the names of our state capitals.

There's no question that for beginning meditators it can be really intimidating to behold the sheer magnitude of the inner craziness. It can also be wearisome to have to start over and over and over. But just know: this is exactly what is supposed to happen. It means you are doing it right. You don't have to reach a special state. Getting lost and starting over *is* meditation, at least at first. And it's also important to know that it gets easier with time. Bear in mind that you are building a new skill here. I'm always struck by how quickly people conclude that they can't meditate. If I handed you a flute, you wouldn't expect that you could rock the flute solo of a Jethro Tull song immediately. Likewise, the first time you meditate, don't expect radiant clarity.

So, again: you don't have to stop thinking, you just have to change your relationship to your thinking. In fact, you can learn to change your relationship to *all* of the mental Visigoths reaving and roving through your head, including thoughts, emotions, and physical sensations.

The name for the new kind of relationship you can create with the contents of your consciousness is "equanimity." This is Jeff's all-time favorite word. In fact, he'd recently started an email newsletter called *The Equanimist*. (I had been rooting for *The Age of Equanimous*.)

In the room with Paula, Jeff explained, "Equanimity is the capacity to let your experience be what it is, without trying to fight it and negotiate with it. It's like an inner smoothness or frictionlessness."

When Jeff's inner chipmunk was active, he explained, he had developed the ability, through meditation, to sit back and "just let it all play out. It's kind of like you're getting a little inner massage with your agitation. It stops becoming a thing that's bugging you, and starts becoming a thing that you're mildly and affectionately curious about. Like, some little critter in your body."

Equanimity was enormously attractive to Paula, who felt pulled in a million directions in her life, balancing her three young children with her more-than-full-time job (aside from anchoring the weekend edition of *GMA*, she's also a co-host of

The View and a reporter for many of our major broadcasts). "What I'm really looking for is level-headedness," she said.

Jeff assured her that this was exactly what meditation is designed to help with: the ability to handle your challenges, both inner and outer, more sanely. "It's sort of like whack-a-mole, you know? In life, normally you're like, *whack! whack! whack!*" he said, pantomiming a kid frenziedly whacking varmints with a mallet. But with meditation, "you're more like, *dum, dum, dum,*" he said, this time wielding the mallet in a decidedly more mellow manner. "It's like you're in a reggae band, instead of an eighties synth band."

"It doesn't change your circumstances," said Paula, "it just changes your reaction to those circumstances?"

"Correct!" I exclaimed. "That's brilliantly said."

I love this stuff. There is nothing more thrilling than seeing the lights go on for someone, especially someone you care about.

The important point about thinking is that you can disembed from it and watch it play out without feeding it. Because the issue of compulsive overthinking is so common, here's a tailored meditation from Jeff.

One of the excellent and admittedly quite counterintuitive mindfulness skills we are learning is the ability to distinguish between thinking and awareness. To use a classic metaphor from consciousness studies, awareness is like the empty stage. Thinking is one of the actors that trots *onto* that stage—along with seeing, hearing, tasting, and touching.

When we are mindful, we watch thinking play out from the vantage point of awareness. Awareness is the wider perspective. Most people don't realize it's the wider perspective because thinking *feels* so similar to awareness. It's perfectly camouflaged.

But when we actually start to pay attention to thinking, we can begin to notice the ghostly details of this important actor. We begin to notice that, actually, thinking is often *tangible*, trackable. It's made up of vague fleeting images and tumbling inner talk and sudden ideas and tugs of emotions that play out as sensations in our bodies. When we're thinking, we may even notice a bit of subtle tension in our face and body as each thought performs its part. Fortunately, we can learn to pan back the camera and notice when any of this is happening. To use the metaphor Dan invoked earlier, we can reclaim our place behind the waterfall. And by the way, this move doesn't prevent us from thinking. It just lets us choose whether we want to reinforce a particular thought-soliloquy or not. The hilarious thing here is thinking itself often tries to convince us how important it is. And sometimes it is. But other times it's unreliable and filled with unnecessary drama, drama that prevents us from seeing what's really going on. The line I like is "Thinking is a wonderful servant but a terrible master." This understanding gets clearer the longer we practice.

For this meditation we're going to stay working with the breath—the feeling of our breath is the focus (or some other home base sound or sensation). But we're going to keep an internal eye on our thinking, and try to notice the moment thinking starts to steal the show. In this way, we slowly learn to counter our lifelong habit of indulging every thought.

CATCHING THINKING IN THE ACT

5 to 10 minutes, although you can do this meditation
in under a minute—there are always thoughts to catch

Start by taking a couple of deep breaths. On the inhale, you can stretch up your spine a bit. On the exhale, imagine you're breathing out any tension, softening the body as you settle down into the chair or cushion.

The first thing we do is set our attitude—a sense of good-naturedness and affability in the way we sit. Not uptight. Curious about this practice—inquisitive about our capacity to be with the breath, but also open to learning about our mysterious and charming thinking process.

So the basic instruction is the same as in our first meditation: focus on the feeling of the in and out breath. Decide the sensation you want to focus on. Maybe the feeling of air tickling the nostrils or the feeling of air moving into the chest, or maybe the tautness of the abdomen as it rises on the inhale. Choose one of these sources of sensation and then commit to it, seeing if you can tune in to the softness and subtleties of the breath. Many people like to use a little note to help them pay attention: *in*, *out*, or *rising*, *falling*. If you do this, let the tone of your noting be calm, at whatever pacing works for you. Breathing in, *in;* breathing out, *out*. Aware of the sensations, aware you are breathing. Mindfulness of breathing.

If focusing on your breath is psyching you out for any reason, then choose another sensation to work with: the feeling of the hands, the contact of your seat on the chair or cushion, maybe a point in the belly or some external sounds. Whatever you choose, the idea is to then commit your attention, lightly and in a friendly way, not straining to make anything happen.

As we progress, it's almost inevitable that we'll forget the breath and find ourselves off thinking about something. Thoughts can be ridiculously subtle: they come up underneath us and carry us away, and before we know it we realize that for the past two minutes we've been fantasizing about walking through a field of golden grass at sunset holding hands with the multi-platinum recording artist Josh Groban. At least, if we happen to be Dan Harris.

> Busted. I am actually thinking about Josh Groban right now.

The point is, there's nothing more normal in the world. The mind secretes thoughts the way the stomach secretes digestive enzymes. It's part of our body's natural functioning. The key for our purposes, as always, is mindfulness— being able to notice when this has happened, so we can catch our thoughts in the act. Each time we notice, we wake up. To help with this, we'll use a little note: "thinking." We say it with friendliness and appreciation, because thinking really can be quite mischievous and wily. And then we go right back to feeling the breath:

In, out.

In, out.

In—image in Dan's mind of Josh Groban pulling him up onstage. His heart leaps! *Me? Is it true? . . . Oh, I'm thinking.*

Notice that you got hijacked there for a sec. Notice what it's like—*snap*—to wake up, to escape thinking's weird gravity. If you are noting it—*thinking*—then you are not *inside* it. Appreciate this tiny moment of sanity, and then return to the breath. Aware you are breathing:

In, out.

In, out.

And so it goes. Never annoyed by our excitable thinking process; rather, we're curious, exploring how soon we can notice that thinking has taken over. Building up this weird new skill of internal discernment, fine-tuning our sensitivity, our mindfulness.

In, out.

When you feel ready—or when the timer goes off—you can open your eyes and head back into your day. As you do, see if you can tune in occasionally to your thinking process. Try to notice when it has carried you away, and also get curious about the exact moment of waking up. What does this moment feel like? Can you notice the contrast between being embedded within the humid interior of your thinking and coming up and out into the more open field of awareness? I can't say enough about how important this is. Again and again, we can wake up from the comparatively narrow trance of our preoccupations into a wider and more spacious perspective. We can learn to live in this place, appreciative of the action, dipping in as needed, but not beholden to any of it. In this way we get more present, more free, more available to life.

CHEAT SHEET

1. Breathe normally, and try to tune in to the sensations of breathing. Let it be enjoyable and relaxed.

2. If you find that thinking has swept you away, note *thinking*, then return to feeling and noting the breath.

3. See if you can appreciate thinking's subtle ability to entrance, without feeding or indulging in the actual content of the thoughts. Get curious about the exact moment of waking up from distraction.

One last note on our encounter with my *GMA* colleagues. As I was holding forth to the gang about the evils of the clear-the-mind myth and cheering on Paula for her emerging understanding of the concept of equanimity, I was struck by an unfortunate irony. This was the moment when I realized I had been a huge hypocrite, albeit an accidental one.

A few years ago, I had my meditation skills tested by neuroscientists. Specifically, they were examining my ability to shut down what's called the default mode network (DMN) of the brain—the regions that fire when we're thinking about ourselves, ruminating about the past or projecting into the future. Instead of tamping down the DMN, I was achieving the exact opposite. Mine was lit up like a Christmas tree.

The problem: apparently I was ignoring my own advice. Rather than gently starting over when I got distracted, I was getting all overheated and self-lacerating about the inevitable wanderings of the mind.

Look, I can pun in French: I've got a soupçon that soup's on.
Did you know that a group of chipmunks is called a "scurry"? And

it's a "dray" of squirrels, and a "business" of ferrets, and . . .
Seriously? What in tarnation is the matter with you?

After spending years assuring people that the whole game in meditation is just to begin again, it turns out I was mouthing the words without truly absorbing their significance. It reminded me of how my two-year-old son, Alexander, would walk around the house, repeating our disciplinary injunctions: "Be careful!" he would cry as he was knocking over a lamp. Or "No circles!" as he whirled like a dervish. And my favorite: the singsongy "No, no, no!" as he inched his hand toward the electrical sockets.

In my defense, it's hard to relax when you have a tangle of wires attached to your skull while being scrutinized by a team of researchers. Still, the results were humbling. I think my problem stemmed, in part, from the very first time I'd heard the basic meditation instructions. I had cockily assumed that I could "win" at meditation and therefore wouldn't ever need to gently begin again. That was for other people, I reckoned. Imagine my surprise.

The larger issue, however, was quite literally in my genes. Paula and Jeff may have struggled primarily with their inner chipmunks, but my principal hobgoblin was an entirely different beast: my inner Robert Johnson.

Robert Johnson was my grandfather—my mom's dad. He looms in my mind as a fearsome figure. He was a cranky old goat, a dyed-in-the-wool curmudgeon, and an unreconstructed fussbudget. He also bore a striking resemblance to the man with the pitchfork in the famous painting *American Gothic*.

He was incredibly smart but also wildly insecure, which could make him unpleasant, to say the least. He was raised by a bitter and violence-prone dairy farmer in upstate New York and grew up to be a disgruntled middle manager at the Yellow Pages with five kids of his own. While Robert himself was never physically abusive, his temper was volcanic and unpredictable. I remember once when he somehow found out that I had gently made fun of him in a letter to my parents that I had sent home from summer camp; he promptly disinvited my mother from her own sister's wedding, which was being held in Robert's backyard. He also refused to speak to her for a year.

That penchant for paranoia and grudge-nursing had undeniably found its way into my bloodstream; it was my inheritance from Robert Johnson. He could emerge, in bolts of self-righteous fury, when I felt wronged at work or at home. He could be unleashed on hapless call center employees who didn't deliver immediate satisfaction.

In fairness, by this point in my life Robert Johnson was making vastly fewer appearances, thanks to meditation, maturation, and marriage, but he was still there, waiting to be coaxed out of his shadowy psychic demimonde.

I saw him quite frequently, in fact, when I would get distracted during meditation. I'd wake up from some sort of mid-meditation daydream, and Bobby J. would come rushing in: *You are as useful as a jar of guano. You have all the personality of a wall sconce, all the sophistication of a spork, all the cultural heft of a Hoobastank record.*

On this Sunday morning, the first day of our road trip, RJ was in full effect. I was exhausted from having been up since 3:45 A.M., I was stressed about all the interviews we needed to get done that day, and I was preemptively missing my wife and son.

I noticed a petty biliousness in my inner monologue. I was criticizing myself (*Why'd you eat so much last night? Now your face is puffy and you'll look bad on all the video we're shooting*), internally henpecking Jeff (*What the hell is he doing using highfalutin terms like "figure-ground reversal" and "parasympathetic response"?*), and getting pissed about unimportant things, like the fact that breakfast showed up late. Like, really pissed. Like, anger coursing through veins. It felt awful.

It wasn't just anger; I was also feeling anxious. I was going on huge jags of what the Buddhists call *prapañca*. I'm not normally one to drop random ancient Indian words, especially in a book designed for fidgety skeptics, but *prapañca* is just too useful and interesting a concept to leave out. *Prapañca* is when something happens in the present moment—a stray comment, a bit of bad news, a stubbed toe, whatever—and you immediately extrapolate to some catastrophic future. My *prapañca* runs would go like this:

> *The singer Josh Groban is supposed to come in later today for an on-camera meditation lesson with me and Jeff, but his publicist seems a bit nervous about it → This encounter is going to be unsuccessful → In fact, this whole trip is going to be a mess → I will be exposed as a fraud → I will end up teaching Jazzercise at a strip mall in Ronkonkoma, New York*

After our interview with my *GMA* co-anchors, the person in charge of filming the road trip, Eddie Boyce, asked me and Jeff to walk through the halls of ABC News so he could record us discussing our first interaction of the journey. I turned what was supposed to be a postmortem on our meditation chat into an extended aria about my own issues.

"It's already been such a long day for me," I said, "getting up at 3:45 and then having to manage all of my colleagues, and everybody from the company, and you." I was also worried about the fact that my wife was due to come in for an interview and she wasn't feeling well.

"That's a lot," said Jeff, with uncontrived empathy.

"I'm definitely more triggered than I normally am," I said.

"When that stuff is all happening, do you find you are able to connect to the meditative principles?"

"Yeah, I am," I said. "More or less. I notice it, and then I try not to be too carried away by it."

"That's the main thing to do," said Jeff, but he then went on to make a key point, one that I largely missed. He said that when he personally was feeling stressed and overwhelmed, he not only tried to see his emotions clearly, but also this: "Can I do it in a way that's sort of more generous?"

Meditation teachers talk about this all the time. It's not enough just to see what's happening in your mind clearly (so that it doesn't yank you around); you should also hold it all with some warmth. Many teachers use terms such as "loving-kindness" and "self-compassion." Jeff, at least, used a less syrupy word: "friendliness." While I knew intellectually that he was on to something, I pretty much brushed past it. Why? Because I am Robert Johnson's grandson, goddammit.

I didn't stop complaining, though. The next thing Eddie, our director, wanted to film was a solo interview with me, in which he would ask about my hopes and fears for the coming trip.

"What are you most afraid of on the bus tour?" asked Eddie. "You're packing in with twelve people on a small bus."

"I'm an anxious guy, so there are a number of things I'm afraid of. My kid has a fever right now, and I'm worried that somehow I'm going to get sick and then infect everybody. Also, I want people to get along. I don't want to work people too hard. I want to make sure we get good material for the book and the app. We really have no idea what we're getting ourselves into. There's no precedent for this. It's not like, 'Hey, we're modeling it on the Great Meditation Tour of '77!' "

Eddie looked on sympathetically. He'd been a meditator since he was eight years old, raised in a Buddhist community. To the cushion born, as it were. It is undoubtedly part of what imbues him with his casual cool. In his forties, he still looks like a film student, with his big glasses, neat beard, and fitted sweaters. He writes poetry and religiously reads *The New Yorker*. And yet there's something boyishly unpretentious and accessible about him. He's the kind of guy who goes surfing in the winter—nearly every day—in Nova Scotia, where he lives with his wife and kids. (When somebody told me that Eddie used to hang out and talk skateboarding with the Beastie Boys back in the nineties, I was entirely unsurprised.) He had started doing freelance video production for the 10% Happier app a few months prior, and had revolutionized our content with his creative ideas. In fact, he was the one who had come up with the whole road trip concept.

By complete coincidence, Eddie and Jeff happened to be old friends; they went to college together. When it was Jeff's turn to do his solo interview, he, too, voiced some concerns about the coming trip.

"I worry that the crew are going to get totally exhausted, that there will be some sort of collective nervous breakdown. I feel like Ed's got his stuff pretty well together, so we'll see."

Jeff also had some personal concerns, so at least I wasn't the only one feeling neurotic. "My energy gets up, and my attention gets totally blown out," he said, referring to those times when he gets so carried away by his enthusiasm and erudition that his mouth can barely keep up with his mind. "I'm worried that will happen on this trip. That I'll get super excited about stuff and get emotionally dysregulated and start saying and doing ridiculous shit."

The fact that both Jeff and I had these active neuroses was deeply comforting to my wife, Bianca. It wasn't that she enjoyed our suffering (well, maybe mine, just a tiny bit), but hearing that experienced meditators still struggle with these emotions helped alleviate her "I can't do this" fears.

She met us in my office. She and I were sitting on my couch, with Jeff positioned across from us on a straight-backed chair. It felt a bit like we'd signed up for couples therapy.

I had been worried about whether Bianca would be up for doing this interview. She had a cold, was exhausted from being on the graveyard shift with our son, and was managing her perennial discomfort with being on camera. Nonetheless, she was in fine fettle. If she were not my wife, it would have been seriously annoying that she could look so pulled together—in her artfully frayed jeans and sporty white zip-up sweatshirt— even when objectively impaired.

It was ironic that Bianca wasn't a regular meditator. You would think a doctor would understand the importance of self-care. Moreover, she was the one who'd gotten me started on all of this, by giving me a book on the subject (*Going to Pieces without Falling Apart* by Dr. Mark Epstein, whom I subsequently forced to become my friend and meditative mentor). Her own personal practice was hindered, though, by a complicated bouillabaisse of obstacles, which we will explore later in this book. (As you will see, Jeff, in full MacGyver mode, came up with a rather ingenious fix.) For now, though, suffice it to say that she, too, wrestled with the fear of not doing it right.

As she told Jeff in my office, "I certainly have high expectations for myself. If I can't do it well, then I'm not going to do it."

However, hearing Jeff and me discuss our own struggles

even after being meditators for many years helped put some cracks in her perfectionism. Turning to me, she said, "Obviously you're much more successful in managing your emotions than you were before, but every now and then it will pop up." In my bad old days—pre-meditation—I had a real temper. Our marital spats were more frequent and vehement. I would carry my stress home from work and too often come in the door scowling and irritable. Although Bianca said I still had a resting face that was a little stern, my bouts of anger these days were exceedingly rare. Neither of us could remember the last time I'd raised my voice.

On the couch, though, I felt compelled to admit my current ill humor. "Right now I'm in a shit mood," I said.

"But I couldn't tell," she said. "Anyway, the point is to know that people can be experienced and still be imperfect. It's very useful."

The fact that the person who knew me best in this world couldn't tell I was in a bad mood was incredibly reassuring. I might have been dealing with a raging internal Robert Johnson, but I wasn't acting on it. It reminded me of an expression I'd heard Jeff use about the way emotions manifest in long-term meditators: "Hurt more, suffer less." In other words, while mindfulness may mean you feel your irritation or impatience more acutely, it is less likely to stick around and you are less likely to act on it—to turn it into true suffering for yourself and others.

As we were wrapping up our chat, Bianca had some words of advice for Jeff when it came to living at close quarters with me for eleven days: "He doesn't really pick up the clothes, just so you know."

"Like being a teenager?" he said.

"A little bit."

By early evening, we were sitting in a radio studio at ABC News, awaiting the arrival of Josh Groban.

Josh and I had come into each other's Twitter orbit a few weeks before, when I noticed that Josh had retweeted one of my many daily pro-meditation missives. I tweeted back, "Do you meditate??" He replied, "Still trying to meditate without wanting to throw a lamp across the room." He seemed like the perfect test case for the Meditation MacGyver.

Josh arrived at the appointed hour, having walked directly off a Broadway stage, where he was starring in a new play called *Natasha, Pierre & the Great Comet of 1812*. It was, of all things, a modern musical update of *War and Peace*, and Josh was getting rave reviews for his performance as the male lead. He had a full-on bushy beard (as the role required) and was wearing a black knit winter hat and dark sweater. He was just as friendly in person as you might think by watching him in his many television appearances.

We were recording an interview so that later it could be included on my podcast. We were also putting it out live on Facebook. I began the interview by saying, "We haven't met formally, and you probably don't remember this, but we actually were next to each other at the urinals backstage at *Good Morning America* one day."

"How could I forget?" he said.

"I didn't peek, just so you know," I added.

I asked him why he was intrigued by the notion of meditation, and he was bracingly frank.

Ever since he had been signed to his first record deal as a teenager, "anxiety and expectation have played a huge part in my existence," he said. "I had a huge amount of pressure on me very, very early on. I had a lot of people around me that made it very clear to me how life-or-death each little thing was as far as the trajectory of my career."

Now that he was thirty-five, he said, those "angst-y beginnings" were still showing up in his life, causing him stress. "The idea of meditation for me was really about centering and really about seeing my life and seeing the world in a wider capacity. Because I get very narrow-focused on things when anxiety kicks in."

In my view, it was incredibly cool and brave for him to admit his anxiety publicly. When Jeff proposed that we try to meditate, however, I thought I saw a moment of hesitation in Josh's eyes. Which, of course, set off my own anxiety. I started to worry that maybe we were forcing him into a live meditation he didn't really want to do.

Jeff proceeded to lead a great meditation, but I could hardly follow his instructions because I was practically vibrating with *prapañca*.

> *Josh Groban is going to launch a Twitter war against me* → *Everybody loves Groban; I can never prevail in this battle* → *Strap on your leotard, motherfucker: Jazzercise*

But when it was over, Josh was totally psyched. "That was great," he said. "That was wonderful."

It was clear he had experienced something of a breakthrough. He had realized that he could, in fact, meditate without throwing a lamp across the room. "It was interesting," he said to Jeff. "As you were saying the things, you were saying them right when I needed to hear them. I think the thing that would make me frustrated in the past is that the control freak in me would kick in. I would notice myself wandering or 'not doing it right,' and then I'd get frustrated. At that point, I would be thinking to myself, 'Okay, I've just got to stop now because I'm just getting frustrated with myself.' I think the friendliness aspect of it, the understanding that you're thinking those things and that's okay, and finding ways to bring it back, is good."

Damn, I was thinking, *I've been meditating for eight years, and this guy, who's been meditating for, like, eight minutes, has already keyed in on the whole friendliness thing.*

Jeff added another important point about giving yourself a break during meditation. "When you get frustrated like that, which is a normal response, what you're basically training your subconscious to say is that, 'Oh wow, this guy's frustrated now. Best not to even notice at all when your mind has wandered.' It actually makes you wander more often." This was the point I had ignored, to my detriment. The most important thing to do when you notice your mind wander is to feel satisfaction that you noticed it in the first place. It is basic behavioral science. If you make waking up from distraction rewarding, you train the mind to do it more often.

"I would imagine this takes practice, right?" asked Josh.

"Absolutely," Jeff assured him.

"It's okay that it takes practice," said Josh.

"That *is* the practice," replied Jeff.

It was hard to call this anything other than a huge win. We had just witnessed Josh Groban grasp meditation in one quick conversation. I was filled with relief and gratitude.

"You're my anxious, half-Jewish brother!" I exclaimed.

"Let's get a drink!" he said.

It was all going so well. Except, as we were saying our goodbyes, Jeff did one of those namaste bows that drive me nuts. "I think of it as coming to center," he said, leaning forward, his hands in prayer position. "When I'm doing this, I imagine I'm gathering in everything, and there's a still point in the center, and I bow to the still point."

Oy, Jeffrey.

I came home from our interview with Josh and found that Bianca had laid out a picnic sushi feast on our living room floor. The kid was in bed. My wife and I sat, chatted, and watched TV before my long journey, which would begin in earnest the next morning.

It had been a good day. Not even Robert Johnson could deny that. We had found many effective rebuttals for the "I can't do this" fear: the impossibility of perfection, the simplicity of just beginning again, the power of friendliness (even if I myself still failed to fully comprehend it).

Tomorrow, though, we would board our bus, hit the road, and confront the thorniest obstacle to meditation of them all: time.

3

"I Don't Have Time for This"

The next morning, I was in the bathroom, scrolling through my emails, enjoying what I thought might be my last visit for a while to a non-rest-stop throne, when my phone rang. The caller ID said "Elvis Duran."

"Morning," I said, somewhat formally, not knowing who exactly was going to be on the other end of the line.

"You're on the radio. We're talking about you." It was Elvis himself, the host of the number one Top 40 morning radio show in America, his unmistakable deep voice resonating through the speaker on my phone and simultaneously out to millions of listeners—all as I sat there helplessly indisposed.

Shit.

I mean, not literally, but . . . *shit*.

I'd first met Elvis three years earlier, shortly after my first book came out. One day my Twitter feed was suddenly clogged with people telling me that someone named Elvis Duran had talked about *10% Happier* on his radio show. I noticed my sales rank on Amazon—which (and I'm not proud of this) I had gotten in the habit of checking compulsively—go through the roof. I told Bianca about this, mentioning that I had never heard of the guy, and she looked at me like I was crazy. "Are you kidding?" she said. "I love Elvis Duran. I've been listening to him since I was a kid."

A few weeks later, I went on his show. It was one of the only interviews I have ever done where Bianca insisted on joining. I was immediately impressed by Elvis. He was a stocky fifty-something with salt-and-pepper hair—and very clearly not your usual morning shock jock. He is openly gay, and the two most prominent figures in his large crew of on-air personalities are women. The team members are nice to one another, as well as to the guests. And they do all this while still managing to be very, very funny.

I was so taken with Elvis that I decided to do a *Nightline* profile on him, during which I came to like him even more. I learned that while professionally he rubs elbows with people like Taylor Swift and Justin Bieber, he is more comfortable hanging out at home on the couch with his longtime boyfriend, Alex, a zookeeper from Staten Island. In part it's because he's shy. "I'm not a glamorous person at all," he told me. "I just don't fit in." But it was also because, at the time, he was deeply insecure about his weight. In fact, during our interview, he revealed that he planned to have a kind of bariatric procedure known as the gastric sleeve, where they take out 85 percent of your stomach. "I haven't seen my penis," he said, peering down over his paunch, laughing. "Can you see my penis and describe it to me?"

As surprised as I was by the early morning, in-the-bathroom phone call, I was also—pun not intended—relieved. I had been worrying about something related to Elvis.

A few weeks earlier, I had asked his team whether it would be okay if my crew came to his TriBeCa studio to shoot behind the scenes on day two of our meditation tour, because I thought that, like *GMA,* it would be a chaotic, counterintuitive environment in which to talk about the practice. However, I did not want Elvis to feel obliged to put me on the air.

And yet here I was, on the air. "Why can't you be interviewed?" asked Elvis. "What's your deal? When are you coming in?"

Say no more. Now I was all in. "Put me on the radio," I said. "I'll talk as much as you want!"

I showered and grabbed the new winter coat my wife had bought me for the trip. Bianca and Alexander came out of the bedroom to send me off. A kiss for Bianca, a groggy snuggle with Alexander, and then I hopped in a cab and headed downtown.

I got off the elevator at Elvis's studio and walked into the spacious reception area. The 10% Happier team—including Jeff, Ben Rubin, the CEO of the 10% Happier app, and the camera crew—was already assembled on the other side of the room. As I began heading in their direction, though, someone grabbed me by the sleeve and pulled me right into the studio. I was whisked to a seat with a microphone and handed a headset. "Dan Harris from ABC News," intoned Elvis, "why are you here on our show?"

"Because you guys are out of your minds," I said, still a little dazed, but trying to be at least somewhat witty. "Every morning I listen to the show, it's a cry for help."

Elvis was barely recognizable after his surgery. He'd always been a handsome fellow, but now, at nearly half his old weight, he looked transformed. He was seated, wearing a black hoodie, at his normal perch in the center of a large U-shaped table, a metallic arm dangling a golden mic in front of his face. He was surrounded by three male producers, who were constantly handing him notes—prompts for jokes, information about callers, texts and tweets from some of the seven million listeners who were reacting to the show in real time. In front of him, seated at a rectangular table, were his two female co-hosts.

Elvis steered the conversation to meditation, mentioning that he had recently resumed his practice, which he often did in the early morning before work with his dog, Max, in his lap.

"I'm finding in my life that I am seeing a change," he said. "I used to get mad and throw chairs."

"You've actually thrown chairs?" I asked, genuinely surprised.

"I used to break chairs," he assured me.

It's easy to forget that, despite his relaxed on-air persona, Elvis runs a complex operation: a show syndicated in eighty markets, with a large staff consisting of lively personalities. Now that he was meditating again, he said, "I do stop and think things through a little more. I am more mindful about people around me and what they're saying. I try to be fair, and I try to be the peacekeeper when I can.

"I'm still moody," he allowed. "I'm still an awful bitch."

After some more chatter, he opened up for callers. This would be our first chance on the road trip to hear from the masses. The very first question was both extremely important and entirely unsurprising.

"Does it need to be a ten-minute session, a fifteen-minute session?" asked Brian, a high school health teacher. "How long does it take?"

This is almost always the first question I get when I speak to people about meditation. Once they grasp the benefits of the practice and realize that it doesn't require clearing the mind, the next big problem is: *How the hell do I fit this into my schedule?*

When it comes to finding time to meditate, I have good news—and even better news. The good news is that meditation does not need to take up much of your time. "I think it's great to start with five to ten minutes a day," I told Brian. The general consensus among teachers and scientists seems to be that if you do five to ten minutes every day, you should be able to derive many of the benefits.

And here's the better news: if five minutes seem like too much for you, one minute also counts. In fact, not only does one minute count, it can be extremely powerful. Getting "on the cushion," to use a meditative term of art, is the hardest part of the habit formation process, and the proposition of a single minute is uniquely unintimidating and scalable. So if the easiest way for you to establish a daily habit is to start with one minute, then go for it. My view—and that of my team—is that, especially at the beginning, consistency is more important than duration.

"The goal is to engineer a daily collision with the a-hole in your head," I explained to Brian. "And then when that a-hole gives you bad ideas, you're better able to resist him."

This one-minute-counts tack is a new one for me. For years I had been somewhat stridently recommending that people start with five to ten minutes a day. My usual argument was: *I don't care if you have seventeen jobs and twenty-five kids, you've got five to ten minutes a day. How much time do you spend watching TV? Checking social media? Is it more than five minutes? Well, then, you definitely have time to meditate.* I loved to quote the Harvard physician Dr. Sanjiv Chopra: "Everyone should meditate once a day. And if you don't have time to meditate, then you should do it twice a day."

I have come to see, however, that this approach is a bit out of touch. To be clear, I really do believe—and Jeff is with me on this—that five to ten minutes a day of meditation is a reasonable and achievable goal. The fact is, the more you do, the more you'll get out of it. (Within reason, of course; no one's arguing you should do it twelve hours a day. Unless you want to go really big and attend a meditation retreat.) Even though I maintain that it's mathematically hard to defend the notion that you don't have the time, I've had to acknowledge that in our overtaxed, overscheduled, overstimulated era, the *perception* of time starvation is very real. I've also learned, through my work with the app company, how difficult the process of establishing a new habit can be.

What follows are nine super-practical pro tips, grounded in scientific research around habit formation as well as the messy reality of daily life. You don't have to do all of these, of course. Just try the ones that seem promising to you. The most important thing to know about behavior change is that there are no silver bullets. The best way to approach it is with a spirit of experimentation. Try things out and then be willing to fail and get back on the horse.

PRO TIP: *Grit Won't Do the Trick—You Need Rewards*

One thing we know from the science is that willpower alone will not get you over the hump. Willpower is an unreliable inner resource that tends to evaporate quickly, especially when you get hungry, angry, lonely, or tired (four classic discipline-killing conditions, often combined in the acronym HALT). A better strategy is to tap into the benefits. Humans are motivated by rewards. Best to co-opt the pleasure centers of the brain if you want to create a sustainable habit.

This became abundantly clear when Jeff and I pulled aside Bethany Watson, one of Elvis's co-hosts, for an interview. We set up our cameras to chat with Bethany, a thirtysomething aspiring actress, in a corner of the reception area outside the studio. I had always been struck by how intelligent, open, and likable Bethany is. As I learned in our chat, though, beneath her easy laugh and fashionable exterior lurks something darker. "I have an anxiety disorder," she told us. "I'm constantly anxious."

Her baseline anxiety, she said, is only exacerbated by her job, which is thrilling but stressful. "You're on all the time," she said. There can be no radio silence; you always need to have something clever to add to the conversation; and everyone's worried about whether the boss is in a bad mood. It was a little like being on *GMA,* only more hectic. No teleprompter, no net.

And then there are all those text messages from listeners, which can get nasty. "At every moment, you have constant judgments on your person, basically?" asked Jeff.

"Yeah," said Bethany.

"It's not just the voice in your own head—" I began.

"It's the voice in everyone else's head," said Jeff, jumping in. We were already completing each other's sentences. "That's . . . intense. It's like being inside a single neurotic brain."

"Yeah, it is," Bethany said.

But when we asked her why she doesn't meditate, she threw the "time" card. "It's just that I am so busy every single day," she said, pointing out that she did the Elvis show for four hours a morning and then went straight into a full day of acting classes. "So then when you come home and you're exhausted, where do you find the time to sit for even five minutes?"

When we pressed her, though, she made an interesting admission: "I think the real reason I'm not doing it is because I haven't fully committed to making it a priority." This is not uncommon. Sometimes when people say they don't have time to meditate, they're actually pointing to a whole panoply of unspoken reservations, some of them quite profound.

This is where reward comes in.

Initially, Jeff tried to sell the reward thusly: "Ultimately, meditation's about enjoying your beingness." To which Bethany nodded politely and uncomprehendingly. Her expression kind of reminded me of when my son tries to share his toys with our cats, or that time when I jokingly offered Bianca a tramp stamp for her fortieth birthday.

Soon enough, however, we got to an extremely clear and compelling potential benefit for Bethany, one that was staring her directly in the face: relief from anxiety. She simply needed to make a more solid connection between meditation and said relief. For example, she knew—and her therapist agreed—that when she exercised, her anxiety was mitigated. "We notice a change in my anxiety levels when I haven't worked out for a while, so I have to make that time." That's what it would have to be with meditation, she acknowledged.

Bingo. I knew there was a decent probability this could work for Bethany, because it had worked for me. Fending off anxiety and depression has been a huge part of what drives me to keep both exercising and meditating. When I am covering a breaking news story and don't have as much time to meditate, I notice that the voice in my head gets louder, more obnoxious, and harder to ignore. "That's my motivator," I told Bethany.

However, humans often need more superficial motivators to help us overcome inertia and indiscipline. Bethany led us in a brainstorming session on features we could build into the app that might help people get started.

"If there was some sort of present at the end," she mused—specifically, she was thinking of a discount card to Nordstrom. "It might have to be that shallow initially."

"No, that's great," I said. "I would do it for cookies, for example."

"Or maybe there's some negative incentive," said Jeff. "Twenty dollars would be taken out of your bank account and given to your worst enemy if you don't do it. Punishment systems."

I could see Ben, my hard-nosed, financially prudent young

CEO, squirming nervously a few feet out of camera range as we tossed out these deeply impractical ideas.

More seriously, Bethany offered: "I need a visual representation of how far I've come." Like a progress line that shows up on your phone, she said—or starbursts that fill your screen if you complete a certain amount of days. This seemed to calm Ben down.

After we wrapped the interview, Bethany headed off to the bathroom. Minutes later she came rushing back to us with the coup de grâce.

"Okay, I have an idea," she said. "What if there was a kitten that I had to keep alive by meditating every day?"

"On the app?" I asked.

"On the app. Like, a little kitten, and every time you meditated, he got a little stronger, and then if you didn't meditate, he withered. That would keep me meditating. The cartoon little paws."

"The adorable big eyes," I added.

"I want a white one with two different-colored eyes."

I turned to Ben, who was now doing full-body contortions. "Do we have the technology to build that, Ben?"

"Too much right now," he said, chuckling and holding his hand up as if to physically repel the idea. "We'll look at it."

"If this happens, we'll be giving you stock in the company," I assured Bethany as she walked back into the studio.

"Namaste," she said, pressing her hands together and giving a bow. The kind I like, with irony.

PRO TIP: *Think Strategically About Your Schedule*

Next up at Elvis's studio, we sat down with Danielle Monaro, a married mother of two with a chewy Bronx accent, tart attitude, and infectious giggle.

Wearing blue jeans and a black sweatshirt emblazoned with the word "LOVE," she told us that, when it came to meditation, she was also simply too busy. "I'm in mommy mode, you know. I don't have time to breathe half the time. You want me to sit down and meditate?"

That wasn't to say she couldn't use it, she conceded. "I feel like I have a lot of anxiety, where I worry about stupid stuff that doesn't matter. I'll honestly be laying there in the bed, and I'll go, 'Gosh, that fan sounds really, really loud. I hope it doesn't fly off the ceiling.'" Not everything that causes Danielle to wring her hands is irrational, of course. "Being a parent, you constantly worry," she said.

I get it. As a parent myself, I understand the sort of nameless unreasoning that can overtake you when, say, your kid is five minutes late coming home, or when you find a swollen lymph node. As Danielle told us, what causes the most anxiety is the stuff you "have no control over."

Jeff assured her that letting go of things you cannot control is one of the biggest benefits of the practice. "You get more laissez-faire. You become more like an old lady, a wise old lady."

"Elvis doesn't want us to be old ladies," Danielle said as we all started laughing. "I could be old on the inside."

"Inside, yeah," said Jeff. "Cool grandma."

"Okay, that's cool. I'll be the cool grandma."

But how to get her to actually do it? Our approach with Danielle—and this is something we recommend to anyone who's struggling with the time issue—was to ask her to step back and take a look at her overall schedule. There were almost certainly points in the day where she could spare a few minutes, and where meditation would slot in nicely.

"I was just thinking as I listened to your schedule," I said to Danielle, "that the best time might be right before you go to bed." She agreed. Jeff promised to make her a short bespoke meditation that could be used anytime she had a free moment, including the moment before bed.

"I hope it works," she said, "because that stupid ceiling fan is driving me nuts."

As you think about your own schedule, bear in mind that some people find that having a set time every day—right before bed, first thing in the morning, just after a workout—really helps establish a habit. Scientists who study habit formation talk about "cue, routine, reward." You can experiment with constructing a cue-routine-reward loop that gets you to meditate. For example, "After I park my car [cue], I will meditate for five minutes [routine], and I'll feel a little calmer and more mindful [reward]." Repeat this loop to ingrain the habit. You can even put it in your calendar, which some people find is a great way to cement the whole thing. That said, if, like me, you have an unpredictable schedule, it is absolutely fine to simply fit it in whenever and wherever you can.

PRO TIP: *Give Yourself Permission to Fail*

It is impossible to overstate the importance of giving yourself the freedom to experiment, fail, and try again. Remember that we are wired to fail. Evolution has bequeathed us a brain that optimizes for survival and reproduction, not long-term health planning. If you get all overheated about whatever tactic you choose first and put too much pressure on yourself to make it work, you will deplete your resiliency. It's helpful to approach habit formation with the same attitude we hope to employ during meditation: every time you get lost, just begin again.

Before we left, Elvis brought Jeff and me back on the air for a quick goodbye.

"By the way," Elvis said, "people were wondering, is this an infomercial? We've given you a lot of free plugs here. I think some cash under the table is perfect."

When we emerged from the building, I saw it for the first time. It was huge and orange, and it would be our home for the next week and a half: our bus.

"This is ridiculous," I said. "I love it."

It had huge signs on each side that read "The 10% Happier Meditation Tour." On the back, a smaller sign said, "We may never arrive!" Passersby were taking pictures.

I climbed aboard and beheld the interior. There were five main compartments. First, the driver's area, occupied by Eddie Norton, a shy, mountainous man who took his job very seriously, which I found reassuring. After Eddie's lair, a living space with ample seating and a tricked-out satellite TV and stereo system. Next there was a mini kitchen and full bathroom. Then came the bunks, twelve of them, arranged in two rows of three on each side of the bus. They looked a little coffin-like, but I briefly lay down in the top bunk that had been assigned to me, and it was surprisingly comfy. (Not that I would have wanted to see it under a black light.) At the far rear, there was another sitting area, which the legendary George Clinton had apparently used as a bedroom suite when on the road with Parliament Funkadelic. No coffin-beds for George.

As I looked around at the preposterous bus and at all of my smiling traveling companions, I was starting to feel a little giddy. Jeff wisely brought us all down to earth with a reminder of the stakes. "Last night, doing that podcast with Josh Groban, and suddenly realizing that a hundred thousand people might be actually finding their way to a practice that might help them, that was a hugely moving experience."

I have met very few people who get more of a high out of service than Jeff. He learned this in part from his parents, who have dedicated much of their spare time to local charities. But it's also just in his character. Some professed altruists annoy me because I cynically suspect they don't actually mean it. In Jeff's case, though, it was clear to me that being useful was like oxygen—especially when it came to engaging one-on-one with meditation students. As he likes to say, "There are no existential crises in those moments."

Back on the bus, I added, "This is fun and goofy, and I love it. I'm obviously P. T. Barnum–esque. But what we're doing matters. If you could actually boost people's level of sanity by ten percent, that's a massive value-add."

Fittingly perhaps, our next stop was a place where I had once been utterly insane—at least, according to my mother.

Several hours after leaving New York City, the bus rolled into suburban Boston and pulled up at Newton South High School, my alma mater, where I could easily have been voted Least Likely to Do Anything Mindful, Ever. Here we were twenty-six years later, and hundreds of people had shown up to listen to me and Jeff speak about meditation.

Before the talk, Jeff and I chatted with my parents backstage. They were both in their early seventies but still deeply engaged in their medical careers.

"Did you guys see the plaque that they put up for my academic excellence here?" I asked them.

"No. Are you kidding me?" asked my mother incredulously.

I was definitely kidding. Suffice it to say I had been neither athlete nor mathlete.

"You were getting D's in math," my mother reminded me.

My dad chimed in, clearly enjoying exposing my miscreant past in front of Jeff and all the cameras. "The irony was, years later, he asked us why didn't we make him study more!"

Now they were really working themselves up into a lather. "One day he said to me, 'Why didn't you guys make me work harder in high school?'" related my mother, grabbing her head in mock exasperation, as everyone laughed. "We were trying to keep you out of jail!"

She was only partly exaggerating. During my high school years, I was a prodigious pot smoker and dedicated class cutter. I also had a robust career spray-painting graffiti onto the walls that lined the local subway tracks.

My mom says she endured a years-long stretch during which she never once saw me smile. "You were so angry," she said.

Too bad she didn't have a meditation practice back when she clearly could have used it. She does have one now, though—because her son, the former delinquent, introduced her to it. She does fifteen minutes a day, often with her cat, Harry, by her side. She told us it gives her "the ability to step back and see what's going on instead of just reacting to it. I always had a pretty short fuse."

I don't recall her having a short fuse. What I remember most is her making elaborate, DIY Halloween costumes for my brother and me, and also insisting that we not watch TV. (For which I believe I have exacted ample revenge by way of my current career.) True, my mother has an intimidating, suffer-no-fools intelligence, but she is by no means as prone to anger as her father, Robert Johnson.

"I'm not as bad as he was," she said, "but I have a tendency to take things personally, worry about what other people are thinking, worry and worry and worry about if I'm doing well enough, if I'm working hard enough, how far behind I am. The usual obsessive, type-A personality stuff."

While my mother had found the practice useful, my father was not meditating.

"He says he doesn't need to," said my mom, chuckling. "He's got perfect equanimity."

"I find napping is an equivalent," said my dad impishly.

Jeff and I took the stage in the auditorium, which was set with an oriental rug and a pair of large potted plants. It looked like an episode of *Between Two Ferns*. In the audience, I spotted a few of my high school classmates, buddies from a group of friends my parents had facetiously referred to as the "Brain Trust." They, too, had managed to stay out of jail.

I held forth for a while about the benefits of mindfulness. Jeff led us in a brief meditation. Then we opened the floor up for questions. Very quickly we got to the issue of time. A sharp young professional named Chris approached the mic, admitting that he was mildly nervous about doing so.

"I hope I don't have a panic attack right now," said Chris.

"You haven't been doing any cocaine, have you?" I asked.

No, he assured me. And then: "I'd like to ask you about time management," he said. He had started meditating as an undergrad and had been sitting five times a week for about twenty minutes. Now, though, he was working at a competitive financial firm and finding that he was only sitting twice a week. How could he find more time to do it?

PRO TIP: *One Minute Counts*

"You should start thinking about short meditations," I told Chris. "I think one minute counts."

As discussed, if you only have the time or the motivation for a sixty-second sit, you should chalk it up as a win. One of the trickiest parts of habit formation is getting the new behavior anchored into your life. Once that is done, you can tinker with the amount of time you sit.

What's more, after one minute of meditation, people often think to themselves: *I'm already here; might as well keep going a bit.* As the meditation teacher Cory Muscara argues, this is a key moment, because you're moving from "extrinsic" motivation (that is, meditating because you feel like you have to) to the much more powerful "intrinsic" motivation (that is, meditating because you want to). The second you opt in for more meditation, you're doing it out of actual interest, which makes it much more likely to have a lasting effect.

So if you're struggling to find time to meditate, look for opportunities for this kind of quickie. After you brush your teeth, after your morning coffee, after you park your car at work, after you sit down on the train, after you put your head down on the pillow . . . You get the picture.

As Jeff argues, one minute counts because it only takes one *second* to disembed from a difficult emotion or thought pattern. Here he is with a one-minute meditation you can use anywhere, anytime.

This is a busy person's meditation. Ten breaths. That's it. A modest one-minute reset intended to take some of the wind out of the sails of whatever story line you've been racing around in. The idea is simple: wherever you are, in any situation or mental state, count ten long, slow breaths.

So the thing my mom told me to do when I was a tantruming kid is actually a meditation?

The only difference is we're adding some adult curiosity about the process, in particular the process of shifting our attention from our mental preoccupations to our breath. We're going to see if we can deliberately let our stories fade out—like the story, say, that some of us tell about not having time to meditate, or the more general "I'm so busy" freneticism inside which a great many of us live. We'll try to let the thoughts fade even as the feeling of the breath gets richer and more real.

TEN GOOD BREATHS

1 minute or longer

Start by stopping, wherever you are: lying in your bedroom, parked in your car, standing in an elevator. Try it with your eyes open, but keep your gaze soft (it's the perfect stealth meditation). In this meditation, we're intentionally controlling the first few breaths, breathing more deeply than normal, exaggerating the airflow to help us feel it more.

Big inhale: "One." Counting breaths helps us pay attention. Make the out-breath nice and long. See if you can let it be a release, your whole body softening as the diaphragm relaxes. For the next few in-breaths, experiment with holding in the air for a moment. As you breathe out, imagine you are breathing out whatever worry or concern may have been spinning around in your head. After three or four breaths like this, move into breathing normally.

As you count each breath, get interested in how fully you can feel the sensation of breathing, its softness and rhythm. Really try to get into it as you stand there in the elevator staring into space, grooving on your breath. Notice how you're able to shift the ratio of your attention, so that your thoughts get less loud and insistent as your breath gets more pronounced. Notice how as we focus in, the visual world kind of washes out. Keep counting—you can make it to ten. If you get distracted and forget where you were, start over from where you got lost, always with a sense of humor. How patient can you be with each breath? No rush, breathing like you have all the time in the world. See if you can enjoy the simplicity of the activity as everything else fades into the background.

When you get to ten, notice any feelings of settledness and calm that may be there. Tune back in to your surroundings. Welcome back. You can come here anytime.

Now: leave the elevator.

CHEAT SHEET

1. Stop, wherever you are. Bring your attention to breathing. Count "one" as you inhale. Imagine breathing out any tension as you exhale. Count "two" on the next inhale.

2. See if you can make it to ten without losing your focus. Explore how fully you can feel each breath, letting the world around you fade out a bit.

3. If you get distracted and forget where you are, start over from where you got lost, always with a sense of humor about your tragic gnat-like attention span.

PRO TIP: *Free-Range Meditations*

The other piece of advice we gave to Chris, the young businessman who spoke up at the Newton South event, was that if you can't find time to do formal meditation, you can co-opt your everyday life activities—walking between meetings, brushing your teeth, doing dishes—and turn them into mini meditations.

Jeff has some advice about how to transform your daily activities into what I like to call "free-range meditation."

So the classic meditation visual is eyes closed, legs crossed, ass planted on a cushion or chair in a quiet room. And that's fine. The cushion is the lab. Or, if you prefer, the gym. It's where you train and experiment in a relatively simple and distraction-free environment. But most people don't pump iron in the gym so they can feel good pumping iron in the gym. The idea is to bring your healthy body into your *life*. Well, the same is true of meditation and the mind. For this reason, some teachers and traditions deliberately emphasize meditation techniques meant to be practiced in the world.

That's what this little section is about. And the good news is, you can pretty much meditate on anything: sounds, sights, tastes, touches, feelings—any sensation. That's because it's less about the meditation "object" and more about the qualities of attention—like, for example, concentration and equanimity—that you bring *to* that object. These qualities are like muscle groups of the mind. They can be *trained*.

The training of specific mental qualities is an important idea, one we'll continue to develop as we proceed through the book. We've actually already spoken quite a bit about the training of concentration. The following meditations tap the same concentration muscle, but they also emphasize the curiosity muscle, which ultimately leads to more clarity about what's going on in our experience. Clarity is like dialing up the resolution knob on an old-fashioned TV set. Here are some simple examples.

FREE-RANGE MEDITATIONS

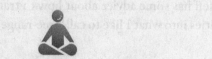

WALKING THROUGH SOUND
10 seconds or longer

We have a full walking meditation in Chapter 8, which focuses on the physicality of walking. This is a meditation that focuses on the auditory aspect of walking. I do it all the time, because apparently I'm a weirdo. The next time you're walking anywhere—inside or out—notice sounds. Part of your attention, of course, is on making sure you don't get run over by a bike courier, but part of it is on the full ambient soundscape: the rise and fall of voices, the distant hum of traffic, the summertime buzz of cicadas. You are deliberately shifting attention away from the inner world of thoughts and feelings to the outer world of sound. Try not to get too caught up in identifying what's making the sounds. You don't need to know *what* you are hearing, only that you are hearing. How weird! Hearing is happening. You are living in ear-world. Round sounds, sharp sounds, crisp sounds: *warblewarble-WHOOTwarbleHOOONKwarblehssss*. Explore how long you can keep your attention on the odd balloon of sound that moves and shifts and undulates along with you. When you get distracted by sights, sensations, or thoughts, notice this. And then notice what it's like to notice this: *electric awareness wake up snap!* "I am mindful," you might say in a droid-like voice, perhaps moving stiffly like C-3PO, to the joy of passing children. Then start again.

SHOWER

10 seconds or longer

Shift your attention to the sensation of the warm water flowing over your body. Can you experience the water as a massage? Zoom in on the little pressure changes, on the individual streams against your skin. Stay with exactly what's happening; try not to get lost in a daydream. Now, this is already a good enough meditation—quite lush and sensual, to say nothing of wet. But I like to add an extra something to test my openness. I'll start by noticing the receptivity of my body to the warm water—pores open, body relaxed. And then I'll switch the water to cold, and see if I can maintain the same open attitude. Not bracing or rigid, but letting the cold flow into and through me. As with cold water, so with life. How long can you keep your composure?

Okay, I need to pop in and comment here that this is a seriously strange and masochistic meditation.

It's equanimity training. Helpful for managing discomfort of all kinds. Zen monks do it under ice-cold waterfalls while a single Japanese flute plays in the distance.

TOOTH-BRUSHING
10 seconds or longer

Who the heck pays attention to brushing their teeth? Normally we're on automatic pilot as we do this, grinding down our gums as we mentally rehearse our day. In this sense, tooth brushing is terra incognita. See if you can slow the whole activity right down: squeezing the toothpaste, first contact, the rhythmic flexion of the bristles on your teeth. How much detail can you feel? How *into it* can you get? Can you brush your teeth like Jimi Hendrix played guitar: eyes closed, hips flung forward, blotter of acid under your terry-cloth headband?

A BUNCH MORE

Meditation is basically the end of boredom. Standing in line at the ATM? Meditate on the feeling of your feet on the ground. Sitting on a bus? Soften your gaze and meditate on the flowing movement of color and form. Bored out of your mind at a dinner party? Meditate on the sound of clinking silverware or the taste of the food—chewing slowly, eyes closed, in a way that is guaranteed to disturb the other guests. Having sex? Meditate on the feeling of stunned gratitude and incredulity.

The possibilities are endless. As you go about your day, look for opportunities to shift the ratio of your attention from thinking and planning to hearing and seeing and touching. If you get distracted, get curious about the experience of *realizing* you've been distracted. This mini realization is a literal rehearsal for bigger realizations that can happen down the line in meditation. Wakeups are all the same; only the size of them is different. And like I've said, it is so important to take a moment to feel satisfaction when you wake up. With mindfulness we are training our ability to choose how we want to pay attention. Each wake-up is a new moment of choice. Many teachers argue it is the only place real choice ever happens.

Last thing: while free-range meditation can be fun and useful—the whole point of having a meditation practice, after all, is to have mindfulness metastasize throughout your whole life—it's easier to make mindfulness-in-daily-life exercises work if you have a base of formal, seated practice, in which you are doing nothing but training your capacity to stay present to what's happening.

PRO TIP: *Adopt an Attitude of "Daily-ish"*

A woman in the balcony at the Newton South event chimed in with a concept I'd never heard before. She said her meditation teacher told students that they should aim to be meditating "daily-ish."

"We might have to steal that," I said. I always worry that if you're overly rigid about dailiness, it can backfire. It sets up a situation where, if you miss a day or two, the voice in your head—that slippery little storyteller—can weasel in and whisper, "You're a failed meditator." Then boom: you're done.

"Daily-ish actually has enough elasticity, I think, to lead to an abiding habit," I said to my new friend in the cheap seats. "Thank you, appreciate it."

Elasticity is a key concept from behavior change research. Scientists call it "psychological flexibility." A related example that Jeff uses, when it comes to his diet, is the "80/20 rule": 80 percent of the time he eats healthy food, and the rest of the time he eats whatever he wants. This way, he rarely feels deprived. It's like a steam-release valve. I liked this concept so much I instituted my own version: the 60/40 rule.

PRO TIP: *The Accordion Principle*

Another way to inject a dose of elasticity into your practice is something I call the "Accordion Principle." It's a combo of "One Minute Counts" and "Adopt an Attitude of 'Daily-ish.'"

If your goal is to do five to ten minutes a day of meditation, one way to give yourself a break on really busy days is to do just one minute. It's another hack that allows you to keep your foot in the game and prevent the turkey in your head from offering up pseudo-wisdom along the lines of "You fell off the wagon, you're a hopeless case. Give up now before you embarrass yourself further."

PRO TIP: *Make Yourself Accountable to Other People*

Behavior change scientists tell us that while some people will not institute a healthy habit on their own, they will do it when other people are holding them accountable.

One way to create that kind of accountability is to join a

community of some sort. This is a huge emphasis for Jeff, who helped start a meditation group in Toronto. As he told the crowd at Newton South, "It can be as simple as this: just get a few of your friends together and start."

Another option is to join a regular sitting group at your local meditation center, assuming you have one in your area. "It's like going to yoga or the gym," said Jeff. "Now you're there; you gotta do it."

Joining a community confers benefits that go well beyond accountability. In my experience, hanging out with other meditators sets up a kind of HOV-lane effect. Being around people who take the meditative principles seriously and are endeavoring to apply these concepts in their own lives can create positive peer pressure. Or, as Jeff says, "it sort of normalizes the whole weird thing."

Speaking personally, while I always enjoy sitting in groups, my unpredictable schedule makes it hard to create a reliable accountability structure. What's more, I've never been much of a joiner. However, I have found that it's enormously valuable to have friends who are interested in meditation. These friendships can run deeper, in part because regular meditators—people who make it a practice to step out of their automatic routines and who are no longer operating from behind such a thick filter of egoic thoughts—have more room to connect with others.

There's a great story about the Buddha's right-hand man, Ananda. One day Ananda was hanging out with some friends, talking about practice. Invigorated, he returned to the Buddha and declared that having friends like these was "half the holy life." The Buddha quickly corrected him, saying, "It's the whole of the holy life." (For the record, I don't think these guys were using "holy" in a metaphysical sense. You could probably just replace it with the word "good.")

Finally, if, like me, you are not a joiner, there is another powerful way to establish accountability: create a relationship with a meditation teacher. Personally, I am lucky enough to have a long-standing relationship with an extraordinary teacher named Joseph Goldstein, who knows my mind well and has managed to keep me on track, even though I'm an attentionally challenged hedonist with trouble sitting still. If you want to find a teacher, I recommend you sample a class at your local meditation center and see if it's a good fit. You can also check online for a teacher who is willing to connect via video chat.

My favorite moment of our visit to Newton came about midway through the event when a woman named Carla, a mom with moxie, came to the mic and let me have it.

Carla was aware of a fact that I have not yet revealed to you, gentle reader, for fear that you might conclude that I am—how shall I say this?—fucking bonkers: I meditate for two hours a day.

Allow me to explain. I made the decision to dramatically increase my daily dosage of sitting after having meditated for several years, and after having written a whole book about it. I did it primarily because I'd had the privilege of hanging around with many people who are long-term, dedicated meditators and seeing how cool and seemingly happy many of them are. This made me deeply interested—both personally and journalistically—in what lies beyond 10% Happier. (In case you're curious, Jeff does about thirty-five minutes of formal sitting practice on most days, but it's worth noting that he's been at this significantly longer than I have, has spent way more time on retreat, and is, frankly, a bit maniacal about peppering his days with all kinds of mindfulness-in-action practices.)

Carla, who'd heard me discuss my two-hour-a-day habit on my podcast, simply could not fathom how, as a fellow parent and busy professional, I managed to squeeze in this volume of meditation every day.

"The biggest obstacle for me," she said, "is I have two young kids and they have this, like, radar. I crawl out of bed so quietly in the morning. I just shuffle one foot over to my cushion. And they sense it—and they're there!" She had a great comic delivery, and the crowd was laughing along.

Then she turned on me. "I think a lot about your wife. I've never met her, but I've heard you talk about how long you meditate each day, and I'm like, 'Wow, she puts up with that?'" Now she really had the crowd. Jeff was beaming with glee and bowing in Carla's direction.

"My husband, I love him," she continued, "but as much as I want him to be enlightened, I want him to unload the dishwasher! If he's like, 'I'm going to meditate for an hour,' I'd be like, 'No, you're really not!'"

Her question was simple: how do I pull this off, and what advice did I have for parents?

I let the laughter subside, and then cracked wise. "One thing immediately that I think would be an easy fix is: have you thought about giving your kids up for adoption?" I will always take the low-hanging joke.

Then I actually answered her question. First I said, "I have a very understanding wife." I won't lie: my decision to go to two hours a day definitely created some tension initially, in part because I made the supremely unwise decision to unilaterally institute my new policy while we had a six-month-old around the house. But by the time of the Newton South event, I'd been doing my two-hour-a-day thing for about eighteen months, and Bianca and I had figured out a system that mostly worked.

As I told Carla, "We talk about it. I often say, 'How can we do this so it's not coming out of your bank account?'" Meaning: how could I do this without making it so that Bianca was constantly left to fend for herself with the child?

I pulled it off largely by being strategic about my daily schedule, as per the pro tip "Think Strategically About Your Schedule." I allow myself to sit whenever I can, wherever I can, and in as many intervals as I want. In some ways, my chaotic schedule has been helpful. I work *GMA* on the weekends and *Nightline* several nights during the week. Plus I travel a ton. So this means I can sneak in quick meditations early in the morning or late at night. I also sit while I'm on airplanes, in the backseat of taxis, or even in my office. When I'm home, I try never to meditate if my son is awake, so I fit it in during the day when he's not around. If, by the end of the day, I have not gotten to two hours, I forgo a few minutes of sleep, or make it up the next day. I admit that it's all a bit nutty, but I seem to be muddling through.

I realize, of course, that not every parent has this option. Which is why I told Carla, "You're at a point right now where you need to write yourself a permission slip that says, 'Okay, I'm not going to get a ton of meditation done right now.' But can you find those little spots?"

A man in the audience weighed in with a tip he'd picked up from his wife. "She meditates in her car, in the parking garage, at work," he said. Her mistake, though: "She finally shared that with her senior management team and now they know where to find her."

Back to my two-hours-a-day thing: There is no question in my mind that it has deepened my practice and improved my life. Sustained sitting time has allowed me to see my inner patterns with finer resolution, helping me better understand my own mind, and giving me increased empathy for how crazy we all are. I also—and this is going to sound a bit Jeff-y—feel that peering inward with greater frequency has enabled me to bump up against fundamental truths (everything is impermanent, and therefore clinging is a recipe for suffering) and universal mysteries (who the hell is the "I," the "Dan," who is observing it all?). Despite the fact that going to two hours created some initial domestic turbulence, Bianca says it has been really good for our relationship. My resting post-meditation face is more open and approachable, I take more of an interest in her day, and I exhibit more patience with the cacophony of parenting. The only potential downside, as she has joked, is that I meditate so much that she feels she doesn't have to.

I don't want to sugarcoat it, though: finding the time can be a serious pain. Which is why my daily megadose is not for everyone. And remember, I started with just five minutes a day.

PRO TIP: *Novel Idea: Try Enjoying Meditation*

There was an even more deeply humbling moment toward the end of the night, when Jeff pointed out that, for all the tips and tricks we were throwing out to get people to meditate, we'd been missing a big one. "How many people here meditate because they enjoy it?" he asked.

A surprising number of people—to me, at least—raised their hands. "There is another thing going on here, which is just the pure enjoyment of sitting in your body," said Jeff. "Everything in our culture is about external rewards," he added, but in fact, "you've got it all right here." He motioned toward his torso. "To be able to just take a moment to sit back and feel what it feels like to be a human being is a privilege."

While Jeff's riff earlier in the day about "enjoying your beingness" had fallen a bit flat for me, this one managed to hit home. Dismiss it as woo-woo if you want, but there is genuine power in tuning in to the blazingly obvious fact that you are alive.

It reminded me of that sketch from *Saturday Night Live* where Dan Aykroyd plays President Jimmy Carter fielding live phone calls on the radio. A freaked-out teenager named Peter calls in and says, "Uh . . . I uh . . . I took some acid . . . I'm afraid to leave my apartment, and I can't wear any clothes . . . and the ceiling is dripping." Aykroyd/Carter responds by telling Peter to take some vitamins, drink a beer, and listen to the Allman Brothers. "Just remember you're a living organism on this planet, and you're very safe."

It also reminded me of how, when I had looked at the videos of Jeff and me from our "wandering retreat" a few months prior, he'd always had this goofy-yet-awesome look on his face when he was meditating, like he was actually having a good time. My mug, by contrast, looked all pinched from the effort.

Sitting there with Jeff on that stage, I realized that while I did have truly pleasurable, fascinating, and meaningful moments in meditation, my daily scramble to get in my two hours had too often taken on the feel of a forced march. I was overlooking what could be the most powerful motivator of them all. And it stung.

I turned to Jeff and admitted, "I don't meditate because it feels good. I meditate because, grr, I'm just supposed to do it."

"I'm noticing that about you," said Jeff. "We've got to work on that."

Ouch. I knew he didn't mean it as a criticism. He meant that enjoyment is something you can train. Good thing I was about to spend the next week and a half cooped up on a ridiculous bus with one of the best meditation teachers in the world.

Jeff, in his role as MacGyver, devised a meditation specifically to help you build the muscle of enjoyment.

For this meditation, we'll continue to work with the breath, but we'll expand to include the sense of our physical body as well. Enjoying the body.

When I hear "enjoying the body," I feel like you're going to start talking about something lewd.

That's because you're a talking head on TV, totally disconnected from your body. I used to be the same: for years my body was just an appendage my mind dragged around behind me, forcing it to do stupid shit. Meditation helped me get back in touch, and enjoyment is a key skill.

So, again, you're saying that enjoyment is trainable, like concentration?

The two are actually related: the more we enjoy a sensation, the more concentrated we can become, which in turn increases the enjoyment. It's a feedback loop, part of working smart. And enjoyment doesn't mean you're blissed-out topless on your cushion covered in massage oil. It's more modest.

Example, please.

Try to notice the sensation of air on the back of your hands right now. Can you find something very subtly pleasant about that?

Sure, I guess. But you are setting the bar very low here.

That's all you need to get on the enjoyment gradient. It's basically an attitude, the capacity to appreciate something a hair above neutrality. You don't need enjoyment to benefit from meditation, but it can deepen the effects.

The moment you say, "This is about enjoyment!" you can pretty much guarantee that half the readers are going to experience annoying discomfort and persistent itches in places they never knew they could have itches.

Totally fine. Enjoyment is simply an option that might be available. Our primary task is to concentrate on the breath or the body, and to accept any other sensations that may be there in the background. Equanimity is a training to face the whole of experience, including any boring or uncomfortable parts.

But then, just for fun, we see if there isn't actually something a wee bit enjoyable about the breath and the body, even with those itches and pains and tensions in the background. Enjoyment is more an attitude than anything else, but our attitudes can radically change the way we experience things. So do the experiment— decide ahead of time to be open to enjoyment. Don't chase it; let it come to you. It's important to *keep it light*. We don't want to compromise our equanimity by getting all hedonistic and pigging out on the good feels. We are learning the delicate art of experiencing pleasurable sensations without grasping, and painful sensations without pushing. This is one of the primary skills of mindfulness, something we'll come back to again and again.

What if it doesn't work?

If it doesn't work, don't worry about it—as I said, you can still get plenty of benefits.

ENJOYING THE BODY

5 minutes or more

Close your eyes (or keep them half open) and take a few deep breaths. Each exhale is an opportunity to smooth out the lines of the face a bit, to relax the throat and shoulders. Try to notice any settling that happens on the exhale—the way the diaphragm relaxes, or the way the body sinks in exhaustion because, frankly, you are working too hard and you should meditate more.

Focus on the sensation of breathing at the nose or the chest or the belly. You can use a note here if you like: *in, out* or *rising, falling.* Breathe naturally, like you've done a billion other times in your life. Except this time you're doing it with the attitude of *deciding* to find this experience enjoyable, instead of practicing within the Dan Harris School of Funereal Endurance. It can feel nice just to breathe—again, nothing dramatic, just a hair above neutrality.

There are different ways to connect to this enjoyment quality. It may be that the sensation of breathing is already subtly pleasurable for you, in which case just run with that, focusing on exactly that soft and subtle quality. Or sometimes a bit of mental reframing helps—for example, you might connect to the idea that the oxygen is filling you with vitality. Or that the breathing is a kind of massage for your insides. Or just that it feels good to be a large bipedal ape with an operational set of lungs. As always, you're allowed to completely fake it until at some point you accidentally find that some understated quality of enjoyment may indeed be happening. And if no enjoyment arises, no problem. It's simply an option.

After a few minutes, shift your attention to the sense of your whole body sitting. Try to notice that the feeling of your breath is rising and falling inside the larger feeling of your body. Anytime you notice any uptightness—about anything—breathe out, and soften through your front. Can you bring a subtle sense of enjoyment to being in your body? The sexy, invigorating animality of it all. Smiling helps, even a noncommittal Mona Lisa half-grin. Appreciating the existential hilarity of sitting with your eyes closed in your living room (or wherever), tripping out on the feeling of having a body.

So you're still focused on the sensation of breathing, only now you've widened the bandwidth a bit so you are aware of your body too. If thoughts and sounds pass through this container, no worries. In fact, screw them. Screw those thoughts, but screw them in a friendly, enjoyable way. Not hating on them—it's more that you don't give a toss one way or another. Sounds and thoughts just passing by, but you are grooving on the feeling of breathing and having a body, like a pleasure-loving hippie truant at Burning Man. No one ever needs to know.

Enjoying the breath, the body, the meditation. When you're almost done, stop meditating altogether, and just sit or lie back with your eyes closed for a few minutes. Relaxing, enjoying the rest. When you're ready, open your eyes.

The real learning with meditation is always how it affects you in the world. You can explore bringing an attitude of relaxed enjoyment to any activity, anytime: walking, moving your hands, exercising, even lying down and stretching luxuriously like a jungle cat. Lots of folks do this instinctively; why not do it intentionally?

We need reasons to reinforce life's easy positives, to counter what some contemplative neuroscientists like to call the brain's "negativity bias" (the near-universal human tendency to overfocus on the slings and arrows of fortune). This is one relatively straightforward way to do this. And, as with everything, it gets easier with practice.

CHEAT SHEET

1. Breathe normally, and try to tune in to the soft feeling of inhaling and exhaling. If it helps, note *in* as you breathe in and *out* as you breathe out.

2. Bring an attitude of enjoyment to the activity. Maybe there's a sense of refreshment as you inhale, or relaxation as you exhale, or some part of the sensation that feels kind of nice. Fake it if necessary. Pretend you're on drugs.

3. After a few minutes, shift your attention to the feeling of your whole body sitting. Imagine relaxing into your body like you're relaxing into a hot tub, opening to whatever body sensations are present.

PRO TIPS

• Be comfortable. Sit in an easy chair if you have to, or a couch. When the body is relaxed, everything is more enjoyable. You can also do the meditation lying down, but know that you may fall asleep!

- Related to this, you can alter your environment to make things more agreeable. Many practitioners create a cozy go-to meditation spot with candles and a plant and whatever sights and smells and sounds please them. I highly recommend doing the same if you can. Or make it a movable feast—sit under a tree, or in a bath, or in bed with a warm cup of tea in your hands.

- Explore a simple visualization. You can use your creativity to make practice more enjoyable—that's totally legit. Imaginative ideas can be a powerful way to frame and shape our experience. So you can imagine breathing up from the ground, or your body becoming suffused with light, or dissolving in a warm bath. What do you think all those ancient forest monks did before they had Netflix?

- Get sensual. You can enjoy the body the way you enjoy any other sensual pleasure. You can either just tune in to a sensation and decide to find it delightful, or you can scan the body looking for subtly pleasurable feelings that may already be there (like tingling in the hands, or the automatic relaxation of the diaphragm on the exhale). To repeat: the key to enjoying sensations isn't to grasp at them, *but to let them come to you.* It's a practice of receiving. For some people this comes naturally; for others it's harder to grok. That's okay—it's one reason we practice.

After the talk in Newton, Jeff and I mingled with the crowd, took questions, and posed for seemingly endless selfies. I sometimes get slightly uncomfortable in these situations, especially if people profess to have liked my book. I feel like I might let them down in person. Also—even though, as a needy anchorman, I enjoy the attention—my emotional reserve can run dry at the end of a long day. (My wife could write a whole book on this subject.) Jeff, by contrast, appears to have a lot more gas in his tank, so to speak. As I peered over at him standing near the other side of the stage, schmoozing with audience members and giving them tips on their meditation practice, he was clearly having a blast.

Later, I walked the halls of my old school with three members of the Brain Trust, Larry, Jason, and Dave. Larry and I had been best friends since age two; we walked to school together every day, and when we were in a fight, we walked on opposite sides of the street. Jason and I used to spray-paint graffiti tags on local train stations. Dave had been captain of the football team back in the day and now worked here at our alma mater, coaching lacrosse.

As Dave showed us around, he pointed out that much of the school had been remodeled. Even the parts that hadn't changed looked utterly unfamiliar to me, though.

"I don't remember anything," I said.

"You didn't spend a lot of time here," said Dave, smiling.

While the physical plant didn't provoke any memories, simply being with my friends did. I recalled the time when we tied Dave to the banister in his front hallway so he couldn't make it to class. Or the multiple times when we used to pull the fire alarm outside Larry's house and then hide in the woods and watch him explain himself to the firefighters. Oh, and my favorite hijinks: calling local fast-food restaurants and claiming to be managers from nearby franchises that had run out of burgers. We would then send in one of our buddies to collect the patties so we could have a barbecue.

As Dave wrapped up his tour, he brought us to the place where our group of friends had kept our lockers. As I stared at the scene of numberless intrigues, alliances, and heartbreaks, I suddenly found myself confronting a completely different issue related to time—not how to find time to meditate, but instead how to come to terms with the fact that so many years had already whipped by in my own life.

"It feels like a long time ago," I said.

"Nineteen eighty-nine's pretty far away, fellas," said Dave, which we greeted with a bittersweet belly laugh.

The 1989 version of me wouldn't have been able to imagine the middle-aged dad who stood here now. In my early twenties, during my first job in television, in Bangor, Maine, where most of the people on staff were right out of college, we referred to one of the other reporters (a guy in his late twenties) as "Jurassic Mark." Now here I was in my old high school at forty-five, slightly punch-drunk from the passage of time, and wincing slightly at my own image in all those selfies I'd just taken because my inner Robert Johnson said my features looked pointy and Tolkien-esque.

But here's the thing about meditation: as Jeff's longtime teacher Shinzen Young says, meditation extends your life—not necessarily by making you live longer, but by boosting your level of focus, so that you're squeezing more juice out of every moment.

It does something else, too. As Jeff had said quite eloquently during the event, meditation "accelerates the 'aging gracefully' gradient."

"You can age badly, and you can age well," he said. "I know affable older folks who sit in the park and watch the kids play, and they've got that good-natured, easygoing quality. A serious practice just makes that happen sooner in your life, so you have it in the middle of your life, or even earlier. You get to have the best of being old while you're still a little more sprightly."

Yes. That's why we do this.

• • •

Shortly thereafter we loaded onto the bus for a long, overnight drive. Susa Talan, a staffer at the 10% Happier company, had instituted a count-off system to make sure we didn't lose anyone. We used numbers, and I was ten. It was fun to listen to everyone call out their numbers; it almost made me feel young again, after having been so powerfully reminded of my infirmity by the visit to my high school.

I was a little worried about the next day, though. Some of the people we were supposed to be interviewing were bailing on us at the last minute—ironically because of the very obstacle we were hoping to confront next.

4

"People Might Think I'm Weird"

Representative Tim Ryan bounded into the room, shaking hands, repeating names, and making eye contact like the seasoned pol that he is.

Jeff and I, with our entourage in tow, had come to the congressman's office because he's a bona fide, out-of-the-closet meditator. He is also, by almost any objective measure, one of the most normal, non-weird American male specimens you could imagine: a hulking former quarterback, a practicing Catholic, and a moderate Democrat who represents a rust belt district in northeast Ohio.

And yet none of that had inoculated Ryan against the barbs of meditation skeptics. *The Atlantic* had dubbed him "Congressman Moonbeam."

Sitting next to Jeff on the couch in Ryan's office, I asked the congressman whether this kind of unflattering headline was hobbling his efforts to enlist his fellow legislators.

"I think so, totally," he said. "You have enough bullshit you have to deal with throughout the course of your political life that answering a question about practicing mindfulness isn't, like, on their agenda."

. . .

Let's just concede from the outset that "people might think I'm weird" is not, sadly, a myth, as the case of Congressman Ryan illustrates.

However, in this chapter, we will show how the stigma is fading as the practice is put to use in some surprising places. We'll also arm you with arguments to make against Neanderthals who mock you for meditating. Finally—and this is the real twist—we'll demonstrate that once you start practicing, you may not care so much what other people think. Mindfulness can help us see into the insecurities, assumptions, and story lines that dominate much of how we act. As this happens, to quote Jeff, "we learn to take a stand in values that are actually truer to who we are." And if that looks weird, who gives a shit?

Not that this is always easy. Despite my status as an advocate for meditation, I have a long and still active struggle with the optics of the practice. During the *10% Happier* publicity tour I wouldn't let any of the news outlets photograph me meditating because I thought it might make me look weird. I have softened on that, but I still get self-conscious whenever I have to meditate in public, as Jeff and I had been doing quite frequently on the road trip. I wear shades when I meditate in the backseat of taxis and hope the drivers think I am sleeping. I even feel sheepish when I run into coworkers at the ABC News meditation room (which, in a sign of how far meditation has come, was established entirely without my input); it feels a bit like running into someone you know in the proctologist's waiting room.

As it happened, the reason Jeff and I were in Congressman Ryan's office on this, day three of our cross-country odyssey, was that the people we were initially supposed to interview had bailed on us—for fear of looking weird.

Our original plan for today was to go to Shenandoah National Park, two hundred thousand acres of protected land just seventy-five miles from the nation's capital. For weeks, everything seemed copacetic: we had eight meditation-curious park workers, one of whom was in her eighties, set to join us for an interview about the obstacles to meditation. Then, four days before our visit, park officials started to get twitchy. "Is there a religious affiliation with meditation?" one of them called and asked. Suddenly we would need clearance from their bosses in Washington. Then yesterday at 4:00 P.M.—right as we were getting ready for the Newton event—a park official called to say they were canceling, in part because they didn't want to show their people, especially park rangers in uniform, meditating. "We can't endorse that," they said.

I frantically emailed the congressman, explained the situation, and asked if he could cram us into his schedule for an interview. He wrote back right away, saying he'd be happy to have us.

Interestingly, even as a kid growing up in Ohio, Tim never thought meditation was strange. He would see football coaches at his Catholic school sneaking into the chapel for prayer and meditation. "Men—role models, for a boy. That stuck with me."

In his twenties, he read a book by legendary basketball coach Phil Jackson, who introduced meditation to members of the Chicago Bulls and L.A. Lakers during their epic championship runs. "So that was an influence," Tim told us. "I said, 'What's this stuff he's doing with his players? What's Michael Jordan doing?' Because as a young kid growing up, you think, 'I want to be like them.'" Intrigued, he asked a priest he knew to teach him how to do "centering prayer," a form of meditation that involves silently repeating to yourself phrases from the Bible or a spiritual word such as "love" or "Jesus."

He didn't get serious about meditation, however, until the year 2008, in his late thirties and five years into his career in the U.S. Congress, when he had a personal crisis. "I was really getting to the point where I was almost burnt out. Elections, Ohio, fundraising—I was just like, 'I gotta do something.'"

So he went on a five-day meditation retreat led by Jon Kabat-Zinn, a former MIT molecular biologist who had designed something called Mindfulness Based Stress Reduction, a protocol for teaching meditation in a secular context. "That's what appealed to me," said Tim. "I didn't have to give up my religion, and I didn't have to join some group, or put on a robe, or do anything funky."

Toward the end of the retreat, as the group was engaged in increasingly long periods of silent meditation, Tim says he had a profound experience. "That's when just—the top flipped off my head. I was just like, 'This is unbelievable.' You could start really seeing your thoughts come. Really understanding what was going on. Then you become aware of why you have high blood pressure. Like, 'I keep thinking these negative thoughts over and over and over again.' And you wonder why you're stressed out!"

This is, of course, one of the prime benefits of meditation: things that have been churning in your subconscious get dragged into the open, so you can see them clearly and not be governed by them. "It's like the person who has road rage," said Tim. "You pull in front of them because you need to change lanes, and they go ballistic. I mean, obviously it's not just about you pulling in front of them. There's got to be layers and layers and layers of stuff that happened that day, that week, that month, that year, that lifetime, that get expressed in that moment. When you stop and calm your mind down, you start seeing those things. You start to respond better to them."

He was telling us this story while leaning back in a comfy

chair in his office, which had the usual American flags, elaborate molding, and Old World drapery, and was also filled with books with titles such as *Where's My Zen?, Options: Meditation and the Classroom,* and *Jesus and Buddha.* Jeff and I were on a couch diagonal to him. From my point of view, the meditation certainly seemed to be working for Tim. He looked exceedingly calm, especially for a guy whose party was currently in the minority in both houses of Congress.

"I don't know how to do it without this, the practice," he said. "I'd be like, 'I'm out. I'm going to go private sector. I'm going to go coach football in Youngstown.'"

Tim had become so convinced of the utility of mindfulness that he, too, had taken on the role of evangelist. He'd written a book, *A Mindful Nation,* about how meditation could transform key areas of government policy, including education, healthcare, corrections, military training, and veteran programs. He envisioned a time when teachers all over America would teach mindfulness to students, doctors would recommend it to their patients, and marines would learn it in basic training.

Along the way, he had hit some real roadblocks. He had established a weekly meditation and yoga session called Quiet Time, which was well attended by a bipartisan group of Capitol Hill staffers. However, his fellow legislators had been loath to hop on board, at least publicly. Meanwhile, a local public school back in his home state of Ohio had decided to stop teaching mindfulness to students, under pressure from parents who feared meditation ran counter to their faith. "Which," according to Tim, "was a real shame."

In the midst of all this, though, he had developed some pretty good approaches for taking the stink of weirdness off meditation.

When it comes to the religious concerns, he pushes back with the science. "Look at the brain research. Don't listen to me. No one has to give up any religion that they believe in, but look at the science. We want to help your kid develop their brain. If we know this stuff, why is it not getting down to the kids in my district? That's unfair. That's unfair for my kids."

For busy staffers on the Hill who worry that, in Tim's words, "you're slacking if you're going to do this," he relies on strategic name-dropping. "You've got to say, 'Phil Jackson.' You've got to say, 'Kobe Bryant did this.' Not exactly slackers. They found it is a performance enhancer."

This is a technique I heartily endorse. When I speak publicly about meditation, I am constantly referring to unlikely meditators, including Steve Jobs, Novak Djokovic, the Chicago Cubs, and employees at major corporations such as Google, Procter and Gamble, Aetna, Target, and General Mills. It's not entirely dissimilar to the way I've long defended myself against people who accuse me of being soft for liking cats. I point to icons of machismo such as Ernest Hemingway, Winston Churchill, and Dr. Evil.

While pushing for greater adoption of meditation can feel slow and frustrating at times, I remain convinced it is the next big public health revolution. I think in the not-too-distant future, mental exercise will be considered to be as important and mainstream as physical exercise. Think about it: running used to seem weird to many people just a few decades ago. Same with yoga and sushi. The arc of history is, I believe, heading in the right direction—on this score, at least.

For his part, Tim seemed utterly undeterred by the hurdles he had faced in spreading meditation. He was resolute about chipping away at an issue that had long concerned both Jeff and me as well—the fact that meditation was largely the province of white upper-middle-class Whole Foods shoppers. That's not a knock on those people. I *am* one of those people. But this health-improving, sanity-boosting practice should be available to anyone who wants it. As Tim put it, "Why is it just wealthy people who can afford to go on a retreat who have this? To me, this is a social justice issue."

After the interview, the team had a convivial, family-style dinner at a delicious Korean fried chicken spot, even though most of us were dragging. Our decision to sleep on the bus the night before had turned out to be a mistake. We drove through a winter storm with whistling winds and pounding precipitation. Despite the fact that the coffin-beds were comfortable, I was up most of the night, worrying that the bus might veer off the icy road. I was enduring extravagant bouts of *prapañca* (that ancient term for spasms of often phantasmagoric prospection) about crashing. And I worried that if we survived, I would be too tired the next day to function. In my own, oft-repeated version of the "fallacy of uniqueness," I had assumed that everyone else was snoozing soundly. But when we arrived in Washington the next morning, it turned out that most of the team was as sleep-deprived as me—including our normally unflappable director, Eddie, who seemed completely drained.

Nonetheless, we had managed to make it through the day on Capitol Hill. We had also resolved not to sleep on the bus again. After dinner, we boarded the orange behemoth for the several-hour drive to our hotel. I went to my bunk for a video chat with Bianca and Alexander. I am not a huge fan of talking on the phone. (Behind the scenes, as my wife has noted ruefully, this professional talker can be downright monosyllabic.) However, I had learned the hard way that calling my wife every day is a must. Many years prior, in the early days of our relationship, I had spent a week on assignment in Haiti and had called only sporadically. I got so caught up in my own work that I left her wondering and worrying about my well-being for days. Let's just say it never happened again. With Alexander now on the scene, I had added incentive to stay in touch. (Although, in a bit of poetic justice, he usually ignores me during our calls.) Jeff and I had warned Bianca that we would be having the film crew record us as we checked in with her every day to ask whether she was meditating. She was prepared, albeit warily, to play along, but I told her the team was too exhausted to follow through tonight. After we hung up, I vegged for a while, alternately watching TV shows and staring at pictures of Alexander, including one where he had ice cream all over his face and looked like the youngest member of the Insane Clown Posse. Meanwhile, other folks were either chatting up front or engaging in a vigorous game of dice in George Clinton's rear cabin. All of us were blissfully unaware that our next interviewees had also considered bailing on us—because they, too, were worried about looking weird.

The next morning, we showed up at Virginia Military Institute. Sometimes called the "West Point of the South," VMI is the oldest state-supported military college in the United States. The campus sprawls over two hundred well-tended acres. There are more than a few cannons.

This is not a place for the faint of heart. Freshmen are known as "rats." They get screamed at all the time, and have to drop and do push-ups on demand. They can't watch TV, listen to music, or use the phone without supervision. The remaining three years don't get much easier.

We set up our cameras in a wood-paneled room in the library. On the wall was a portrait of the Confederate general

Stonewall Jackson, bearded and with a heavy brow, who taught natural and experimental philosophy at VMI back in the 1850s and was said to have been a "strict and inflexible teacher." One of my producers pointed out that the general was also known to eat lemons like apples. He looked like he might have snacked on gravel as well.

As we were milling about, waiting for the cameras to roll, we learned that the administration had nearly scrapped the whole shoot. The school's communications honcho explained that VMI had been through a public relations debacle a few months earlier, when news broke that officials had given out coloring books as a way to help cadets deal with stress—a move that was perceived by some as too touchy-feely for one of the nation's premier military academies. The press had a proverbial field day. Alumni were up in proverbial arms. The school now feared our on-camera session might devolve into a gooey celebration of the cosmic benefits of meditation, and they'd be exposed to further criticism and mockery.

Enter Colonel Holly Jo Richardson, PhD, a physical fitness instructor with short red hair, and Major Matthew Jarman, a baby-faced assistant professor with a doctorate in psychology. The two strode into the room wearing impeccably pressed uniforms. Both Richardson and Jarman had recently begun teaching meditation to the cadets in their respective classes. They disclosed that when they had first begun doing so, they were a little apprehensive. To sell the practice, they relied on the same tactics Tim Ryan employed: an emphasis on the science that suggested health benefits (including increased resilience to post-traumatic stress disorder, a scourge of the modern military) and a spotlight on the aspirational figures who were meditating themselves, especially professional athletes.

Jarman added a fresh twist to the sales pitch. As a pushback against the argument that you are a wuss if you meditate, he essentially argued that you are a wuss if you *don't* do it. "Meditation isn't this soft, fluffy thing. You're facing your fears. You're facing your stresses head-on. You're kind of leaning into them. And it's giving you the tools to do that more effectively, and to not be swept away by them."

The approach appears to have worked: the classes in which meditation was taught were well subscribed. Richardson said there was widespread recognition that stress is "endemic" at VMI. Specifically, she thought cadets could use mindfulness "so they could withstand their first year here."

Jarman acknowledged that concerns about teaching mindfulness in a military context come from two sides. Some meditation purists consider it a perversion of their beloved practice. "Is it ethical to teach meditation practice to people who might be killing others?" asked Jarman. From his perspective, yes. He said mental training helps you make better decisions, "which hopefully results in as few casualties as possible." Further, in his class, called Modern Warriorship, he defines a warrior as "one who creates change of some sort." He added, "You can trace the word 'war' to creating disorder and change." Jarman sees warriors as actors not merely on the battlefield but also in schools, businesses, and families. Their primary focus, he believes, should be on helping others—and mindfulness, he says, is an essential skill for this kind of fight.

"Some cadets tell me that their roommates kind of make fun of them," said Jarman. But this, he said, is a good test. Part of being a change-maker, he said, "means that you're going to be going against a lot of people. If you can't do something as simple as meditating and be okay with the fact that others might think it's a little weird, then you're not really getting into the training yet. It's such a minimal threat, as far as the grand scale."

Jeff chimed in, "And part of being a warrior is going against the stream."

That term speaks to the revolutionary message at the heart of the meditative endeavor. To "go against the stream" is to refuse to be swept up in the dominant culture of unconsciousness, to carefully examine the conventional narratives and assumptions of the day. As Jeff explained, "The momentum of everyday life is to just continue tumbling along unheeding. To actually stop and pause and take stock of your life and decide to not go along with that is considered to be going against the momentum of the culture. So there's a warrior quality to that, very much."

I had seen this play out, to a certain degree, in my own life. I've noticed my lifelong susceptibility to the opinions of others diminishing somewhat. The act of sitting and witnessing the insane torrent of my own mind somehow helps me not take so seriously the clamor of the collective mind. Worrying about what people think of you, comparing yourself to others, falling prey to social media-induced FOMO (fear of missing out)—these are all painful mental states. It's a relief to have the wherewithal to see them arise and then let them pass without getting overly entranced by them.

Jeff often spoke about how meditation led to more spontaneity in himself and in friends and students who practiced. "You get less caught up in self-judgments and endless concerns about what other people think. It's very liberating; you feel lighter."

To be honest, I still care what people think. I'm a TV news anchor, after all. On bad days, one mean tweet can preoccupy me for hours. For example, when something like this comes over the transom: "your [*sic*] an idiot." Or this: "Why are @paulafaris & @danbharris SO full of themselves?! Stop talking over your cohorts, you are neither one that interesting."

I maintain that a certain amount of vigilance about the opinions of others can be healthy. Sometimes those mean tweets contain a grain of truth—and if I can get past my instinct to be defensive, I can home in on the constructive part of the criticism and use it to improve. Similarly, when I am contemplating what my wife or brother or parents might think of a particular action, it can prevent me from doing something dumb. The trick is to separate signal from noise. Meditation has helped me to do that—to see whether there is genuine reason for concern or whether I am stuck in a cul-de-sac of pointless angst.

Something else I've observed: even though most of us spend an inordinate amount of time worrying about how we appear to others, the hard truth is that they really don't care that much about you. I remember obsessing over what the public reaction might be to the embarrassing personal revelations in my first book. While there was some blowback (the *Daily Mail* ran the following headline: "Redemption of a Bald, Miserable Egomaniac"), it became clear to me that people were only somewhat interested in my baggage. What they really wanted to know was: "What do you have that may be of use to *me*?" An old boss of mine—a man who had been the subject of a few negative headlines—used to say that enduring embarrassment is a little bit like being seasick. For you, it feels like the world is ending; for everybody else, it's only mildly amusing.

Four cadets who'd been taught meditation joined the conversation: three men and one woman, all seemingly out of central casting. They wore uniforms that had been compulsory at VMI for decades: crisp black shirts tucked neatly into pressed wool pants, with black shoes shined to a mirror finish. Just days earlier they had been on a twenty-mile march in extreme humidity, during which some of them had lost toenails, but no one looked the worse for wear. They exuded an easy, uncontrived confidence in the utility of meditation, public opinion be damned.

Eilana, a quietly confident cadet, said that the practice had helped her set personal records in her shooting competitions. Jared, a strapping junior, said he had used meditation to calm himself down before baseball games, quoting Yogi Berra: "Baseball is 90 percent mental. The other half is physical."

I was particularly struck by Anthony, an imposing senior who had recently enlisted in the special forces and looked like he too occasionally enjoyed a lemon for a snack. He said he had learned about meditation from his girlfriend, "who's kind of a wannabe hippie." After she told him how it helped her with stress, he started doing ten minutes at night in the library. "It definitely changed my evenings and how I felt centered in myself. The voices and the narrative that I was constantly going through in my head just kind of faded away. I was more present in myself."

To sit there and listen to this archetypal badass so accurately describe the benefits of meditation made my heart sing.

"We're taking you on our tour," said Jeff.

Finally, there was Al, the quarterback of the football team, who said he had heard about the practice from one of his receivers. Al had decided not to enlist in the armed services after graduation. He was planning to go into ministry. I asked whether he thought meditation might in some way run counter to his Christian faith.

"Previously," he said, "my thoughts on meditation were: it's a Buddhist kind of thing, or an Asian, Eastern kind of thing. Now I really just see it as a practice. I don't see it as a tie to being any kind of faith. I don't think that Jesus looks down upon finding who you are, and really just finding your focus and your calmness. I don't think that's anything that conflicts with my beliefs."

After our chat, Jeff led a meditation where he discussed the true "ninja move" of mindfulness: leaning into—and learning from—whatever story lines and emotions we encounter when meditating, rather than playing our usual game of avoidance.

As mentioned earlier, there's a classic progression in meditation. First we work on building up concentration: focus on breath, get distracted, come back. Then, once our attention is a little more stable and balanced, we move away from the breath and get curious about the distractions themselves, which are loaded with information about our go-to thought patterns, preoccupations, and triggers. This stuff is extremely useful to explore. It's like pulling back the curtain on the mind's hidden dramas.

I like where you're going here, but please resist your temptation to get too weird. Thin ice.

Is nothing I do ever good enough for you, Dad?

I'm . . . Dan.

And I'm a defensive son who apparently still feels the need to prove himself to his seventysomething parental units. This clichéd hangover from my kiddo years continues to live and simmer under the surface. It once caused me to lash out, or to lose hours stewing and muttering. I still do this, but less often, and in a less escalating fashion. Meditation has helped me notice this pattern — or, more precisely, it has helped me get familiar both with the typical triggers that set me off and with the early warning signs that I'm beginning to get hijacked: a besieged hunch in my shoulders, a vibratory urgency through my core, and a twitchy combativeness in my hands.

I'm more likely to notice this stuff now, and once I've noticed it, I'm less likely to go along with the pattern. The whole thing is easier to laugh off.

I assume you are planning to connect this to a human being other than yourself?

Ha ha—just laughing off the criticisms!

It turns out our patterns are getting activated all the time, including when we sit with our eyes closed. Fortunately, the more practice we have noticing them, the less likely we are to automatically get sucked in. And that's what this meditation is about. It's pattern-noticing school. Once something is seen, it can't really be unseen. It can still be overlooked, and ignored, and temporarily forgotten. Hell—it can be triggered and retriggered another five hundred times, so that we despair of ever actually learning anything in this confounding life! But at least it will never again be totally unknown to us, and—if we keep practicing— there's a very good chance it will eventually be so known to us that it will no longer be a "problem" at all.

So for this meditation, we'll begin with a loose focus on the breath, but as soon as we get distracted by something, we'll get curious about the nature of that particular takeover. What hidden drama is happening here? For this, noting helps—using little silently spoken descriptors like *spacing out, stewing, tension.* The idea is to keep the words simple and accurate, and to try not to overthink the whole thing.

Some folks get tripped up on this concept. After all, noting is thinking, right? In fact, it's thinking about thinking. Which leads people to ask, "Isn't this the opposite of what we want to be doing in meditation?"

Noting is the skillful use of thinking in the service of insight. It shows that you are mindful of what's happening. The idea is to just name the distraction—with a calm tone—then return to the breath. Doing this can actually be very helpful for overthinkers, because it co-opts a bunch of your thinking bandwidth. There's often a bit of a learning curve. Usually after a while the mind stops playing games and the noting just becomes automatic. Until that time, just do the best you can. Or don't note at all. That is always an option. Noting is a useful tool only if it actually helps you stay on track. But give the tool an honest chance before you abandon it.

Of course, in keeping with the whole investigatory spirit of this meditation, the ultimate deft move if you find yourself in a thinking storm is to note *overthinking*. Overthinking is also an extremely useful pattern to notice! Noting it can pop you right out of your downward ruminatory spiral.

There are so many potential patterns to discover, it's shocking. For example, you might be with the breath and nothing else seems to be happening and then you realize you are kind of *waiting* for something to happen. That's a pattern. Note *waiting*, note *expecting*. The layers are often very subtle and we never think to notice them because we're *inside* them. But patience and curiosity are amazingly effective—they can illuminate a pattern like a shot of iridescent dye in a pool of murky water. When we notice

and name a thing, we immediately pan back the camera—
snap—to a bigger picture. From this place, we can respond more
sanely. Sanity, it turns out, is a trainable skill.

INVESTIGATING PATTERNS

10 to 20 minutes

Get in your meditation position and bring your attention to
your breath.

Take a few deep breaths and begin to calibrate yourself a
bit: relaxing on the exhale, straightening on the inhale, and
generally setting the intention to not be uptight about this
whole potentially very uptight-making meditation.

Your breath is your starting point—your home base, the
place to come back to. The idea is to let the sensation of
breathing pull you in, but not pull you in so far that you lose
any sense of a wider perspective *around* the breath. As always, noting helps: *in, out.* If the breath bothers you, note
bothered and choose a different anchor: maybe the feeling
of warmth in your hands, a point in your belly, contact with
the ground, or even external sounds. Once you've chosen a
direction for your attention, lightly commit to it.

So here we go, business as usual, noticing the nice cool
sensation of breathing in, and then . . . *WTF!* Where did I
go? Who did that? You look around for someone to blame.
Only yourself—apparently you suck at meditating. Note:
judgment. We have a new object of meditation: a grumbly

critical inner voice, a sudden uptightness in your posture, the hint of an exasperated scowl. *Judgment.* Call it what you want, but be nice. Friendliness is key—we are not trying to cultivate any weird schizoid inner antagonisms here. "Judgment," you say, like judgment is the most charming fellow you've ever met. "How excellent to make your acquaintance!" Who *is* this rather dashing sharp-tongued part of you? Where does it live—what body feelings are associated with it, what story lines, what parental timbres in words and tone? Note any part of it: *judging, thinking, tension.* Welcome it, feel it, explore it, and—when you're ready—return to the breath.

Of course, nothing like this may be happening, and that's fine. Just stay with the breath in a relaxed and easygoing manner. But it may happen that, in a very secret way, some pattern rises up below you, unannounced, like a large invisible whale. *Gulp*—in you go, swallowed whole. Maybe the whale is resignation—you realize you have already decided that nothing is going to happen. Note *resignation.* Or irritation—"That idiot teacher has no idea what he is talking about." (True in most things). Note *irritation.* Or boredom—"Really? This is meditation? My life isn't changed yet. I don't see any magic iridescent dyes. I could be watching television." Note *boredom.*

Back to the breath. You get the idea: it's about staying curious, and seeing our distractions and discontents as learning opportunities. It may be that most distractions are simple physical or external ones: *indigestion, itching, pain, sound.* That's fine too. Or maybe you brought them with you into the meditation—*sourness, anxiety, speediness*—and you could benefit from getting some perspective. The general rule is if it's strong enough to pull you away from your breath, note it and then explore it for a while. Where are you experiencing this distraction? In your body? Your mind? What part? How tight is it? Where does it grip? Can you let it go? Follow this strange pattern like a private investigator of consciousness. When you're ready, go back to feeling the breath.

But of course, most of meditation isn't this cut-and-dried. It's more like we are half paying attention to the breath and half doing this other thing that we do that we don't really know that we do. Right? Can you notice *that* thing? Can you name it, open to it, gently trace it out? Curiosity is king here.

There are no "problems" in this meditation. Only things to exist with and around, in a good-natured exploratory way. The ninja move of this practice is to let everything be there, sitting like a champ inside the full sensate surround, from the most delicate and understated sensations to the most coarse and insistent. Work smart: if something gets too intense, you can always return to the breath, to your home base. It's up to you to decide how much you want to go into an uncomfortable pattern, a dynamic we'll explore in more detail in Chapter 6.

When you're ready, take a few moments to just relax and drift, and then open your eyes.

CHEAT SHEET

1. Choose a home base for your attention, somewhere to start and return to—the breath, hands, seat, belly, sound. Do this for a while.

2. If something pulls you away—or if you happen to notice something subtly interfering with your experience—get curious about that something. Note it: *thinking, anger, discomfort,* etc. Try to have a welcoming attitude.

3. Make this distraction the new object of meditation for a while. Where is it happening? Is it familiar? What happens when you observe it? Does it get more intense or less? Does it change or stay the same? Explore for a minute or two, and then return to the breath.

When we opened our eyes and started talking about what we had just done, the cadets seemed genuinely enthused. Eilana mentioned that she had leaned into some mild indigestion during the sit, and that doing so had "helped tone it down a lot." Al, the quarterback and aspiring pastor, reported something more psychologically significant.

"The thing that I really focused on was people's thoughts about me. That's one thing I've always struggled with," he said. "Even my comments earlier about me thinking that Jesus is okay with this and he's not going to look down upon this, I was like, 'Oh gosh, the whole Christian world is going to see that on ABC News, and I'm going to get flak about it.' Then I was like, 'No, that's what I believe, and I think that's what I have to stay true to.'" He concluded, "I guess it's just kind of like a revelation."

There is a revelation here for all of us. The kind of meditation Jeff just taught is a revolutionary way to approach being alive. As I explained to the cadets, most of us live our lives like this: "Something comes up that we don't like, we do everything to get rid of it—think about something else, eat something, go shopping, take a drug, whatever." But with meditation, the approach is entirely different. "If I'm pissed off about something, or I'm scared about something, or I'm bummed about it, I'm going to be a warrior, and I'm going to feel it fully. I'm just going to lean into that thing. And you see, in many cases, that this isn't going to kill me. Or it's not as bad as I thought it was. Or actually I can handle it."

Jeff added that if you live your life refusing to feel certain things, you're essentially closing a series of doors in your mind. "It's like you live in a mansion, but now you're just going to live underneath the stairs. You're not even going into those other rooms, because that's where I broke up with my ex," he said, by way of example, or "That's my feeling of besieged inadequacy around my parents, and—man, stay out of there!—that's my embarrassingly low self-esteem!" This is not easy to do, of course, but Jeff said, "If you can just open up each door and face it, you may find out there is actually no monster in there. It's manageable. Bit by bit, you start to get more and more free in your life, so you can just live bigger and bigger and more and more fearlessly and with more and more freedom."

This strategy can be applied to all kinds of worries, including worries about people thinking you're weird for meditating. (For the record, I am referring here mostly to run-of-the-mill mental churn. We will still have more to say about deeper struggles, including trauma, soon.) If you are encountering challenges in meditation, know that you are not alone. Difficulties in practice are so common that ancient masters went to great lengths to exhaustively categorize them. They called them "the hindrances," or sometimes "the defilements" (which Jeff thinks sounds like a middle-aged R&B band from Belfast).

There are five main hindrances: sloth/torpor, desire, aversion, restlessness/worry, and doubt. These categories are broad enough to cover most of the big issues that can arise in a practice.

FAQ: *The Hindrances*

Help, I'm bored out of my mind while meditating. What do I do?

Boredom is related to sloth (a superb word), as is sleepiness. They are variations of mind-body lethargy where you have no energy and feel dull, heavy, and uninterested in things. Or we can be totally spaced-out and numb. One way to combat this is to get energized: to first notice what's happening, and then to try to summon up some curiosity about it. Curiosity is energizing.

The opinionated side of boredom—the judgment that something is boring—can be looked at like anything else. Where is "boring" in this sound, this sensation, this situation? You bring it with you. So get curious and see if you can find where this feeling lives. The curiosity itself can dispel the boredom, and it is very liberating to no longer be yanked around by what can be a chronic sense of dissatisfaction. We'll get more into this in a minute.

Of course, if you are really bored, you can also just stop meditating and go for a fast walk, or jump up and down, or dunk your head in a sink full of ice cubes.

Those tactics would probably also help with another common problem, sleepiness.

For sure. Here are a few things you can try when you feel sleepy. One, meditate when you're most alert—that is, first thing when you get up, or after your morning workout or coffee. The timing will be different for everyone. (It's probably not a good idea to meditate after a meal, though—the digestion process can make you feel a bit dozy.) Two, a few big inhales can help oxygenate the body, as can deliberately stretching your spine. Three, meditate with your eyes open. Four, you can note, out loud, either *sleepiness* and/or the breath—*in, out*. Five—probably the most effective intervention—you can meditate standing up. Or six, you can do a quick walking meditation as per above, to get the blood moving. If you are persistently sleepy, it is also quite possible that what you really need right now isn't meditation but a nap.

What about desire? Not infrequently in meditation I will find myself wanting to check my phone, yearning for ice cream, or planning my next TV binge.

I know it well. During many meditations I've been lost in lustful fantasies, or visualizing a cheeseburger, or—for this I repent— both simultaneously. Often we don't even know *what* we desire— it's just all-purpose wanting, like the feeling of walking down the street and wanting to buy something, or that pervasive teenager sense of wanting *something*—anything!—to happen, even if you have no idea what.

Using noting here can really help: *wanting, wanting, wanting*. If you can stay with this feeling, a very liberating and powerful moment can sometimes happen: the wanting passes, and you realize you are actually fine. More than fine: happy. Content with how things are. And you realize how many *hundreds* of hours you have been—and will be again—lost in this pattern, robotically indulging your novelty-seeking, when, had you just thought to look, the urge would eventually pop like an empty soap bubble and you could relax.

This is called an "insight" in Buddhism: an experience of truth. Insights make an "aha" noise as they pass through your heart, and then they land in your belly with a thunk. In this case, you realize (1) "Wow, this pattern has influenced a *lot* of my life," and then (2) "But much of the time there hasn't really been anything wrong." So you sit with that for a while, digesting. And then you get up, and twenty minutes later you're hopelessly fixated on your Facebook feed.

Meditation works. But it can take time for the bigger insights to sink in.

How about desire's Janus-faced opposite: aversion?

Variations of pushing away, from fear and subtle dislike all the way to hate, repugnance, and anger. All are aversion. You can work with them the same way: note *fear,* or *dislike,* or *anger.* They're all part of our natural fight-or-flight response.

I've definitely struggled with anger in my life and practice, and I can say I've been consistently amazed at the number of things a person can find to get angry about in a silent sit: anger at discomfort, anger at the teacher for clearly being a fool, anger at yourself for being a bad meditator, and even irrational Homer Simpson–style anger at the object of your focus—"Stupid breath!"—so that you convince yourself there is something much better to be meditating on. It turns out we can get into furious fight-or-flight spirals *with ourselves.* It's like evolution imploded backward into our brains.

Is there an antidote to anger?

The classic one is loving-kindness meditation. Basically: when you notice you are mad, you try to do a meditation that is about deliberately evoking feelings of care and friendliness for yourself, your pals, strangers, and the whole creaturely shebang. Dan loves these practices. Sometimes he floats down the street and imagines throwing his golden lasso of love around everyone he sees. We'll explore a few variations of these meditations later in the book.

It's like you almost know me.

Unlike Dan's aversion to loving-kindness, many of our aversions are unconscious. When we look closely, we can sometimes detect a faint layer of friction or tugging around what we're thinking and feeling and hearing and seeing. *I like it, I don't like it, I like it, I don't like it. Push, pull, push, pull. Want, don't want, want, don't want.* All of this struggle, this lack of equanimity.

It's there in a conspicuous macro way in terms of our opinions and judgments and likes and don't-likes. And it's there in an understated micro way in terms of our tiny winces and bracings and averted gazes, as well as our little pulses of zeal, of grabbiness, of indulgence. You start to see how desire and aversion are like two paddles in a giant pinball machine, launching and relaunching your spinning little head around the game board of life.

This seems like a good place to say more about how to work with physical pain, where aversion is the natural response.

Physical pain from sitting—in the knees, the legs, the hips, the back—is one of the classic meditative training grounds for how to develop equanimity or lack of resistance. Obviously if you're in pain it's fine to move. But if you are feeling ambitious, you can also learn a lot about how aversion works. You can learn to ob-serve and open to your pain in a way that actually makes the pain less of a problem.

I have to give a shout-out here to my teacher Shinzen Young, who wrote an excellent book about how meditation can help with chronic pain. His formula is one every human being should memorize: Suffering = Pain × Resistance. Pain is an inevitable part of life. Suffering (in his definition) is not. It comes from fighting or resisting some uncomfortable sensation or emotion or whatever. When we do this, there's a snowball effect: tension spreads, and the original insult starts to reverberate through the whole mind-body tract, leading to even more discomfort, stress, and reactiv-ity. The suffering amplifies.

You can literally watch this dynamic play out when your knee starts to hurt when you meditate. There is the pain of it, but there's also your panicked judgment of the pain—*Oh, man, this is only going to get worse;* there is bracing in the body and the face; there may be a slight holding of the breath; and there is almost always that subtle aversion layer being activated. So one medita-tive solution is to counterintuitively focus on the center of the sensation of pain itself, relaxing and breathing into it, trying to let go of your aversion and develop a kind of field naturalist's curios-ity and acceptance instead. You watch your pain like it's an intriguing little animal. When we do this, the pain itself can di-minish dramatically and sometimes even disappear.

Next hindrance: restlessness, worry, and anxiety. How to deal with these?

I am happy to be the poster boy for this particular defilement. This is partly an *energy* issue. Too much juice, too much excitability—"full of beans," as my grandpappy used to say. In the body this manifests as fidgetiness, agitation, and sometimes the desire to bolt or (I've actually had this) punch yourself in the face. In the mind it manifests as scattered or persistent thinking, being distracted by everything, landing nowhere, always worrying and making plans. Plans! I love plans. Plans about how to get away from here so I can immediately make a new plan about how to get away from there. These and other derangements of "the monkey mind" have occupied a large portion of my adult life.

So: what to do?

Well, first of all, give yourself a break. You've got beans! It's a good thing. Those beans just need to be channeled or discharged, and there are many ways to do this. Number one: if you have *crazy* energy during a particular meditation, then for God's sake stop. You need physical activity, like martial arts or pole vaulting or trench digging. Get outside and get into the dirt and let Mama Earth ground your zing. You can go back to sitting when you're feeling more settled.

Number two: long exhales. Your breath is your best friend in life and in meditation. Breathing in and up can raise your energy when you are low, and breathing out and down can lower your energy when you are high. So if you're really agitated, try taking some deliberate long slow exhales, and as you do, imagine your energy settling and draining into the ground.

Number three: be a ninja of equanimity. Notice agitation or excitement or anxiety in your body, imagine yourself as a wide-open container. Be distantly curious about how the vibrations play themselves out. Note that the big trick here is not to feed the energy, not to get too curious and thus accidentally entangled. I tell my students: *Do not feed the beast.* So much of my own practice has been about learning to breathe out, back off, and return to a grounding sensation. We'll come back to this theme in Chapters 6 and 7.

Finally, number four: find stillness. Stillness is very healing. The good news is, we don't always have to wait until we're relaxed to find it. Often a subtle quality of stillness or silence already exists in some part of our experience: under the softest part of our breath, or at a point in the belly, or as a noticeable quiet around us or even inside us.

If you have strong energy or agitation, do a little survey: Is there something unchanging somewhere in your mind and body? Some quality or sensation you can deliberately focus in on? Even if it's just a hint. Hold yourself still and try to delicately make contact. Not in any rush. Breathing calmly, soothing yourself. This kind of exploration can be a game-changer. It is the path of self-regulation.

Last hindrance: doubt. I have this in spades.

"Am I doing this right?" "Am I wasting my time?" "Am I forever unfit for all meditations?" Note: *doubt, doubt, doubt.* There is nothing wrong with healthy questioning; this hindrance refers more to a chronic inability to commit, which can actively prevent the full experience from unfolding. It's a bit like romantic relationships: if you're always on the fence, you'll never know the depths of connection that total acceptance and commitment bring.

Clear instruction helps, as does a teacher you feel confident in, and an understanding of both the dynamics involved and your reason for practicing. So can having a mature patience with the whole process, which inevitably includes periods when you're going to be confused and unsure and thickheaded. That's okay—that's life. Everyone who has ever meditated has gone through periods of being terrible at meditation and doubting themselves—that's why they named a hindrance after it. Be like Kurt Vonnegut: "So it goes."

One final thing to say. Hindrances don't just happen in meditation. They happen in life, and it's useful to at least try to notice them. We start to see how pervasive they are, how they can distort our view of things and prevent us from being present and available to the people around us. And sometimes a hindrance can mask a deeper issue: desire can mask loneliness, agitation can cover fear, sleepiness can be a form of avoidance. Many possible permutations. The meditation teacher Gil Fronsdal calls these "strategies of resistance"—patterns of reactivity that our unconscious uses to dodge uncomfortable feelings and situations. The Buddhists are masters of noticing this stuff. They have a fine phrase: "guarding the sense doors." It means being good-naturedly vigilant about what we spend our time doing and thinking about, because these things have a pervasive effect on our moods and dispositions. In the words of another teacher, Steve Armstrong: "The hindrances can become our personality." But not all of it, and hopefully not for long as we become more skilled at the practice.

On the bus that night, as we headed to the next stop on our tour, I decided to check in with Jeff about something that was worrying me.

"Have you felt criticized at all when we pick on you for getting all mystical-shmystical?" I asked. Ben and I had been teasing him for dropping phrases such as "enjoying your beingness" while we were trying to appeal to skeptics.

"Sometimes it feels lonely to be hanging out with a bunch of secular folks when you know the most important fucking thing in the world is to understand the sacred fact that you're alive," he said, his face radiating geniality, notwithstanding the f-bomb. "Sometimes I get reactive around that. There's a defensive quality that can come up. Which doesn't do me any good. It doesn't help the cause. On the other hand, I'm pretty easygoing. My relationship with my friends has always been a teasing one; we bust each other's balls. I kind of enjoy it."

Apparently even Meditation MacGyvers care what other people think of them.

In fact, while I was spending this concentrated time in close quarters with Jeff, the complexity of his personality was coming into focus for me. I was starting to realize that many of his core personality traits—including a sensitivity to criticism that was seemingly at odds with his external insouciance—could be traced back to the ADD. When he was a boy, the condition had contributed to him being hyperactive, impetuous, and basically a pain in the neck for his exhausted parents. Jeff often felt criticized, a dynamic that had residual impacts even now.

It also led to what I considered to be a strange resistance to raising his public profile. During our "wandering retreat" several months before, I had encouraged Jeff to be more ambitious. I couldn't understand why a teacher as brilliant as him wasn't better known. At first he pushed back by insisting he liked to keep things simple. But then he admitted that part of his reluctance was connected to his ADD. He had a habit of popping off and saying things he later regretted and a propensity for taking on too many responsibilities and then getting overwhelmed. Both of these behaviors undermined his confidence. He didn't know how to ask for help and felt embarrassed for even having these problems as a meditation teacher (i.e., "someone who is supposed to have his shit together on every level").

All of which goes to show that just because you start meditating doesn't mean that every one of your deep patterns and mental habits will evaporate. Even people who teach meditation for a living suffer. But the great ones, like Jeff, harness their neuroses in ways that allow them to better connect with the people they're trying to help.

For my part, even after years of meditation, I still notice plenty of anger, impatience, and other distractions in my own mind. For instance, while meditating with the cadets earlier in the day, I was besieged by all sorts of random thoughts:

What's the funniest name for a historical military encounter? That's easy: Battle of Salamis. Really happened. Big fight between the Greeks and Persians in 480 B.C. Would've been awesome if it was followed by the War of Pastramis, the Siege of Mortadella, and Last Stand at Pimento Loaf.

When I find myself thinking about nonsense, or getting angry for no readily apparent reason, I often add an extra layer of suffering by telling myself: *You're a meditation advocate now— you have no business feeling this way.* This is a complete waste of energy. You can't control what arises in your own mind—it comes out of a mysterious void. You can only control how you respond. The move isn't to artificially squash your emotions; they will only reemerge elsewhere. No, the move is to use the tools that Jeff just taught us: lean into whatever is coming up and try to see it without judgment, so that you can respond wisely. Do this enough and, over time, you may even starve your unwholesome patterns of oxygen by not feeding them with compulsive thinking.

As our orange bus headed south through the inky Virginia night, Jeff expounded on the extra ingredient that speeds up this process of handling your emotions. The true warrior move is not just to see your hindrances clearly but also to send them a little friendliness.

By way of example, he revealed one of his own neurotic patterns. As a result of feeling chastened as a kid, "I internalized this voice that I now call 'El Grandioso.'" The voice would compensate for perceived criticism by telling Jeff how well he was doing. "It was kind of pathetic, but it would be like my own personal cheerleader in my corner." El Grandioso would exaggerate and distort what was really going on around him, goading him into riskier and ever more ridiculous behaviors. This contributed to Jeff's various excesses (lots of partying) and injuries (broken neck, climbing and biking accidents) through his teens and twenties, to say nothing of how it prevented honest and direct connection with other members of *Homo sapiens*. But through meditation, he said, he'd developed the ability—most of the time, at least—to notice this voice before it overtook him.

Now when El Grandioso pops up, Jeff deliberately sends the voice a wave of friendliness. "I'm like, 'Oh, there you are. Haven't heard from you in a while, buddy. How you doing?'"

Jeff studied me carefully across the bus's small dining table. "I've noticed something about you, Dan," he said. "You still have an asshole in your head." We were back to talking about the joyless, airless, eat-your-vegetables nature of my practice.

Jeff suggested that I try to see my inner crank as lovable. "The asshole is basically a protective program. You internalized an asshole at some point in your life," he said. "It was trying to help you. It was trying to make Dan have the best life Dan could have. So it was working for a while, then it outlived its use. Now it's an anachronism." He said I should give the pattern a name—he recommended "Robert Johnson"—and send him a little love. "Whenever Robert Johnson's coming up, be like, 'Hey, Robert, what do you have to say now, buddy?'" When you remove the reactivity, he said, "it just defangs Robert."

I was intrigued by this, but it also seemed a little corny. I was fine identifying the fact that the ghost of Robert Johnson would continue to show up in my interior life, but I wasn't so sure I was game for naming a bunch of my inner characters and systematically sending them good vibes. I said I'd take it under consideration.

I was actually a bit distracted during this conversation. As Jeff and I were discussing our alter egos in the bus's dining area, the camera crew was on the bench opposite, recording the exchange. My eye was repeatedly drawn to Eddie, our director, who seemed distracted, staring unhappily at his phone.

Why wasn't Eddie having fun? I knew he was a little tired, but this is the meditating-since-he-was-eight surfer dude! Plus, this whole road trip was his idea, after all.

I was worried about Eddie. But there was also, to be frank, a touch of Robert Johnson lurking: *How dare someone not fully enjoy my road trip?*

I didn't realize it at the time, but we had all been ignoring one of our core principles, and it would soon come to a head.

5

"Meditation Is Self-Indulgent"

On the morning of day seven of our cross-country meditation peregrinations, I was standing in the lobby of a hotel in Nashville, contemplating the fact that "continental breakfast" is a misleadingly grand name for a basket filled with half-stale bagels, when I ran into Eddie. He was lugging the gear he would need for our first shoot of the day. Again he was looking harried and exhausted.

By contrast, I was feeling peppy, since I'd had a full night's sleep and had managed to get up early and sneak in a workout. As we waited for the rest of the team to join us, I inquired gingerly about his mood.

He sighed deeply. "I'm just not getting much sleep," he said. As we talked, I quickly began to realize that he had every reason to feel run-down. Eddie was genuinely being put through the wringer. Each day, when the rest of us headed to bed, he would stay up for several hours more, recharging the gear and loading all the video we had shot onto a hard drive. He and the crew would also have to rise earlier than the rest of us to get their equipment ready. Then they had to run around all day with heavy cameras or an audio kit. (Both Eddie and our director of photography, Nick Lopez, were shooting during the trip. We also had a soundman, Dennis Haggerty.) And it didn't end there for Eddie. As the creative director of this project, he was also in charge of the "look" of each of the many shoots we would do, often on the fly.

It wasn't that Eddie disliked any of his responsibilities, per se. The opposite was true—he approached his work with an earnest and seemingly effortless zeal. The real issue was that our movable meditation feast had become a rather shambolic affair. The trip had been planned carefully in advance, but now that we were actually on the road, some sizable logistical issues had emerged. Turns out crossing the country in eleven days requires covering a lot of ground every day. Since we had resolved after the first night never again to sleep on the bus, we didn't have much time to get the day's shooting done. In order to make the schedule work, we needed military efficiency, which we manifestly did not have. Part of this was due to a communications mix-up. Eddie thought Ben, the 10% Happier CEO, would be playing the role of Julie the cruise director, making sure everything ran on time. Ben did not share this impression.

The leadership vacuum created disorganization, which left us constantly running late. This meant the crew would often get screwed on sleep. And that's what was really frustrating Eddie. Though he was sleep-deprived himself, he was more concerned about the welfare of his team. In fact, on this morning, Eddie was shooting solo, so his crew could sleep in.

So Eddie was tired. And if Eddie was tired, it was a real problem. This guy is no malingerer. Having spent much of my career out in the field shooting stories, I knew firsthand how morale problems can metastasize and poison the atmosphere. However, when I tried to get under this particular hood, Eddie, in his low-key manner, basically shut me down. He assured me that everything would be fine, that he was a team player, et cetera. Before I could query him any further, the rest of the gang showed up, and we were off on our tight schedule for the day.

As we headed out to meet our next set of interviewees, I was struck by the irony of the situation. Here we were, tromping across the country trying to convince people to conduct regular mental maintenance, and all the while we were inadvertently putting Eddie and his team in a position where they couldn't take care of themselves.

The unfortunate situation in which we'd placed Eddie and the crew brought into stark relief an issue we had been encountering throughout the trip. People are burned out—from their jobs, from their family responsibilities, and from all the pressures of twenty-first-century living. Either they are unable to take sufficient care of themselves (as in Eddie's case) or they actively resist doing so. The latter was our next big obstacle: the belief, among so many, that self-care is self-indulgent. And, of course, the most self-indulgent flavor of self-care imaginable is sitting with your eyes closed, doing nothing.

This psychology was articulated by a speech-language pathologist we met on our trip named Leslie Wandemberg. She told us she felt awful every time she took five minutes to meditate, because she would immediately start contemplating all the other ways she might have used that time. "I could have been maybe coming up with more things to do with my baby. I could have given my husband five minutes of 'How was your day? Let's talk about your things.' So guilt has been my biggest barrier. As soon as I start to relax, I think, 'Oh my goodness, I shouldn't be relaxing. This is so bad. Why am I so selfish?'"

Let's not sugarcoat it. Meditation *can* be self-indulgent. Like anything else, it is certainly possible to use this form of self-care to the detriment of other important things in your life. However, it is also true that if you want to take care of other people, you simply cannot do so effectively if you are not taking adequate care of yourself. It's the old cliché from the airline safety instructions: put your own mask on before assisting others. In fact, neglecting to engage in a little bit of smart maintenance may leave you so bedraggled and resentful that it ends up having a negative effect on the people you are ostensibly trying to help. Researchers have found that mindfulness practice can reduce burnout among health professionals. Moreover, despite the supremely solipsistic optics of meditation, Jeff and I are of the view that the practice can both sensitize you to the challenges of others and help you respond with greater suppleness and care. It's what VMI professor Matthew Jarman argues in his Modern Warfare class, and it's what meditation masters have been arguing for millennia: the whole point of the practice is to prepare you to be of service.

Jeff has personally wrestled with this issue. "Self-care is my insulin," he says. "If I don't take small chunks of time for myself—to meditate, to be in nature, to rest—then my whole system very quickly gets out of whack." Running his meditation community in Toronto involves helping students with intense emotional challenges. This combined with his own ADD-fueled difficulties with organization and boundaries sometimes brought on burnout. It is the shadow side of Jeff's commitment to being of service: he sometimes pushes himself too far and gets resentful. In those times, it is not uncommon for his better half, Sarah, to direct him to the meditation cushion, or push him out the door "to go hug a tree."

I, by contrast, have no compunction about taking care of myself. Ask anybody in my orbit, and they will tell you it is tricky to expect too much of me if I haven't gotten enough sleep, food, meditation, and exercise. I'm like a delicate ficus. Does this make me selfish? Or self-aware? Where do you draw the line?

Whether or not you're susceptible to the "meditation is

self-indulgent" myth, in this chapter we'll explore a few different practices that are explicitly about caring for ourselves and others. The first of these is a self-compassion meditation, which is one way of getting people to learn, in Jeff's words, "how to give a shit about themselves." I will admit it took me a while before I could bring myself to do these kinds of practices. I considered them irredeemably sappy and forced—like celebrating Valentine's Day with a knife to my throat. However, there's a growing body of science suggesting that compassion meditation can confer both health and behavioral benefits. In other words, it can make you feel better and *act* better. While these practices are sometimes presented in an insufferably saccharine fashion, Jeff has a unique talent for making them relatable and practical.

I have a writer friend with chronic back pain. She's a very caring and generous person, but the pain, she says, makes her selfish. When it gets bad, all her thoughts are for her own survival. The same thing can happen to people with serious emotional pain—it's me-me-me problem-solving 24/7. It is much harder to be there for others when you're in that state. We're not even really there for ourselves. Half the time we end up grasping after half-baked solutions, or numbing or distracting ourselves with booze or work or social media, so we don't have to feel our hurt or anyone else's.

Support is there in the form of self-compassion. It's the most important medicine in the world that half the people in the world don't think they need. But everyone needs it sometimes, because everyone goes through tough times.

It can be hard to accept this. When I was younger, I'd be having a hard time, and then I'd get angry—at myself—that I was having a hard time in the first place. It didn't fit with my family's ideal of being stoic and uncomplaining. My life model was Sylvester Stallone from *Rocky IV*, whose Russian opponent remarked, in an appreciative monotone, "He is like a piece of iron." Except I was more like a piece of cheap IKEA particleboard, all warped and trailing sawdust. There's nothing like holding yourself to some other person's standard of engagement, fitness, or "happiness" to make yourself well and truly miserable.

That reminds me of a famous Buddhist parable about "the second arrow." A man is walking through the woods and he gets hit by an arrow. He immediately engages in a round of self-pitying thoughts: "Who shot me with an arrow? Why am I always the one who gets hit by an arrow? Is this going to totally ruin my dinner plans?" Those painful thoughts are the second arrow.

I think many of us experience some version of this. We suffer a legitimate wound—a physical blow, a difficult emotion, a professional disappointment—and then we compound the misery with our secondary stories about, say, how we don't deserve this, or how thoroughly screwed we are. We literally add insult to injury.

Obviously, important learning and problem-solving can happen after an injury, but other times there's a lot of painful resistance and rumination and mechanical self-laceration. We can have really old stories too: some arrowhead got snapped off years before, and it's still festering in our chest, radiating out into our experience in the form of grudges and avoidances and lifelong convictions about how things are and should be. These patterns are *reactions*. We can live inside them without any memory or awareness of what they once reacted to.

Fortunately, this compassion meditation is refreshingly direct: you don't need to figure out who or what hurt you. You can leap over all that and go straight to acknowledging that you're not feeling great in the first place. Because if you're feeling lonely or angry or overwhelmed, then, my friend, hurt is there. It's already a done deal.

The other piece of good news is that this practice doesn't require feeling any specific emotion for it to work, although of course feelings may happen and can be wonderfully gratifying. The definition of "compassion" in Buddhism is the *intention* that suffering be relieved. As my fellow CEC teacher and friend Avi Craimer says, "An intention is not a feeling, nor is it a plan." It is more like a simple wish, in this case for someone's hurt—i.e., your own—to diminish.

One of the learning curves of this practice is maintaining your intention without being attached to a particular outcome, including the outcome of feeling better. Which sounds counterintuitive, but it's important. We are not concerned with "the how" in this practice—we do not want to get bogged down in a new round of worrying and strategizing. The equanimity training here is genuinely wishing for our—and everyone else's—hurt to end, *while being okay with not knowing whether it will actually end or not.* This allows us to practice compassion even in cases that seem hopeless or intractable. It is a practice of caring independent of conditions.

Ultimately, self-compassion is a strategy that is implemented in the moment. Again and again, whenever you need it. Once you get the hang of it, it doesn't take long. You stop for a moment, notice and accept your discomfort (big or small), and then connect to a crisp intention for that discomfort to ease. Something magical can happen in that simple acknowledgment and intention. The situation gets a little more bearable. You have more room around it, and you have more room for other people too. You find yourself gradually expanding the range of conditions in which you see that compassion is applicable.

Ready?

Only if you promise not to say the word "heart."

I feel like I'm trying to sneak a love scene past the NC-17 film censors.

GIVING A SHIT ABOUT YOURSELF MEDITATION

*1 to 15 minutes, can be done in a few moments or
as part of a longer practice*

Start in the usual way: eyes closed or half closed. Relaxing into the posture as you breathe out, straightening up the spine as you breathe in. Setting an intention here to not get too uptight about things, to go along with the experiment. Take a few breaths to get settled.

Get curious about what's going on with you in this moment. Is there any way in which you aren't totally fine? Maybe there is some rushy anxiousness, or a dull heartache, or a feeling of stress. Or maybe there is some clear physical discomfort happening. Or maybe there is nothing like this at all. Sometimes we're just idling along in neutral. All of these states are fine. All we need to do here is sit with exactly what's happening inside us, not trying to fix anything. The beginning of compassion is allowing: allowing ourselves to feel what we feel, to be this exact person at this exact time. Just breathing into our bodies and sitting in this accepting way with ourselves.

Now for the self-compassion part. Start by connecting to a simple intention inside yourself to be well. There's nothing necessarily sentimental here—we're talking about the extremely reasonable desire to be healthy and not in pain. A short phrase here can help: *May I be well.* This is different from noting or using a mantra; it's using a short phrase to highlight your intention. If that language sounds lofty or artificial, use a different one: *It's okay,* or *Feel better.* Choose words that feel natural to you. The key is to connect to your own sensible aspiration for your discomfort to pass. You are not trying to fix the problem or think about all its permutations. Put that all aside. You are going below it, to the most simple and uncomplicated intention: *Obviously, I'd prefer not to suffer.* Who wouldn't?

Some people recruit an image to help with this, for example, the image of themselves as a little kid. This can help kick in some nice warm feelings, although warm feelings aren't required. You can imagine yourself as a four-year-old running around in a park with ice cream smeared all over your face and then you wipe out and start bawling. *"Oh, man! May you be well, little lady/dude/gender-nonbinary kiddo."* Can you connect to the reasonable feeling of wanting that kid—you—to be happy, to no longer be in pain? You can use any scenario, real or imagined, that works for you. And of course you can use an adult version of yourself too, because that kid is still inside you, nested like a Russian doll inside your years of learning and living.

May I be well. The practice is returning, again and again, to the simple intention for you to be well, and then sending that intention to yourself. You can use an image to help with the latter, or—if images are tricky—you can simply focus on the embodied sense of yourself sitting. *May I be well.* It helps to smile. Notice what feelings come up. All are fine and natural—the specific feelings are secondary to your intention. You may feel loving or calm. If so, great—enjoy. Or you may feel annoyed or self-conscious. Also no problem. If the latter occur, have a sense of humor about the backfiring hilarity of this meditative situation, and send that sense of humor down and into your black, black heart. Compassion by another name. There's always a workaround.

May I be well. Connect to the reasonableness of the intention behind your words. *May I be well.* For real. Like everyone else on the planet, you're doing the best you can. *May I be well.* May all of us be well. Recognizing our shared human condition. There can be something very poignant about this.

So that's the main part of it. You're sitting there repeating your phrase, and as you do you're continually reconnecting to the simple intention for your suffering to ease. Sending this to yourself, with maybe an extra visual or feeling. It's okay if it seems awkward at first—you're like an actor rehearsing your lines. It gets easier with time. *May I be well.* Eventually your focus will be less on the words and more on the intention behind them, which gets stronger and clearer and more obviously commonsense.

There's one more thing you can do: if some specific part of your body actually hurts, then imagine sending your caring intention directly into that part, opening the channel, sending in healing vibes. *May I be well.* You are practicing giving a shit about all parts of yourself. And then feeling what you feel. Feeling and fellow-feeling: *May I be well.* May all of us be well.

A good way to finish this meditation is to expand the circle of compassion out: to imagine others in your life, others like you, people doing the best they can. Connect to your intention for them to also be well. *May you be well.* Find a phrase that works for you, and silently repeat it if you like, maybe visualizing faces near and far. *May you be well.*

Think of it as a final act of generosity, sending out your intention and your care and the benefits of the practice to others. Maybe there's some gratitude there. *May you be well.* It's basically the best training program a human being can enroll in, ever. It's worth the effort.

Finish up by feeling the breath and the body. Solid in your posture, supported by the ground, chilling on your stoop like a little Buddha. A final couple of breaths into the chest, feeling that area fill with air and warmth. When you're ready, open your eyes. Yes, you just did that. You are now a beautiful marshmallow of compassion.

CHEAT SHEET

1. Take a few breaths to get settled, and then check to see if there is any physical or emotional discomfort present. It may also be that you feel perfectly fine and normal. All possibilities are okay.

2. Connect to the simple and reasonable intention for yourself to be well, to not be hurting. *May I be well,* or *It's okay,* or *Feel better.* Find a phrase that works for you and repeat it, continually reestablishing that simple intention.

3. To help with this, you can draw on images and feelings, although you don't need to. It helps to smile. One image people use is themselves as a little kid.

4. Finish by sending some good vibes out to your friends and family and the whole alive planet. *May you be well.* Paying it forward.

• • •

My wife, Bianca, presents with an interesting variant of the "meditation is self-indulgent" myth. She not only resists prioritizing her own needs but also adds to it a distinctive streak of rebelliousness.

When we interviewed her at the ABC News studios back on the first day of the road trip, Jeff and I tried to get at the root of why Bianca wasn't routinely meditating. Part of it was finding the time. "I'm just so busy doing things for everyone else," she said. "I'm in a caretaking profession. I have a child." Then, side-eyeing me, "Or two."

In her job, she often has extremely busy periods at the hospital, where she goes into what she described to us as "intense survival mode," taking care of patients around the clock. As she explained, "The problem is, there is nothing more important in those stretches. I will sacrifice whatever I have to sacrifice about myself." She made it clear, though, that she was not necessarily suffering during these times. Turning to me, she said, "It's like you, covering war. My adrenaline is sky high, I'm invigorated, I'm interested, I feel good at my job, and I feel really relevant."

But then she would come home and have to put our toddler to bed. (Because of my unusual work schedule—a combination of late nights and early mornings—the job usually falls to her.) This is where the aforementioned rebelliousness would kick in. Instead of meditating for a few minutes at the end of her day—which she had long acknowledged would be a smart and healing move for her—she would often make a different call.

"At ten o'clock when the kid is finally asleep," she said, "I would admittedly rather indulge myself in some bad TV for ten minutes before I go to bed than anything else."

Talking to Bianca, it became clear that she viewed meditation not only as self-indulgent but also as a chore she resisted with particular ferocity because, as she had once put it, "I am married to the happiness guru." Despite the fact that I was careful never to lecture her about meditation, merely living with me was a form of finger-wagging all its own.

Even if you don't live with a semipro meditator, the practice—or any kind of self-care, really—can be massively guilt-inducing. As Jeff says, "It suggests that if you're unhappy or stressed, it's your fault for not doing anything about it." It's another form of the second-arrow stuff we discussed earlier. "You have the original stress," says Jeff, "and now the knife you keep jabbing into yourself for not meditating. You end up in a whole aversion cycle with meditating, pushing away the thing that will help you because merely thinking about the thing that will supposedly help you—that you are of course not doing—makes you feel even worse."

This is why, when he's teaching, Jeff often avoids the "meditation is good for you" emphasis and focuses instead on the exploratory fun of doing it for its own sake. "Exercise is good for you," he says. "In contrast, dancing or hiking is pleasurable in a way that creates its own motivation. When we get instrumental about meditation, we can lose touch with its intrinsic 'just because' goodness."

Bianca's version of the second arrow was that, after sheepishly turning on the TV at the end of her long day, she often would not even allow herself the luxury of simply watching whatever show she had chosen. Rather than truly give herself some rest, she would multitask by tidying up or ordering groceries. "I think I'm feeling better. I think I'm entertained. I think I'm more organized. But then I'm twice as spent the next day."

As Bianca laid all this out for us, I knew enough to keep my mouth shut and let Jeff work his magic. He pulled what may be his most ingenious MacGyver move yet to get Bianca over the hump.

He started by empathizing. He related the story of how he, too, had spent many years neglecting himself. "I was helping a lot of people, and I would put all of my energy into that. But when it came to my own situation, I was constantly . . . whatever," he said, shrugging. "Now I have a practice where I check in with myself," he said, looking down at himself. "I'm like, 'What's up, little dude? What's going on in there?'"

As Bianca smiled, Jeff suggested a plan for her.

"I was thinking, what about a reality TV meditation? Your job every day is to watch ten minutes of reality TV."

Basically, his idea was to co-opt her current routine. "You hack the existing structure of your life," he said. As mentioned earlier, scientists who study habit formation talk about "cue, behavior, reward." For Bianca, the "cue" had been reaching the end of her day, the "behavior" was to watch TV, and the "reward" was zoning out. Jeff's proposal was to take the same cue but slightly alter the behavior, which would transform the reward.

He promised to make her a bespoke guided meditation that would combine self-care, self-compassion, and restfulness without feeling like yet another item for the to-do list. "It's not another injunction," he said. "Actually, it's the opposite of that. It's like being lazy in a way that's actually good for you."

She seemed sold. She liked the idea of a guided meditation. (She said she liked "answering to someone else, as opposed to myself—as long as it's not Dan.") She was also enthusiastic about the fact that the practice Jeff described seemed a lot less regimented than the one I do.

"I will take your prescription and try it," she announced.

Below is a version of the meditation Jeff made for Bianca.

This is the most over-the-top self-indulgent meditation I can think of. It's about *reveling* in rest and taking care of yourself. Own it! You're allowed to do this, by the way. Call it self-care, call it basic maintenance, call it escaping from Dan's meditative gulag. Take fifteen minutes to do nothing on a porch, or go for a walk, or lie on the grass. You probably already have go-tos of your own here. This meditation is about being a bit more clear and intentional about it all.

Whatever you do, do *not* get into the trap of comparing yourself to some martyr partner/friend/relative. Everyone has a version of the badass Italian grandmother who raised twelve kids and eighteen grandkids, cleaned every home in the neighborhood, and made phenomenal pasta e fagioli, all while apparently never taking a break. These people make us look bad and are actually demons.

The point is, everyone has different capacities, *and everyone has different capacities at different times.* The more rested and healthy and supported you are, the more you have to give. This obviously goes up and down depending on many internal and external variables. One of the trickier aspects of being human is balancing the amount you need to give others with the amount you can afford to give yourself. Your body can help you make these decisions if you listen. But give yourself a break too—there are times when it's going to be unbalanced. That's just life. But we can be smart and make up for it where we can.

For those who imagine this is somehow a lesser practice, I know excellent meditation teachers who *only* teach rest. They teach you to find it while you sit, while you lie down—even while you walk. We think we know what rest is, but many of us have no idea. Rest is on a continuum. You think you're resting, but then you realize you're actually holding your breath, holding your body tense and quivering at the edge of your meditation cushion like you have a giant pickle up your ass. And so you sigh and let go, and your whole body drops. We learn in meditation that it's possible to do this again and again and again. Each time we let go, our body seems to shed another layer of tension and gripping. They come peeling off us like ghosts, an exorcism for our secular age.

TAKING BACK LAZY,
OR ESCAPING DAN'S MEDITATIVE GULAG
2 minutes to 2 hours—yeah, revel in it!

The first thing to do is get yourself in position. By "position" I mean crash on your back on the living room floor with the TV on in the background. Or flop down on your bed, or porch, or couch. It can be slovenly. It *should* be slovenly. This practice can also be done with somebody, particularly a child, a pet, or a sluggish roommate who watches too much TV and is covered in potato chip crumbs. Curl up next to them if it feels good to you. The idea is to hack whatever natural life situation you find yourself in and turn it into a perfect meditation.

    Close your eyes and take a few deep breaths. Make the out-breath a nice, slow, and enjoyable settling. Soften the face. Slowly bring your attention to the feeling of the body lying on its back or on its side. The feeling of relaxation. Can you imagine sinking even more deeply into the ground? If you like, you can lift each arm and each leg and one by one let them flop down. Really let go here, rag doll style. Every time you think of it, imagine you can let go of another layer of tension. If there are any thoughts, just let them be in the background, like the far-off hum of a radio or television, or traffic in the distance. Not a big deal.

Bring your attention to any feelings of rest in your body. The simple feeling of lying there, relaxed. If there's somebody next to you, send your attention out and notice the physical connection with that other body. Your own body rising and falling with the breath, the other body rising and falling with their breath. The idea is to include this full loop of sensations, you and the other, into the meditation. Enjoying this connection and enjoying your own animal feeling. The attitude here is "Yeah, all right, nothing to do." Nothing to do but rest in your own body and your own relaxed awareness. That's the main meditation instruction.

If you fall asleep, then sleep. I guess you needed it. This is all about the drowsy pleasure of lying on your back on the floor with no agenda. Like when you were a kid. The innocence and simplicity of this. Relaxing, giving yourself this time, not needing anything else.

In this meditation we're emphasizing relaxation and letting go and not trying to constantly control our situation. It doesn't matter if your mind wanders. You don't need to implement some special meditative technique, although you can if you want to. You don't even need to be "mindful." Forget mindfulness. You just have to be a gorgeous lazy slacker.

In fact, let's do some more deliberate lazification here: if you feel like it, sigh and flop down a few more times, settling even more into the ground.

As per the self-compassion meditation we just did, a caring piece may emerge naturally on its own. Caring for yourself, caring for the human or animal next to you (if there is a human or animal next to you). If caring is there, let it be a pleasurable feeling in the background. Your attention is primarily on the lush laziness of the body and maybe this other body next to you, although you may drift too and that is fine, that may be part of it. Notice any feelings of simple fulfillment and comfort. This is a complete practice, exactly the one you need. Taking back lazy.

If you have more time, keep meditating in this way. Enjoy this stolen moment. It's good for you. When you're ready to wrap up, slowly open your eyes, and see if you can bring some of this relaxed vibe into the rest of your day. Oh, and tell your roommate to get a job.

CHEAT SHEET

1. Flop down on the floor, or couch, or anywhere, in a relaxed and perhaps slovenly way. It's okay if a kid or animal is next to you—we'll make their presence part of the meditation.

2. Close your eyes, if you like. Big relaxation on the exhale, letting go of any tension. Imagine sinking more deeply into the ground. Lift your arms and legs a bit and then flop them down

a few times. Your attitude is "Yeah, nothing to do." Nothing to do but rest and drift. This is the main instruction.

3. If you fall asleep, that's fine. If there are thoughts, let them be in the background, like noise from a distant radio. Just lying on the floor of the room like when you were a kid.

4. Open your eyes when you're ready, and then slouch-walk-groove into your day like a young John Travolta. Taking lazy to the street!

After simmering for days, our crisis of team morale came to a head in, of all places, the Big Easy.

It happened, ironically, on the heels of one of the most absurdly delightful gambits of the whole trip. Jeff and I had brought along a rickety $400 "meditation booth," a sort of contemplative kissing booth, which we had ordered online. We set it up on a bright, bustling morning in Jackson Square, right in the center of town.

I love New Orleans. Even after—perhaps especially after—having covered the horror of Hurricane Katrina. I adore everything about the place: the people, the architecture, the history, the life-altering music, and the life-shortening cuisine. Tennessee Williams is reported to have said, "There are only three great cities in the United States: New York, San Francisco, and New Orleans. All the rest are Cleveland."

Ben, always looking to eke out every iota of performance from the team, went to the iconic Café du Monde and picked up containers of coffee and several bags filled with their legendary beignets—diabolical, pillow-like pastries covered in powdered sugar. I had been abstaining from sweets during the road trip, because they inflame my inner crackhead, disrupt my sleep, and make me generally insufferable. In what was, for me, a colossal act of self-control, I managed to limit myself to half a beignet.

Wiping the powdered sugar from my face, I joined Jeff at the booth. As excited as I was about our social experiment, I was also feeling mildly anxious and self-conscious. Ever since I was a cub reporter, I had always hated "MOS" (man on the street) interviews, which entailed corralling strangers and trying to get sound bites out of them. Our booth, with its banner proclaiming "Free Meditation Lessons," was an exponentially more embarrassing version of MOS.

Farther down the square, there was a large crowd surrounding a guy who was performing acrobatic stunts using an enormous, sparkly hula hoop. Someone with a tuba set up shop right next door to us on the promenade. "It's possible," I said to Jeff, "that we will be here for a long time and nobody will take us up on this offer."

"Absolutely possible we'll be rejected again and again," said Jeff, although he didn't seem to care. As a younger man, he had struggled with self-consciousness, but had found an unusual way of dealing with it: by going to nightclubs and forcing himself to dance. It's harder to boogie when you're locked in your own head, and Jeff had developed the ability to cut loose with full-on, goofy abandon. Yet another thing I admired/envied about him. Back at our meditation booth in Jackson Square, he noted with something bordering on enthusiasm, "I think that we're going to find all kinds of permutations of humiliation. They're all available to us."

Things began inauspiciously. A lady in a purple coat and sunglasses walked by and mentioned she had read my book. "Thanks," I said. "Want to learn how to meditate?"

"No thanks," she said, walking away.

Jeff cackled.

"Parenthetically," I said, "she's saying: 'I read your book— not that good.'"

Then the floodgates opened. Suddenly there were loads of people excited to meditate with us in public. Older married couples on vacation, middle-aged businessmen in town for conventions, even a local, bowler-hat-wearing magician who stopped by for a session before performing elsewhere on the square. Craig, a stressed-out salesman, mentioned he'd recently bought my book: "I thought, if this guy can relax, I can relax." Our new friends would belly up to the booth, in groups of two or three at a time, where Jeff would have them rest their hands on the faux wood countertop while giving short courses in mindfulness, enveloped by the clang and clatter of the city.

A funny thing happened for me as we stood there, meditating with total strangers in the middle of a noisy public space: I started to really enjoy myself. Perhaps because it was such a "bad" meditation spot by most traditional measures, I found myself just surrendering. As Jeff instructed, I let the noises flow through me, felt my feet on the ground, and tuned in— when I could—to my breath. I experienced an upwelling of gratitude toward Jeff for a virtuosic performance. Even though I make fun of him for waxing oracular at times, I know of very few other meditation teachers who could wade into such an unusual environment and truly connect with people in this way. At one point, as we were meditating with a pair of nurses who worked in a local psych ward—and who used meditation as a form of self-care—Jeff suggested that they open to all the physical sensations, the sounds, and "the strange, self-conscious weirdness of this random situation of meditating with two middle-aged dudes in the middle of a square in New Orleans."

We concluded our afternoon by meditating with Jerome, a performance artist who made his living by covering himself in silver spray paint and posing as a living statue with picture-taking tourists. He could sit with such superhuman stillness and silence that he made us meditators look like amateurs. It was awesome.

However, as we packed up to leave, the beignets were gone, the booth was back in its cardboard box, and Eddie's baseline affability had fully curdled. Yet again, Ben had failed to step up and make sure that we were running according to schedule, and Eddie was justifiably upset. The two of them exchanged some sharp words on the street, which produced for me the following bout of *prapañca:*

> *Eddie and Ben are going to come to blows* → *The tabloids are going to run stories about how this sweet, sensitive meditation road trip devolved into acrimony* → *My mindfulness career will be comprehensively and panoramically fucked* → *Jazzercise*

It was time to have it out. We couldn't let this fester any longer.

At a truck stop about an hour out of town, I convened a meeting. Eddie, Ben, Jeff, and I commandeered the front cabin of the bus, while everyone else retired to the George Clinton suite, no doubt speculating about whether there might be a homicide in the offing.

As soon as the doors closed, wham—roundhouse to my head. I didn't even know who hit me. As I went down, I saw Ben throw himself up against the window. Jeff started chanting. Eddie tore open his shirt and shouted, "Who wants some of this?"

Nah. The whole thing transpired in exactly the reasonable

way you might expect. Eddie got a chance to vent, we listened, and we admitted we had been pushing way too hard. He teared up a bit, and we all hugged it out. Then we made a bunch of changes to the schedule, canceling some of the planned shoots so that we had more breathing room in the itinerary. We also got Ben to agree to truly take on the job of maintaining and enforcing the daily plan, ensuring that everyone was getting enough rest and food. All in all, it was one of the single quickest and most congenial instances of conflict resolution to which I had ever been a party.

Afterward we called in the rest of the gang, briefed them on the schedule changes, and did a postmortem. Eddie was still choked up. "I felt really good about our conversation," he said. "We're meditators. There wasn't a ton of ego to smash through to get down to the kernels of the problem. There was some weird silver lining of delight in being totally ground down to revealing demons," he said. I felt like reaching out and giving the man another hug. No wonder Jeff had been so close with him for so long.

There was a lot to be learned from this situation. For Eddie, it wasn't just "a simple self-care lesson." It was also, he said, an allegory about what happens when "mindfulness meets capitalism." It was a lesson in leadership, boundaries, and also the challenges of taking care of yourself. As we talked it through, some of our fellow travelers weighed in with their own stories about how they had put others first, failed to implement self-care, and had it all blow up in their faces.

Carlye Adler, who had come along to help Jeff and me turn this journey into a book, discussed one of her inner demons. As a woman who balances being a wife and a mother with a busy writing career servicing a bunch of high-octane clients, she sometimes finds herself taking on too many commitments.

"So it's like, 'Yes, yes, yes yes yes.' And I mean it. It's not with resentment that I say yes and take things on," she said. But at some point she will encounter an unseen internal trip wire, "and then it turns into the Rage Fairy."

"Rage Fairy" is a term Jeff had apparently coined during a separate conversation with Carlye about the issue. As Jeff explained, it's like Carlye starts off as a "pink fluffy unicorn" who is "all peace and love." But when triggered, she "turns into this psychotic unicorn and rips the shit out of everybody."

"Yeah," Carlye agreed as we all laughed. "Unfortunately I can be a little destructive to the people around me when willingness turns to resentment. The switch flips."

"And it's exactly what it feels like for me too," said Jeff. "It feels literally like a switch has flipped. I guess like Jekyll and Hyde. I'm just super 'Yes, yes, yes, happy to be helpful.' And then all of a sudden my answer's like, 'Fuck you forever.'" (I've seen this phenomenon at play with Bianca, who will have rare but piquant episodes of what the writer Gretchen Rubin calls "obliger rebellion." For example, I often eat off her plate at restaurants. Usually she's happy to share. But if I have the gall to go for the last bite of her favorite orecchiette dish, I might get a fork in my eye.)

For Jeff, those moments often turn into opportunities for self-judgment. "It is very hard to see that stuff, because you think, 'I'm a dick and I'll always be like this. This is the real me.'"

I was experiencing my own self-judgment during this group discussion, because I couldn't really relate to much of it. "I'm definitely not an accommodator the way you guys are, where I whirl around saying yes to everything. I have fears about being self-centered and about my capacity for compassion."

This is a deep issue for me. For most of my life, my friends, family, and I have made a running joke out of the fact that I can be a bit of a jerk. My parents love regaling people with tales of my epic adolescence, like how I used to torture my bookish younger brother by throwing ice at the ceiling over wherever he was reading, to "make it snow." In college, my roommate had the habit of leaving a dictionary open on my pillow with the word "ethics" highlighted. In the early days of our marriage, when Bianca would confront me over an infraction, I would often smirk and proclaim it to be her fault because "you married poorly." There was, unfortunately, some truth undergirding these jokes. I have a long history of being prickly. (It's not that I was Genghis Khan, but there were certainly times when I escalated conflicts at work or at home into shouting matches.) Part of it was congenital; I am Robert Johnson's grandson, after all. Part of it was learned; my sharp-edged sense of humor earned me friends (although, admittedly, not everyone was into it), and my competitive spirit propelled me forward professionally. However, even as I have outgrown much of my tendency toward being irascible, it has remained a painful part of my self-image, especially when I compare myself to softer and more effortlessly altruistic people like Bianca, Jeff, and Carlye. It is not uncommon for me to notice a selfish or angry impulse arising, and then launch into a whole second-arrow story about what a terrible person I am.

The point—as I have learned, and as we have been saying throughout this book—is not to feel guilty about whatever you're feeling. It's to see it all clearly, so that it doesn't control you. As Jeff explained to the group of us on the bus, the smart strategy is to work through your issues with equanimity and friendliness, which—and here's where he lost me—would clear the way for the emergence of a more "loving heart."

"When you use terms like 'loving heart,' can I go puke?" I asked.

This quickly devolved into a debate about whether we

should call this book *The Loving Heart by Dan Harris*, featuring a gauzy picture of me on the cover, with the wind blowing through my hair. Someone offered the alternative title *Awakening to Your Inner Douche by Dan Harris*.

Even though I am an avowed anti-sentimentalist, I really do believe in the power of compassion practices. As cloying as I may find them to be on some levels, I have been motivated to explore them precisely because I have found them to be an antidote to some of my perceived deficits. In this meditation, Jeff moves from generating compassion for ourselves to generating it for others. As we've said, you can't do the former without the latter.

Compassion makes the world go round—or its good parts, anyway. It's helpful to understand the difference between feeling someone's pain, on the one hand, and more active compassion, on the other. Social neuroscientists call the first "empathic resonance"—our own bodies can literally resonate with another person's sadness and hurt and fear. Empathy is an important building block of compassion, but it can also lead to becoming overwhelmed and to what's known in the caregiver world as "compassion fatigue." We end up bailing on the person in front of us, because we can't handle their pain. Mature compassion, by contrast, is more sustainable. What's more, the intention and presence it generates are arguably more helpful and comforting for the other person.

How many times in our lives have we been frozen in the face of someone else's grief or loss, with no idea of how to respond? Most of the time all you need to do is shut up and show you care. Here's how.

SMART COMPASSION

30 seconds or more

This meditation can be done when you're alone, or it can be done on the fly, when you're actually with someone who's hurting in some way. It's always good to begin with a few long deep breaths, just to help relax and cool out the nervous system. Right at the start we are looking to establish an inner composure and calmness in the way we hold our experience.

If you're in a sitting meditation, you can do this for a couple of minutes, feeling the breath as your anchor, settling and breathing out tension on the exhales as usual. If this is happening in the company of someone, these long breaths are still good to do—as you settle and get more present, you help them settle and get more present. This is part of empathic resonance. The vibes we send out and the vibes we receive are contagious. We work skillfully with this understanding.

Now bring to mind the image of someone you know who needs some love. Someone who's having a hard time physically or emotionally. Maybe say their name at the start here, bringing them more fully into your experience. If you're doing this live, you obviously don't need to do this—they're right there. Notice if there are any sympathetic emotional responses in your own body and mind as you connect to their situation. That's fine—breathe into any feelings that may be there. We'll use this as a springboard as we move to the main part of the practice.

Try to connect to your sincere aspiration—your intention—for this person's hurt to end. As with the self-compassion meditation, a short phrase can help. Something like *May you be well* or *May you be strong.* Or maybe your language is more direct: *It's okay* or *I'm here.* Choose a sentence that works for you, and repeat it silently. Don't spend too much time deliberating—if nothing suitable comes to mind, use one of these. It's the intention that matters.

The idea is to connect to the very reasonable desire for this person's hurt and challenge to end. We are not looking to create an emotional response, although emotions can happen and are welcomed. Nor are we trying to fix the person or "the problem." Your compassion isn't dependent on any kind of outcome. It's caring for its own sake. We simply wish for the person to be well. It's a concentration exercise, which means continually reestablishing the intention, and letting yourself feel what you feel.

For the next few minutes—or for as long as makes sense if you're with the person—repeat your phrase, *May you be well,* at a pace that's comfortable for you. If your mind wanders, start again with your simple intention: *May you be well.* Patient—not in a rush. A steady expression of calm seeing and presence. *I'm here.* There's an understanding here that everyone goes through tough times, that life's ups and downs are beyond our control. You sit—or stand—solid inside all of this.

May you be well. This is a fundamentally active practice—you are not passively submerged in feeling. Rather, you are actively offering your intention and your presence and your caring. It is a *doing*. We are practicing how to respond to others in a supportive way. As with every meditation in this book, it is both an exploration and a training.

Stop when the time feels right. Connecting to your breath and body, feeling your feet on the ground, breathing deeply but naturally. *May you be well. May all of us be well.*

CHEAT SHEET

1. This meditation can be done live, in front of someone who's having a hard time. Or it can be done while you're sitting and imagining a person in a tough situation. Either way, take a few deep breaths to get settled.

2. Try to connect to a sincere intention for this person's hurt to end. Repeating a silent phrase in your head can help: *May you be well,* or *It's okay,* or *I'm here.*

3. If emotions happen, no problem. Let them be present. But they're not required. This is all about the intention, which for some people feels very reasonable and calm.

4. Repeat your phrase—*May you be well*—at a pace that's comfortable for you. If your mind wanders, start again with your simple intention. Not in any rush. This is all about your steady, mature presence and your compassionate intention for this person to be okay.

The day after our group reconciliation session, everyone had time for themselves. We'd decided to cancel all the shoots and take a mental health day. In the morning, I bumped into Eddie in the gym at our hotel in Austin, Texas. He was jumping rope in an incredibly fluid way. As it happened, I had learned to jump rope myself a few months earlier and had all the grace of a blind howler monkey. Eddie, by contrast, seemed to be floating.

Our man was back.

After lunch, we all hopped back on the bus for our daily drive. With no real work to be done, I had a chance to sit back and appreciate the experience. We were just past the halfway mark of our trip, and I wanted to savor it all. The infelicities of the bus bathroom, which had really started to smell. The crazy souvenirs (a jar of spicy pickled okra was a standout). Nick, our hilarious director of photography, singing karaoke and doing eerily spot-on impersonations of George W. Bush. Dennis, the sound guy, wearing his perennial grin (perhaps because he was newly single and spending much of the trip using Tinder to arrange assignations in the various cities we visited). Mack Woodruff, the youngest member of our team (coincidentally the son of Bob and Lee Woodruff, who had introduced me to my wife), who with his good looks and fashion sense made us look cooler in public than we deserved. Our long group bull sessions, led by Jeff, who was starting to remind me of the coolest camp counselor ever.

The prior day's intervention, as tough as it was, had had a magical effect. The air was cleared. News flash: the mechanism for this kind of conflict mediation is not complicated. Talking about your emotions in a supportive environment is a time-honored tactic for working through them. Meditation is a way to provide that service for yourself, to drag your neuroses out from under their little hiding places in your mind's backwaters and expose them to the light.

Of course, there are many people who do not want to do this kind of inner work. They don't want to face their emotions and deep-seated patterns. They're afraid, often justifiably.

At our next stop, we would meet some people who had every reason to feel this fear.

6

Pandora's Box

—————

It is simultaneously one of the most hilarious and appalling scientific studies I have ever seen. Researchers from the University of Virginia Department of Psychology asked subjects to sit in a lab room for fifteen minutes with only their thoughts. There were no phones allowed, and no other people around. However, the room was equipped with a button that the subjects could push and give themselves an electric shock if they wanted. The results were astonishing: many of the people, including two-thirds of the men, were so uncomfortable sitting quietly alone that they opted to zap themselves.

The study authors weren't quite sure what to make of this. There are many theories. You could draw the conclusion that we live in such a hyperstimulated age that we get bored very quickly. You could also surmise, as the lead author does, that part of what is going on here is that humans evolved to scan for threats and opportunities, which can make idling excruciating. Both of those theories have merit. But I suspect—based on zero evidence beyond my layman's gut—that there could be an additional process at play. In my view, this study speaks to one of the deep and often subconscious reasons some people avoid meditation. They are afraid to be alone with how they feel. They worry that if they look inside, they will open up a Pandora's box of potentially paralytic emotions.

This is a fear Jeff and I heard in a powerful way when we visited Aprendamos Intervention Team (AIT), a company in Las Cruces, New Mexico, that serves mostly low-income children with developmental disabilities and delays. The management had been trying, with mixed results, to introduce mindfulness as a form of self-care that could help the staff better handle job-related stress.

Jeff and I sat down with roughly two dozen employees.

"Opening yourself up to vulnerability is hard. It's scary," one staff member said.

Said another, "Some days I just don't really care for being in my own head."

A physical therapist named Zoe Gutierrez said, "I get people all the time asking me, 'How do you do what you do? You work with kids that've been abused, and they have brain damage because of child abuse. How do you go into that home and deal with that parent, knowing it was the dad that did it?'" Zoe said she loved her work, but that when it came to handling the psychological issues the job produces, her main priority was simply to move past it all. "I think the hard part is coming home and shutting off that side, and then focusing on your family and what you have to take care of, and getting back to life."

We also heard from Lidia Mendez, a boisterous and likable woman who works with autistic children. At first she told us her mind was simply too busy to meditate—a classic "I can't do this" sentiment. Upon further probing, though, she admitted that, despite her ebullient exterior, she suffered from anxiety and had deep reservations about sitting with herself. "I'm scared of what I will find if I actually let everything out." She laughed a bit nervously, perhaps surprised by the weight of her own admission.

It is true that meditating can bring up our deep fears. However, anxieties tend to surface sooner or later anyway. Meditation gives us a way to work proactively with our emotions, enabling us to see them clearly rather than having them sally forth from their dank mental redoubts at a time of their choosing.

There is an important caveat here. If you have trauma in your personal history, if you suffer from mental illness, or if you experience any psychological difficulties upon starting a meditation practice, it is prudent to consult a mental health professional before going any further. This does not mean that meditation isn't the right move for you, but when it comes to addressing our mental health it's rarely one-stop shopping.

That said, both Jeff and I have suffered from mild bouts of depression and/or anxiety, and we have found meditation to be enormously useful, often in conjunction with traditional psychotherapy. In my own experience, when the fog of gloom descends, meditation helps me step off the hamster wheel of obsessive thought, so that I don't get so caught up in the stories barfed up by the voice in my head. In fact, research appears to back this up, suggesting that meditation can be beneficial for depression and anxiety. The *Journal of the American Medical Association* published a study led by the Johns Hopkins School of Medicine that found daily mindfulness-based meditation was roughly as effective as antidepressants in providing relief from some symptoms.

No one is suggesting that the process of confronting your emotions through meditation is easy. In our exchange with Lidia, Jeff spoke candidly about encountering some of his own issues, in particular those created by his ADD. "It was scary when I realized I had to start facing some of these things," he said. His first few years of meditating were mostly peaceful and interesting. "Then, maybe five years in, all this aggression and shame and hurt started to bubble up out of nowhere. It would last anywhere from a few minutes to a few hours. Even once it calmed down, I'd feel it simmering under the surface in my day-to-day life. I realized it had been there a long time, I just had never seen it clearly. Eventually it worked itself out."

Jeff also pointed out that sometimes what you're avoiding is not as bad as you might fear. "Often I've had this experience: 'Oh God, I don't want to go in there.' And then you open the door a crack, and it's a little mouse. There's no monster in there."

For many of us, the natural inclination is to run from our difficult emotions. (As Stephen Colbert joked when I appeared on *The Colbert Report* to promote my book, "I used to not be happy all the time and then I just grew a pair and manned up. I do what men do: we stuff it down!") Meditation offers an alternative, although, as Jeff points out, it's important to pace yourself; it can be delicate work.

There is a popular acronym that many people, myself included, have found useful as a guide for leaning into emotions, RAIN: recognize, accept, investigate, non-identification.

RAIN is a way to explore any sensation, thought, or emotion—even the hard ones. It's a very useful tool to have in your meditator's tool belt. Other meditations in this book that can help with difficult emotions are Taking Back Lazy (Chapter 5), Smart Compassion (Chapter 5), and Walking Meditation (Chapter 8).

The practice helps in a couple of ways. First, it boosts your emotional literacy. Instead of being lost in an emotional reaction, you stop and get curious about what's happening inside you. Although we can obviously have emotionally loaded thoughts, our bodies are the real epicenter of our emotions. Massage therapists like to say, "Our issues are in our tissues." It's true. And not just any tissues—*your* tissues. You may experience anger in your jaw, or in your forearms, or in your ears, as they throb and shoot cartoon flames. We're all uniquely configured, but there's overlap too. With RAIN, we get curious about our own idiosyncratic "tells," the many subtle tics and quirks and contractions that are our particular body's way of saying: *I'm feeling over here! Feeling is happening!* In this way, we can learn to catch our emotional reactions early, and not, in teacher Sharon Salzberg's excellent words, "fifteen consequential actions later."

And there's a second way it helps. The fruit of meditation isn't just less emotional reactivity. *It's also having fewer negative emotions in the first place.* The more we practice observing our emotional habits, the less potent they become. Over time, they can begin to heal. This can happen with even our oldest and most private emotions. The process is slow. But it's effective.

How does this happen? What does it *feel* like to be inside this undertaking? That's what RAIN is about. It's the gift inside Pandora's box.

RAIN

5 to 15 minutes

Start by taking a few breaths. When we work with emotions—which can get very strong—there's an important preliminary step of identifying some subtly comfortable or settling sensation or simply seeing if you can tune in to an underlying stillness. Like a home base you can come back to. It might be the breath, or a peaceful feeling in the body, or a sound, or an image—even an external picture you can look at. Take a couple of minutes to find this place and to meditate on it, noticing its qualities, getting familiar with it. This is a place we'll come back to over the course of the meditation; you can visit it anytime you need a break. Note it, if you like: call it *home* or *rest*.

The first step of RAIN—the "R"—is **recognize**. Can you recognize any emotions happening in your experience right now? Sadness, happiness, anger, frustration, curiosity, boredom, impatience, anxiety—any emotion. If so, note it: *sadness, boredom,* whatever.

A feeling may not be obvious. Sometimes when we look we realize that, actually, we've been carrying around a kind of background emotion with us all day. Maybe it's a hollow hurt feeling in the throat, a shaky excitement in the chest, or a band of tension in the neck and shoulders. There are many permutations of these, often expressed through some trackable body sensation in the face, throat, neck, chest, or belly. If you think there's some emotion happening but you don't know exactly what it is (or even where it is), just note it as *feel*.

If you happen to be emotionally neutral at the moment, you can try to deliberately evoke an emotion. You can bring to mind some idiotic YouTube video of a guy farting in a freezer bag and notice any feelings of hilarity or weary disappointment in humanity. Or you can think of a situation or person that angers you, or saddens you, or fills you with well-being. Whatever is here, the first thing is to see it clearly.

Our next step is "A"—**accept.**

That means, whatever the emotional sensation, you let it be there. Instead of trying to ignore or suppress it—which we often do—you open to the whole complicated feeling of it, with great tenderness and care. You are cultivating a feeling of self-compassion as you do this, which hopefully means you will also naturally pace yourself and take it easy. This attitude provides a new way to experience these sensations, so the emotions behind them can start to get expressed and even metabolized. The neuroscience of this is intriguing: we are essentially integrating our emotions with our cognition, marrying what we *feel* with what we *know*.

Acceptance may seem unassuming, but it is the most important move a human being can make. It has dozens of near synonyms, described in different ways in every culture and tradition: forgiveness, love, equanimity, maturity, being present. It is a radical act of coming into the world by letting go of what's in the way and welcoming exactly what's emerging. There can be a bracing existential quality to this act: it's as though when we accept every part of this moment, we synchronize with it.

Acceptance isn't easy when we're inside a challenging emotion like anger or fear or sadness. But the alternative is either grabbing on, which can make the emotion more painful when it leaves, or pushing away, which may work in the short term but ultimately amplifies and drags the emotion out. The expression is "What you resist persists." It's like trying to win a wrestling match with a giant blob of melted toffee. The harder you press, the more entangled you get. Sometimes you don't even realize you are subtly fighting with a feeling or sensation. Your body might be tense, like you're braced in some way against a thought or a feeling or a sound. It's a kind of friction that we can sometimes detect if we look. If you realize that you actually don't want to accept a particular emotion, then the kung fu move is to pan back the camera and accept your aversion. It's always the same move; only the scale changes.

Which brings us to the "I" of RAIN: **investigation.** Investigation is expanding and deepening the volume of what we are accepting. It's getting interested in whatever we are feeling, and exploring it at a pace that works for us.

There is a learning curve here around how to do this skillfully. We want to be curious and aware of our emotions without feeding them. This is so important. Some of our chains of emotional reactions are on a hair trigger: guilt leads to critical thoughts, which lead to sadness and negative images of yourself and sudden catastrophizing about the future, and before you know it you're curled into a ball in the basement under an old tarp, inconsolable and covered in petrified mouse droppings. We can go from zero to TILT! very quickly. When this happens, we're no longer mindful—we've almost always lost our ability to keep track of what's going on.

We're working with emotional feedback loops that want to complete their circuits. It's like the energy in them can't quite discharge, so the pattern keeps playing out again and again. And every time it plays out it gets more entrenched. How to work with it, then?

With a light touch. The key is to observe our emotions in the most relaxed possible way, friendly but also objective. It's more important here to be relaxed in our attitude than to see every part of an emotion clearly. We let the sensation come to us; we let it show itself. We are never in a hurry. The clarity will emerge from the equanimity, less so the other way around. This kind of openness is the ideal medium in which to absorb an emotion's momentum.

It is exactly in this moment that change can happen. When you see and open yourself to a feeling—particularly one that comes around again and again—then it's less likely to escalate or chain forward. The mindfulness somehow takes the wind out of its sails. If you do this enough times, you create a new and healthier habit. The entire emotional-behavioral response can be rerouted. It is a way of slowly and patiently taking responsibility for ourselves.

What's the move if we're doing this meditation and a strong emotion spikes up and gets super intense, and we find ourselves en route to that tarp with the petrified mouse droppings?

There are a few options. One, you can deliberately zoom in on one small part of the emotional sensation—the very center of it, maybe, or one of its edges. You breathe out and keep the body relaxed as you lightly track this one small part, noticing how the sensations—the throbbing, or tingling, or aching, or tension—either move and change or stay the same. When we isolate one part of the emotional sensation it becomes more manageable, and by staying clear and mindful we can prevent the emotion from amplifying into what can become an overwhelming chain reaction. So it may surge, but if we stay with it in a mindful way, the wave can also quickly recede, leaving us feeling lighter and calmer.

Another strategy is to swing back to the home base sensation we identified at the start. Everyone should do this anyway, as a matter of course, throughout the meditation; it is part of working smart. Every few minutes, practice shifting your attention to the comparative comfort of this other place: your breath, an image or sound, or some peaceful grounding quality in the body. Meditate here for a while. Or do a compassion practice—that is also a good option. This is how we pace ourselves—we swing into a feeling, lightly observe it for a while, swing back to home base, relax there, then return to survey the activation for a little longer. That's the process, moving at a rhythm that works for us, a bit deeper with each swing of the pendulum.

Of course, it's also important to say that at any time you can just stop meditating and go for a walk or talk it out with a friend. There are many ways to work with our emotions.

The fourth and final step of RAIN, the "N," is **nonidentification**. Non-identification is less an action than an attitude, the attitude of not taking your emotions personally. However counterintuitive it may sound, it's something to try, to explore. How does it change your experience to note *anger is happening*, the way you might note *a thunderstorm is happening*? Emotions are the atmospheric conditions of this human moment, part of the natural flow of things, a product of untold causes and conditions that roll out quite on their own. So give yourself a break. You don't have to constantly judge yourself for feeling a particular way. It's okay: we're all part of this much bigger process. And guess what? When we stop compulsively claiming every passing emotion and thought as *I-me-mine*, then something beautiful may happen: we feel more connected to everything and everyone else. Very slowly, we start to get over ourselves.

Non-identification is actually implicit in RAIN's previous two steps. It's a deeper kind of allowing. If you want a "move," try lightly noting each sensation as *not me*—or, even better, *be free*.

We're liberating the butterfly conservatory over here. Free all the little sensations! *Not me! Be free!* Let all experiences come and go. What's happening now will be different soon enough, and what a privilege it is to be here at all. *Sub specie aeternitatis:* the view from eternity.

And that's the practice. Make sure to finish back at your home base, at the breath or some sound or sensation that feels comfortable for you. Before you open your eyes, take a few minutes to relax, maybe even lie down. Let the work integrate.

CHEAT SHEET

1. Close your eyes and first find **home base:** some sensation that feels comforting. Maybe it's the breath, or a relaxed place in your body, or a picture in front of you.

2. **Recognize.** Now ask yourself: are there any emotions happening? If so, note them: *anger, sadness, exuberance.* If you can't find the exact name for what you're experiencing, note it as *feel.*

3. **Accept.** Open to the feeling and let the sensation of it do exactly what it wants to do. See if you can find a quality of caring and friendliness for this emotion that just wants to express itself.

4. Investigate. Now we get curious about our emotion, about where it's happening and what it's doing. Is it centered around a particular part of your body? Is the feeling staying the same, or is it changing? See if you can lightly follow the sensation, like you're a field naturalist. If the emotion starts to get too intense, you have a couple of options. One is you can try to zoom in on one small part of it and notice just that, which makes things more manageable. Or you can swing your attention back to your comfortable place, noting *home* or *rest*.

5. Non-identification. Can you let the emotional feeling do its thing without taking it personally? Try to see your emotions like you see the weather: not as something to judge yourself for but, rather, as part of the natural atmospheric conditions of the moment. This is a deeper form of allowing. After you've let this happen for a while, go back to the breath or to your *home* or *rest* sensation for a bit. Before you open your eyes, take a few minutes to relax and do nothing.

Jeff, a few questions on RAIN. I want to home in on the "accept" piece because it seems to be so central, and yet also so subtle. How do you know if you've really accepted something?

Usually the emotion gets less intense, although not always—feelings have their own arc and lifespan. There can also be dramatic experiences, in which you get a noticeable release. It's a bit like when you suddenly realize you've been holding your breath—or tensing some part of your body—and you let out this long exhale and everything relaxes and you're like "Man, why didn't I let go of that sooner?" Or you finally give someone a piece of your mind, and afterward you feel this big weight come off your shoulders. It's cathartic—in fact, "catharsis" is another word for this dynamic.

The more we accept, the more the energy bound up in our

previous gripping or aversion or fixation gets freed up. As a result, we often feel calmer and lighter and generally more sane. And of course, when we let go, we also make space for new things to come in. So each release is also an update.

I know you're interested in the idea of "updating" the mind, like we do with a software program. Except the total disappearance of a pattern only rarely happens, right? How much can chronic feelings of anxiousness or sadness or anger really change? Isn't meditation more about mitigating our suffering rather than resolving it altogether?

I think it's both. One way to think about it is to ask what is the relationship between in-the-moment experiences of catharsis— which are pretty common—and long-term change and transformation? It's the million-dollar question. There's definitely a relationship. I've had meditators tell me about seeing and releasing some deep pattern in the moment and they say it's gone for good, *poof!* Which is completely bonkers if it's true, and has serious implications for how we think about learning and behavior change. I think it's one of the most important things meditation has to share with neuroscience.

But my sense is that these kinds of sudden transformations are pretty rare. And, actually, contemplatives say this too: it's more about gradual change. Most practitioners I've spoken to say the patterns come back, just a little less insistently each time. This has been my personal experience. I see this stuff again and again, and the more I do, the less it owns me. Eventually I've had emotional patterns get so worked through that it's like they become transparent—still there, but hardly influential. But then, other times, this thing I thought I had dealt with comes back and bites me in the ass ten years later. Especially if I'm stressed.

It is worth mentioning here that the *permanent* disappearance of all patterns of reactivity is one of the central claims of Buddhism. They say it can be done. Although most of the senior teachers I know say it's more like you are always halving the distance to zero, but never quite getting there.

As our encounter with the folks from AIT was wrapping up, we took some group pictures in front of the bus, and then the 10% Happier team clambered aboard, did our count-off, and set off for our next destination. Amazingly, we were on schedule. It wasn't luck or divine intervention; it was Ben, who was now officially running this road show. He had initially resisted the assignment, but now that he was actually in the role, he loved it. This didn't surprise me at all—Ben really enjoys bossing people around. A more polite way of saying that would be: he's a natural leader.

I was well acquainted with the benevolent dictatorship of Ben Rubin. Despite being nearly ten years my junior, he had essentially been running significant chunks of my life for quite a while as the CEO of our 10% Happier meditation enterprise.

As I do with everyone I like, I mock Ben mercilessly. He dresses in what might charitably be called geek chic. His hair reminds me of that scene from the movie *Knocked Up,* where Katherine Heigl asks Seth Rogen whether he uses product in his unruly mop of curls, and he replies, "No, that's, ah—I use 'Jew,' it's called." Ben toggles back and forth between an all-business C-3PO-like chief executive and, when he is letting his figurative hair down, a florid goofball who insists on telling jokes that only he finds funny. In spite of his lack of comedic chops, Ben has become one of my closest and most trusted advisors. He's like a younger version of me—except more disciplined, more thoughtful, and way better at math.

Among our shared interests: making good-natured fun of

Jeff when he goes off on his mythopoetic jags, waving his arms wildly like he's conducting the universe or Rolfing reality. Among our shared aversions: pretty much everything touchy-feely. In fact, Ben—even though he, too, is a dedicated meditator—has this particular allergy even worse than I do. So you can imagine how excited he was when Jeff, on board the bus, proposed a group discussion about our go-to emotional patterns and how meditation could help. It was a voluntary opening of Pandora's box.

We were in our usual configuration. Jeff and I were seated at the small dining table in the front cabin, with Ben, Carlye, and several others arrayed on the bench across from us.

"So maybe I'll just start," said Jeff. "If indeed Ben has any emotions, they may even emerge."

"Unlikely," said Ben, smirking.

Jeff then walked us through an account of some of what he had excavated when he turned the meditative microscope on deeper and deeper levels of his own psyche. Early on in his practice, he noticed a "go-faster pattern" that was, he said, "the secret life of my ADD—a stream of images of places I'd rather be and things I'd rather be doing, along with a continuous agitated buzzing through the core of my body." This chronic dissatisfaction caused him to push for ever more stimulation, which in turn activated him more (and satisfied him less) until eventually he'd crash, only to repeat the cycle again. Meditation helped him back off and observe this process without indulging it.

The practice also enabled him to see deeper emotional elements, including one of the sources of his sharpest pain. "I learned that as a consequence of feeling like I didn't belong"—in life, in his family, anywhere—"I had a lot of judgments about that, which I internalized, about not being good enough. I could see—way down—this part of me that would just put the knife into myself." That feeling of insufficiency, he said, had created mindless behavioral patterns. "There's one that's about being compulsively super-nice and wanting to help everybody all the time. It's this acting out of my own insecurity that is just so ingrained. And another one is anger that I have this embarrassing insecurity in the first place."

As moved as I was by Jeff's honesty, when it was my turn to speak I felt a surge of discomfort. Hearing my friend hold forth in such a raw manner reminded me that I had thus far been spared so much of the difficulty that other people have had to endure. The truth is, I was born on third base, the recipient of an incalculable amount of unearned privilege.

"I had a kind of idyllic childhood," I said. "I have two really loving parents who never got divorced, and I was totally supported. They were hippies, and there was a lot of lovey-dovey stuff. So I think the result was a spoiled kid."

Yes, I had endured the trifecta of panic, anxiety, and depression, but my struggles were rarely rooted in personal trauma (and, in fact, were sometimes self-manufactured). And yes, through my years of meditation, I had faced some difficult interior phenomena, including anger, impatience, boredom, and fear. But, truthfully, none of it felt that heavy. Maybe this meant I was a terrible meditator. Or maybe there simply wasn't a lot of Mahler music playing in the backdrop of my psyche.

I found it embarrassing that so much of my internal bandwidth was occupied by material that was, relatively speaking, petty and selfish. Even as we sat there on the bus, most of my thoughts were swirling around whether all the greasy road food we were eating was going to require me to wear Spanx, and whether my ongoing email negotiations with the musician Moby, who was supposed to lead a sound meditation at our culminating event in L.A., would prove successful.

This discussion tapped right into my ongoing story line

about having some sort of internal frigidity. "I definitely have stuff I don't want to face," I offered to the group, adding that I suspected it was "around capacity for compassion and stuff like that, which I think is a source of shame for me." Intellectually, I knew I wasn't a sociopath, and yet I still struggled with this story about myself.

I was not alone. Ben weighed in, explaining that, like me, he struggled with feelings of selfishness. "I feel like I get locked. Instead of feeling compassion for all of these people who need help, I just squish it down and put it in a box because if I feel the compassion for them, then I might have to help, and that would hurt me." It would hurt him, he said, because the voice in his head was saying, "I can't help. I don't have the time. I don't have the energy. I don't have the money. I don't have the . . . whatever."

Sitting there, I felt empathy and compassion for Ben's perceived lack of empathy and compassion. I knew from prolonged personal exposure to him that he was actually extremely helpful, and also that he viewed leadership as a source of service. His words also helped me realize that I had actually made real progress since I was his age. Despite the sometimes selfish nature of my inner dialogue, having a child had opened up heretofore unseen reservoirs of feeling. Moreover, through meditation, I had actually come to enjoy helping others, because mindfulness had revealed how good it can feel to be nice. As a tiny example of this, bring to mind how pleasant it can feel when you do something as simple as holding open a door for someone. Meditation had shown me how scalable this behavior is. I call it "the self-interested case for not being a dick."

When we catch ourselves thinking or acting in unkind or ungenerous ways, it can produce a running dialogue of second-arrow self-reproach. Such was the case for Ben. "There's the layer of shame on top of that that's like, 'Oh you're a shitty person. What a shitty person. You can't be bothered to help, or even feel compassion when you can't help. You're kind of a broken human.'"

"When you're in a pattern it feels like fate," said Jeff. He had seen it play out in his own life. He said he would occasionally get into "a mood where my life is completely fucked and everything is screwed up, I don't know what I'm doing." But that's when his years of meditation practice would kick in. "Anytime I go into that space now, which I still do, I always have a little bit of perspective around it. I can always say, 'Oh yeah, I've been here before.'" That is the kind of invaluable perspective we are training in this practice, using RAIN and other meditations to boost our inner radar. We can learn to track our emotional storms before they make landfall.

As the bus drove west from New Mexico into Arizona, passing fantastic rock formations that looked like gigantic, Martian versions of the Play-Doh sculptures my son makes, I recalled something Jeff had said during our visit to AIT. When confronted with difficult emotions or distractions, he said, "the first move" is to say, "All right, welcome to the party."

Welcome to the party: it seemed like the perfect way to introduce equanimity when confronted with emotions we don't want to face. Moreover, it struck me as something that might help me in my own practice. Perhaps "welcome to the party" was the antidote to my seemingly intractable habit of beating myself up every time I got distracted. "What if," I asked Jeff, "at that moment when you wake up and you're having judgment about everything, you just use that as a mantra right there?"

Jeff was jazzed. There are few things MacGyver loves more than minting new meditations. "Why don't we do a 'welcome to the party' meditation?" he exclaimed.

WELCOME TO THE PARTY

5 to 15 minutes

Start in the usual way: a couple of deep breaths, relaxing on the exhale. Make a decision here at the start not to get uptight about *anything*. That's the whole principle of this meditation: no secret biases or preferences, everything that rises is welcomed, including your most neurotic judgments and unholy feelings and seething resentments. All perfect. "So happy to see you, welcome to the party of my direct experience. Would you care for an aperitif?" Like that.

If you're a breath person, start there to get settled, zeroing in on the soft feeling of it. Or choose another body sensation: heart, belly, bum, hands. Note, if you like, *feel*— or, if you are working with the breath, *in* and *out*. Enjoying the full feeling, committed to this direction in our experience. Mind wanders, bring it back.

And . . . here's the fun part. There's one more note: *Welcome to the party.* Really say this in your head. Whenever you're getting pulled into a thought, or you get distracted by something and you notice it, say, *Welcome to the party.* Make it your mantra. Welcome the insistent thought, welcome the annoying sensation, welcome the distracting sound. Then return to noticing the breath.

There are no enemies in this meditation, there are no problems, only new things to notice and welcome. And, as usual, it's okay to fake it. Welcome your fakery. Welcome your suspicion. Welcome the smell of fried chicken floating in from the neighborhood. Explore how this attitude affects the tone of your meditation. Try this for a while. If your mind wanders, welcome the fact that your mind wandered and go back to the breath. There is no traction here for feeling bad.

After you've done this for a while, if you like, try experimenting with a wider expanse of mindfulness. To do this, let go of your focal attention on the breath or body, and send your awareness out to include any sounds coming and going, and also the wider sense of space in the room, the volume of air above and behind and around you. Note *sounds* if you like; note *space*. Let your mind get big and soft. Welcome your big soft mind to the party.

If you find this open focus challenging to maintain, you can return to the breath at any time. But the idea is to explore what happens when you expand the stance of your welcoming. Now there really is no such thing as a distraction. All sounds and sensations are welcome, all of it rising and falling within the broad space of your awareness. *Welcome to the party*, you say to anything you happen to notice, and then you kick back, aware of sounds, aware of space, maybe aware of the body and the breath and whatever else. Aware of it all. No limits.

When you're ready, come back the body, to the breath and the feeling of contact with the ground. Enjoying the body—its solidity and presence. Re-combobulating. Rest here for a minute or two, then slowly open your eyes.

CHEAT SHEET

1. Choose an anchor for your attention—breath, belly, bum, hands—something you already know works for you. Use a note if it helps: *in, out, feel.*

2. Whenever you get distracted, notice this has happened, and then good-naturedly note *welcome to the party*. Notice it with welcoming amusement, and then return to your anchor, letting the distraction fade or stay in the background or do whatever it wants. You are a generous party host.

3. After five or ten minutes, experiment with a wider field of mindfulness. Let go of focal attention on the breath and expand to include the sense of sounds and space around you. Note *sounds,* note *space,* note *welcome to the party* for all of it. If you don't like this broader stance, you can always return to your original focus.

4. At the end, bring your full attention back into the body, and then let yourself rest and do nothing for a couple of minutes before opening your eyes.

"That was a great meditation," I said as Jeff wrapped up.

To be clear, it wasn't magic. Big Eddie (that's what we called our driver, to distinguish him from regular Eddie, our director) was blasting the radio up front, and it was continually annoying me. I would try to greet both the noise and my reaction to it with a hearty "Welcome to the party!" It didn't work every time, but it was comforting to hear Jeff say that it didn't have to; this was a training. As Jeff often said, "Fake it until you make it." In those tiny little moments where the mantra did work, where I was being less uptight about my less-than-perfect concentration, I got a glimpse of how powerful this practice could be—how it could make my meditation less fraught and perhaps even transform my relationship with my own emotions.

Yeah, yeah, yeah. Isn't all this getting-in-touch-with-your-feelings stuff, not to mention the maudlin, *Girl, Interrupted*–style group therapy, just going to turn you into a navel-gazing softie? Maybe Colbert was right about the utility of stuffing it all down?

At our next stop, we were about to see if meditation could survive in one of the most difficult and dangerous jobs imaginable.

7

"If I Get Too Happy, I'll Lose My Edge"

The first time I was in the back of a police car I was four-teen years old and the 5-0 had nabbed me and my fellow Brain Trust wastrels for (allegedly) vandalizing a train station.

I vastly preferred the ride Jeff and I took late on day nine of our road trip, when we hopped (voluntarily) into the back of a police SUV piloted by Sergeant Raj Johnson, a supervising officer on the midnight patrol in Tempe, Arizona.

Tempe is just outside of Phoenix, with a population of about 165,000 that soars to 265,000 when the local college, Arizona State University, is in session.

Raj, as he insisted we call him, is a sturdy former college football player with a shaven head and meticulously courteous manner. I had a hard time imagining him in his former life working undercover in narcotics, with dreadlocks down to his shoulders.

As we sped down the freeway, Raj regaled us with stories from his SWAT days and spoke openly about the strains of the job. "It can be very stressful to come out here and know that you can go to a call and you could get injured. Or you might have to use force that could injure somebody or take their life." He talked of seeing horrific car crashes, acts of domestic violence, and suicides. He mentioned the rising antagonism toward the police, and a troubling uptick in ambush attacks on officers. And he told us how he'd recently come close to discharging his weapon for the first time when confronted by a man, high on meth, who kept reaching for his waistband as if he had a weapon, all the while shouting, "Shoot me!"

"I thought my job was stressful," I said.

"Yeah, but the other side of that coin is . . . man, I love this job. Do you know what I mean? It's awesome to go to work with people who think like you and believe in the same mission. Where you truly do want to protect, you want to serve."

As if to accentuate the perilous nature of his work, a call came over the radio indicating a pursuit in progress. "Sounds like there is a unit trying to stop a car—or a car is fleeing from them," said Raj as he pulled a U-turn and started heading quickly in that direction.

I could feel a little surge of adrenaline, an echo of what I used to experience when things got hot while I was on patrol in war zones. I was curious to know whether Raj felt it, too. "I wonder, is a part of you also a little excited?" I asked.

"Oh, absolutely." This is what they train for, he said. "It's exciting to go get some bad guys."

When we arrived, it seemed like every police vehicle in Tempe was there, lights blazing. The cops on the scene reported that a DUI suspect had initially refused to stop. When he finally pulled over, he fought with the responding officers, who proceeded to tase him.

Back in his SUV, Raj told us that when it came to handling the psychological ramifications of their work, police officers traditionally didn't have many options. He listed the most popular coping mechanisms: "Drinks, stuffing it down, or talking to your buddy about it."

I asked, "Do you think, on the force, meditation is considered socially acceptable? Or would people make fun of you a little bit?"

"Um," he said.

"You can be honest."

"You know," he said, looking at me and Jeff a little sheepishly in the rearview mirror, "I think people are going to make fun of you just a little bit."

As he made clear, however, the concern went well beyond the "people might think I'm weird" obstacle. For police officers, the more pressing fear was that meditation might be downright dangerous.

Raj came right out and said it: he worried meditation would make him soft. "You have to be on your game every day," he said. Faced with the demands of a high-stakes job that required tough, split-second decisions, what he needed most was speed and strength, both mental and physical. His question about meditation was: "Will it slow me down?"

The "lose my edge" fear is one with which I have struggled mightily. Before I started meditating, I assumed the practice would hinder my ability to compete in the sometimes cutthroat world of TV news, and also that I might be required to wear my wife's yoga pants to the office.

I have come to firmly believe that, applied correctly, mindfulness enhances rather than erodes your edge. Increased focus helps me get more work done in less time. Decreased emotional reactivity sometimes allows me to stay calm during heated meetings. Having compassion for colleagues can lead to more allies, which in an intensely collaborative atmosphere like ABC News is incalculably valuable. (Of course, having positive relationships with your coworkers happens to feel good for its own sake.) Full disclosure: if you ask anybody who knows me, they will tell you I retain the propensity to be a multitasking, Twitter-checking, temper-losing dummy. Not for the last time, I will remind you that this is a game of gradual improvement.

Even though meditation has taken off in all sorts of hard-charging, high-profile professions, from law enforcement to athletics to entertainment, I still encounter people who fear the practice will render them ineffective. Not long ago, I was invited to do an interview at the last place on earth I thought I'd ever talk meditation: Fox News. It was a radio segment with an amicable anchorman named Brian Kilmeade, who posed a question along the lines of, "If I get too happy, won't I end up like Rocky from *Rocky III*?"

I hadn't seen the movie since I was a kid, so I went back and watched it. The film opens with a montage of the boxer, fresh off winning the championship, signing autographs, shooting TV commercials, and gamboling around his mansion with his wife and son. These scenes are intercut with images of a vaguely psychopathic-looking Clubber Lang (played by Mr. T) training hard and drubbing his opponents. By the second round of their eventual encounter in the ring, Rocky is on the mat, bleeding and unconscious.

Message received: my new friend from Fox was worried that meditation would leave him vulnerable to leaner, hungrier opponents. But this conflates happiness with complacency. Just because you meditate does not mean you have to abandon stress and lazily rest on your laurels.

I still experience plenty of internal churn. *Why doesn't our app have more downloads? Why is Eckhart Tolle selling more books than me? Why is my son refusing to brush his teeth, and will he eventually look like he has meth mouth?*

My meditation teacher Joseph Goldstein once gave me the single best piece of advice I've ever received when it comes to the management of worry. When for the eighty-seventh time you find yourself chewing over, say, an impending deadline or your rival's promotion, maybe ask yourself one simple question: "Is this useful?"

I employed this mantra quite often on our road trip whenever I found myself carried away by anxious thoughts. *Why isn't Moby answering my emails? Is my next book going to be a classic case of the sophomore slump? Will it end up like that second, critically panned Strokes record? I actually liked that record. "Meet Me in the Bathroom" is my jam.* . . .

Whoa, whoa, dude. At some point, maybe after I had stress-eaten a bag of pretzels, the mindfulness would kick in. *Is this worrying useful? Probably not.* Then I'd go back to listening to whatever interesting thing Jeff happened to be saying at the moment.

The "Is this useful?" mantra has not only helped me waste less energy on internally generated distress but has also allowed me to clear up bandwidth for new and different kinds of thoughts. For example, I am in closer touch with my more positive professional motivations—such as wanting to work on incredible stories with cool collaborators—as well as my gratitude for what I already have. (There's an expression I frequently call to mind: "These are the good old days.") I used to spend the final moments before drifting off to sleep mulling over, for the umpteenth time, all of my current problems. Now I perform a somewhat corny ritual where I list everything I'm grateful for, including my wife, my son, and my job. The litany gets so long that sometimes I nod off before I come to the end.

Turning down the volume on my unproductive mental nattering has given me the space to reckon with an indisputable fact: I am not fully in control. None of us is. We inhabit a chaotic universe. I try to adhere to the concept of "non-attachment to results." It's great to work your tail off in service of a goal, but best to never forget that the end result is often dependent on much larger, often impersonal causes and conditions. If you keep that in mind when your grand plans are subject to force majeure, it can drastically increase your resilience.

In this way, meditation leads to edge without as much edginess. Mindfulness has helped me to see more clearly what really matters, which has made me much less focused on advancement for its own sake. Fair warning: it is possible that increased self-awareness may lead you to conclude that some career goals you've been rabidly pursuing may not actually provide true satisfaction, which may in turn lead you to pursue new and different goals. To me, however, that's not losing your edge, it's losing your delusions. Don't worry, though; if being heedlessly acquisitive genuinely makes you happy, meditation probably won't stand in the way.

Nor, for that matter, do I think it will stand in the way of your creativity. People whose livelihoods depend upon being creative often tell me they fear increased happiness could come at a cost. There is a widely held belief, fed by tales of such miserable masters as Beethoven and Van Gogh, that you need to suffer for your art. I'm struck by the paradox that people come to meditation with two irretrievably irreconcilable fears. On the one hand, there's the fear of opening up a Pandora's box of enfeebling emotions; on the other, the fear that meditation will lead to some sort of bovine neutrality or blissed-out blankness. In my experience, though, it works like this: meditation simultaneously puts you in closer touch with your emotions while making you less of their marionette. Believe me, I'd love it if the practice miraculously erased all of my neuroses. Instead, I think it allows for greater intimacy with the pain and poignancy of life while providing the wherewithal not to drown in it.

When we interviewed the singer Josh Groban back on day

one of the road trip, he asked about the interaction between meditation and creativity. Jeff's response: "If you're just crowding your head with the violence of your own anxious and neurotic preoccupations, how are you ever going to mine a deeply fertile experience? You're blocking it."

Josh seemed to resonate with this concept of accessing the muse. "Honestly," he said, "some of the times when you feel like you've written the best thing, you say, 'Well, I didn't write it; I was quiet, and it came.'"

Or, as one of my favorite rappers, Schoolboy Q, once rhymed:

Metapho'
How I come up with it, I don't fuckin' know.

While I do not consider myself an artist—my rapping and beat-box skills haven't advanced much since seventh grade— I have found that being less tied up in knots of fruitless worry gives me better access to good ideas, wherever it is they come from.

It has helped me immeasurably with extemporizing in live situations, a big part of my job as a morning news anchor and traveling speech-giver. The most vivid example of this may be my aforementioned visit to *The Colbert Report*. I was more nervous about this appearance than any I'd ever done in my TV career. The idea of discussing my personal failings and my belief in the power of meditation with a fictional cable news bloviator was unsettling, to say the least. Colbert is one of the most quick-witted and fearsomely intelligent comics of our age, and his whole job in this role (before he went to CBS, where he appears as himself) was to mercilessly play his guests for laughs.

Before the show, the producers would take the guests aside and advise them not to try to be funny. Just play the straight man, they would say. Colbert himself would pop into the green room and deliver a rapid-fire, rote speech about how his character is a buffoon who will mock everything you hold dear. When he delivered the speech to me, I could feel the blood drain from my face.

Moments later, I found myself in the surreal situation of being seated across from one of my pop culture heroes on the set of a show I had so often enjoyed from the comfort of my couch. My strategy was simple: fall back on my meditation training. Drop all of my plans. Deliver no canned lines. Just be in the moment and respond to whatever happens.

A few minutes into the interview, we got to the issue of drugs. "Were you, like, a club kid on the ecstasy? What were you doing? Did you have a pacifier in your mouth and glow sticks?" he said, waving his hands like a raver. This was exactly the moment I had feared. I could hear the rising roar of the laughing crowd. I felt like I was in the Roman Colosseum, and I was the gladiator about to get nixed. I have no memory of saying the following, but, seemingly out of nowhere, I replied, "You're making me realize I did it wrong."

Colbert paused, leaned back in his chair, and said, "Okay, that was good."

Thank you, meditation, for enabling what was one of the most validating moments of my public life. I really am sure the conversation would have gone down very differently had I not been able to let go, listen, and trust the moment. This is a whole different kind of edge, one that is available to anyone, whether or not you have built a career as a talking head. And it applies well past the workplace, enabling more spontaneous, authentic interactions in all aspects of your life.

• • •

If you're a cop in Tempe, Arizona, however, your needs are significantly more urgent than the ability to ad-lib on camera, write a catchy song, or navigate office politics. When I make a mistake on air, it's embarrassing; when Raj or his colleagues lose their edge, people could get hurt or die.

The day after our ride-along with Raj, Jeff and I went to visit his boss, the city's new police chief, Sylvia Moir, who has made it her mission to introduce meditation to her officers. Latterly of El Cerrito, California, she'd been in Tempe for about a year. She combined NoCal earthiness with the crisp, authoritative demeanor of someone who had spent decades in criminal justice. Sitting in her large, light-filled, impeccably neat office, decorated with both law enforcement memorabilia and tasteful throw pillows, she said her job required a tricky balance. "Dan," she told me, "try being a woman in police work. There's a lot of risk of not looking hard-core."

Chief Moir had initially written off meditation as a "crunchy granola thing," but the science convinced her mindfulness could help her cops be more effective on the street and more resilient in the face of a torrent of stressors. Indeed, despite Raj's fear that meditation might slow him down, studies of people with dangerous jobs, including soldiers, firefighters, and police officers, have shown that meditation produces such benefits as improved working memory, reduced release of the stress hormone cortisol, and quicker recovery times after high-pressure incidents.

But the PR problem remained real. The chief described the usual pushback from fellow officers: "They're like, 'What are you talking about? This is going to make you lose your edge. You're going to be soft. What about the tactical necessity of

the job? You have to make split-second decisions and be tactically sound.'" She argued the opposite is true. "I offer that it
makes us *more* tactically sound."

The chief's argument appeared to be having an impact.
When Jeff and I sat down separately with a group of eight of
her officers, many of them were either open to the idea of meditation or were already practicing.

We were situated around an empty square of tables in a conference room at police headquarters. Sergeant Rich Monteton, a former marine, was the first to speak up. With his
close-cropped blond hair, black golf shirt, and tattooed biceps,
he had what the writer Emily Nussbaum once called "vinegar
charisma." Sergeant Monteton had been on the force for eighteen years. In his current role as the officer in charge of skills
training for the department, it was his job to execute the new
chief's meditation agenda. He acknowledged the stigma
around meditation, but argued that members of the force were
already practicing a form of it nearly every day—breathing exercises that officers would perform while en route to potentially dangerous calls or in the middle of tense confrontations.
Deep breathing can mitigate the impact of adrenaline on fine
motor skills and information processing. In fact, this is what
Raj had told us he had done when confronted with that suspect who was high on drugs and demanding to be shot. The
department called this exercise "combat breathing." Sergeant
Monteton noted drily, "Now you're on board, because I called
it combat, right? I painted it black. It's tactical. You'll buy it."

What emerged from the group discussion was that officers
were craving the ability to build on combat breathing. Specifically, what they were seeking was the ability to "reset" both
during and after stressful events. One of the biggest challenges
of police work is not to take the anxiety and anger from your

previous call into the next one. The men and women in the room with us saw this ability to reset as a way to sharpen their edge while out on the street.

This notion was nicely summed up by Officer Jake Schmidt, a newbie on the SWAT team who looked so young that everyone called him "K-Through-8." He said, "You go to a call, there's shots fired. And you leave that call, and the next one usually, you're going to someone with a barking dog. The citizen's really upset, and you're kind of like, 'Really? You're upset? I just went to someone who just got shot.' You just kind of gotta hit that reset button."

Equally as important, he said, was to not carry the disquiet of the day back into your personal life. Jake had a newborn and a toddler at home. "I want to be a good father to them and also be a good husband to my wife. So I think doing this kind of puts me in the present, and not so caught up in replaying the day or worrying about tomorrow."

Jeff was nodding vigorously. "You start to see how you're always bringing stuff into these situations. You're bringing your aggression, you're bringing your fear." But the smart move, Jeff explained, is to mindfully let it all be there, without fighting it. "Instead of white-knuckling it through your experience, you're actually opening to the experience, and that's what allows you to reset."

There were several questions in the room about how best to apply this skill in real time. Jeff had at the ready another simple but game-changing acronym, SURF: **stop, understand, relax, freedom.** Actually, he got it from me; I came up with it. I think of it as a free-range version of RAIN. You can use this as a way to bring mindfulness into moments when you're fighting the urge to lose your temper, send an impolitic email, or eat a fistful of french fries.

Psychologists use a version of this meditation to help people through their addictions, including our technology addictions. The idea should be a familiar one by now: the faster we are at noticing our urges, the less likely we'll be to helplessly act on them, and the more quickly they will pass—thus allowing us to reset. It is extremely hard to reset fully. As with everything about mind, body, and behavior, we are talking about a continuum. You can get better and better at disembedding from your urges and not acting on them, but we're still going to miss some of them, and catch others late. And even with the ones we *do* catch, the feeling of wanting to act on them can linger for a long while, sometimes causing us to act out all over again as soon as we lose mindfulness.

All of which is fine. Forty percent better, 20 percent better, even 10 percent better—that's *still* better. As someone with life-long impulse control issues, I can definitely say that meditation has reduced my ratio of high-risk behaviors, to say nothing of the blurting-out-stupid-shit-at-dinner-parties ratio.

Obviously there is good automaticity and bad automaticity. You want to be able to trust your body's training and knowing. It's important to make a distinction between the urges we want to immediately act on and the ones we don't. Like if we are about to get run over by a bus, we want to act on the urge to move and not be in some kind of death-inducing deliberation about it.

But in the more nuanced world of health and society, where context and thoughtfulness are important, there are definitely urges and impulses that are better left unrealized.

SURF THE URGE

1 to 5 minutes (meant to be done on the fly;
once you get the hang of it, can be done in a few moments)

Step one: **stop.** When you feel the first stirrings of an urge, try to use that feeling as an early warning, a reminder to pause and breathe for a moment. In, out. Breathing out the *go-fast* tension and urgency. You can still act on the urge—you are just trying to insert the tiniest space between stimulus and response. This battle, by the way, is practically the whole battle, so I'm not saying it's easy. But it doesn't need to be perfect. You can stop even once you've already given in to the urge a little bit, or even a lot. There is still damage control. It's not like stop and go are your only two options.

Another thing that's helped me deal with urges— especially the urge to share some half-baked opinion—is something I learned from the Zen teacher Bernie Glassman. When you go into any situation, he said, "think: don't know." As in, don't pretend you know what's up or what's really going on. Chill for a bit in the situation, watching, learning. There's a humility here that is really helpful. It's kind of a natural "stop" that you can learn to bring with you into all of your life.

Next is **understand.** This just means: "Oh yeah, I got this urge that's about to pop off. I know what urges are about. They're those things that make me act like a dysregulated idiot and lead me into long chains of self-flagellation and regret." That's the minimum "understand" move: being conscious enough to know an urge when you feel it.

The more in-depth move is to get curious about where you feel the urge in your body, what the sensation feels like, how it moves. Is it in your face? Your hands? Your chest? Is it prickly or smooth, concentrated or spread out? This is so important. Knowledge is power. If you have an urge that you struggle with a lot in your life—to smoke, to punch, to binge, to blurt—get to know where in your body this drama plays out.

You can also start to understand the life cycle of your urges. Generally our impulses have a bell-shaped curve, which means they come up fast and get real intense but then taper off. Once you've learned to find the epicenter of the urge, the next step is riding it, riding the wave.

Relax. "Relax" could also be called "ride." Except for me it feels like I am riding the urge *backward*. It's like you notice the surge that wants to propel you up and forward into doing or saying, but instead you do the opposite: you breathe out, and deliberately relax down and back. Take a moment to actually feel this scenario in your imagination. Someone says or does something, and instead of spasming forward like a puppet on a string with your knee-jerk objection or action, instead you pause, breathe out . . . *ahhh* . . . and settle back *through* whatever urge has come up. Like you and the urge are two ships passing in the night.

The "action" is this settling back *into* yourself. From the outside you don't move a millimeter, but from the *inside* it's like you've just sat back into a fat armchair. As you do, watch the original urge pass through you like a ghost.

Last one: **freedom.** This is about noticing the feeling of the urge passing and you not acting—and taking satisfaction in this. Once again, we are back in equanimity, inside this quality of things moving through you and you not fighting with them, the feeling of the energy draining from an urge or an emotion, so you can move toward a reset.

The accessible end of this is just noticing you didn't act and taking satisfaction in that. Notice your mindfulness, the mindfulness capable of seeing all this. When you notice and appreciate the mindfulness you reinforce it. This is what it feels like to be centered, to have autonomy, to be free—or at least *more* free. Noticing that freedom. Now, whatever's going on out there, it's from *this* place that you want to respond, with the full measure of your intelligence and care.

And that's it. I went through it slowly, but once you get the hang of it we're really talking about a single motion: noticing, pausing, and then settling back into yourself as you breathe out and the intensity of the urge passes. Pretty soon you're settling back automatically, metabolizing life's temptations and provocations on the fly. Over time it's like you live in that settled place more and more, better able to choose what bit of conditioning you want to follow along with.

CHEAT SHEET

1. **Stop.** When an urge comes up, notice it, and pause instead of hurtling along unheeding. Catching the urge is the hardest part.

2. **Understand.** Be curious about where this urge lives in your body. Where exactly do you feel this clutch of urgency? In your face, your chest, your hands? Explore for a bit.

3. **Relax.** Settle back into the urge, breathing out, letting any associated sensations spike and then taper off. Try to let the urge pass through you without either fighting it or acting on it.

4. **Freedom.** Take a moment to feel satisfaction that you didn't act on the urge. Notice any sensations of the urge dissipating, and any other attendant feelings of freedom, openness, and sanity. This "noticing with satisfaction" will reinforce the SURF habit.

Not to nag, but it really is much easier to apply mindfulness in moments of acute stress if you have a foundation of formal practice.

Officer Lindsey Fernandez, a twenty-two-year-old rookie, illustrated the point perfectly. When she first started on the job, she had experienced considerable anxiety, especially because she had been assigned to patrol the neighborhood where she grew up, which at times entailed arresting people with whom she'd gone to high school. She had recently started meditating and claimed it had made a big difference. "I'm five foot two. I'm about 110 pounds. I'm a tiny officer. So when I show up to scenes, it's essential that I'm calm, my mind is in the right place, and I'm able to talk to people." She said meditation had made her less scattered and better able to de-escalate situations. "For me, it's a big thing, especially when I'm first on the scene, being a female."

For these officers, keeping a level head was especially important at a time when tensions between police and the community were running high all over America.

Officer Denison Dawson, a jacked but genial patrol cop, weighed in with a surprising take on this subject. "We see it on some of these videos of confrontations with police, how the officer's interacting with the community. If he was calmer, if he was more caring, it goes a long way." Meditation, said Dawson, could not only help officers reset but also provide them with more compassion. "If you can express that caring, and they can see that love coming from you, it's totally a different experience."

I was struck by the use of the word "love." Playing devil's advocate, I asked whether exhibiting love for people out on the street could "hinder your ability to be an effective police officer."

"No, it actually increases," he said. "I practice this daily in the community. There's been times where people have cried with me. I've cried with them. I've been vulnerable. I'm able to be intimate and vulnerable with them, even though I have a uniform on."

Amplifying the point, Jeff added that meditation helps us see that everyone is caught up in their own baggage. "There are no true enemies. They're just people in screwed-up situations."

For Officer Dawson, this wisdom was hard-earned. "My mom was a crack cocaine user. Never around. All my siblings have different fathers. My father raised me. He was very abusive." As a younger man, Dawson had "a lot of anger management issues, a lot of pain." But now, in part through meditation, he had learned how to harness the energy in constructive ways. "You can never completely wipe your past out, but I've learned how to control it and focus it and center it, to where it's now my motivation and my drive, not a hindrance."

"Wow," said Jeff. "You should be teaching this meditation."

Let's not let Jeff off the hook. Here he is with a meditation that plays off a key cultural aspect of police work: skills training. Cops constantly run drills to maintain skills such as shooting and driving. Mental skills are no different. As Jeff explained to the officers, there are six mental muscle groups that we train in meditation. We've talked about these skills throughout this book, but here Jeff ties them all together.

My favorite description of the Buddha is "the unexcelled trainer of the animal in the human." Meditation practices train the mind and they train the heart (sorry, Dan).

The core training—the one that sets the stage for all others—is mindfulness. Dan talks about mindfulness as the capacity to notice our stuff. I also like an older definition: "to remember." Mindfulness is remembering that we can wake up and smell the coffee at any moment. We can snap out of our trances, and from that place of wider awareness we can choose both *how* we want to pay attention and *what* we want to pay attention to. In this sense, mindfulness isn't neutral; we bring to it a preference for reinforcing healthy patterns and qualities. Our own ethic is built right into it.

Other trainings roll out from here. My teacher Shinzen Young emphasizes three: concentration, clarity, and equanimity. To these I would add: enjoyment and friendliness. Because we're trying to help Dan thaw the imaginary block of ice in his rib cage.

The baseline levels of all of these qualities can increase over time; as they do, they spill out of our meditations and into our lives. I've already described mindfulness; here's a quick recap of why each of the other five qualities is important, and what they feel or "taste" like when they're present in our experience.

- **Concentration.** If you've ever felt focused and in the zone, then you know what it's like to be temporarily concentrated.

Concentration is the ability to choose and then to hold a direction, to get absorbed in some activity and to see it through. Not only are we more effective when we are concentrated, but there is good science showing that a concentrated mind is a happy mind. Concentration feels like you are merging with the action. It can be very pleasurable, with a feeling of internal stillness and quiet. There can also be a slight—or strong—sense of buffering from the external world.

- **Clarity.** This is the ability to discern and tease apart the details of our actual experience. It balances the dullness that can sometimes happen with concentration, and has other benefits as well, from boosting the vividness of life to giving us better information about our thoughts, our emotions, and our particular patterns of bias and activation. Clarity is clean and bracing, with an aha moment's subtle electric snap. It's the satisfaction of seeing an old thing in a new way, or of finding the right focus with your camera so the image is suddenly bright and crisp. It is recognizing what is true in our experience, and for this reason clarity tastes like sanity.

- **Equanimity.** The learned capacity to be smooth with our experience, to not push and pull on sights, sounds, feelings, thoughts, and sensations. Equanimity feels like letting go, like openness, like the world is falling through you. It is the weird and paradoxical skill of getting out of your own way. If you've ever had the experience of being braced against some uncomfortable feeling or sensation, and then suddenly accepting or relaxing into your discomfort, then you've been temporarily equanimous. Usually when this happens our discomfort diminishes, and some or all of the energy bound up in our resistance gets liberated, to be reapplied in whatever direction we choose (service, creativity, medieval jousting). Equanimity is a peerless life skill that has the potential to turn us all into frictionless ninjas.

If our first three skills help cultivate a steady and balanced mind, then our next two deliberately skew to the positive. Friendliness and enjoyment are part of the attitude we bring to meditation.

- **Friendliness.** The compassionate part of us that decides to treat all visitors—all thoughts, feelings, sounds, and sensations—with care and good-naturedness. Friendliness is primarily an *intention*. It doesn't require some big emotion, and in fact the feel of it will be a bit different for everyone. For myself, it feels like affectionate amusement, like smiling on the inside. Friendliness acts as an insurance policy against subtle inner antagonisms.
- **Enjoyment.** Another intention, this time to be open to the hedonic dimension of experience. If friendliness is smiling, then enjoyment is deliberately enjoying the *feeling* of smiling. Although optional, it does make meditation more pleasurable. The key skill here is balancing enjoyment with equanimity, finding pleasure in experience without subtle gripping or dependency.

In this meditation, we'll let the mindfulness be implicit and make these five other skills explicit. I'll try to point out each of their "tastes" in situ, as it were. I can't say enough how important this is. The single greatest accelerator in a meditation practice is noticing the "reward flavor" of each of the attentional qualities you are training. So noticing the vaguely enjoyable feeling of being concentrated allows you to get even more concentrated, which in turn increases that enjoyment, and so on. Ditto with clarity and equanimity and friendliness. All of these qualities mutually support and reinforce one another, and all of them feel like *something* when they are present.

TRAINING THE MIND

10 to 20 minutes

We start with our familiar breath meditation here, the one we've used as the standard through this book. If not the breath, then choose something else you find relatively easy to concentrate on—maybe some part of the body, or sounds. Don't worry if you suck at concentrating. Sometimes I do too. You're simply exploring what it might be like to suck marginally less. It's a training exercise. So take a few minutes to get as focused as you can get on your chosen sensation, in a light and good-natured way. We're looking for a balance of concentration and easygoingness. The first skill of concentration is the directedness, the ability to choose what you want to pay attention to. Explore what this is like: to center your attention on a chosen object, and then to re-center it every time your mind wanders. Explore this.

Sustained concentration builds quickly in some people, and more slowly in others. At a certain point, the mind settles and you get into the zone, or at least more of a zone. It's this feeling of being more in the zone—of being "into it"—that I want you to try to notice. Sometimes it just feels like the external world has faded a bit and the breath or other sensation is more vivid and present and full. Other times it feels like there is more quiet inside, more stillness, that it is a tiny bit easier for your attention to stay where you want it. Try to stay relaxed as you proceed. You aren't trying to drill into the sensation, you're just trying to hold your mind lightly in a particular direction. How *into it* can you get? Can you find something enjoyable in the object of your focus?

Although sustained concentration is helpful, concentration also happens in little pulses—pulses of paying attention to something deeply for a moment or two. You can notice that if more sustained concentration is less available. The instruction is to meditate and be curious about both the experience of directing your attention and any feelings of absorption or into-it-ness that may emerge. No rush, nowhere to get to other than easily being with your chosen sensation.

Sometimes the stabilization of attention leads to dullness or a loss of vividness. There is less novelty, so we may find ourselves moving toward sleep. We need to actively train ourselves to stay clear once attention settles, thus clarity is our next skill. Clarity is the ability to discern the details of our experience. Curiosity is king here. If you're working with the breath, see if you can get very still and steady and notice the subtlest part of it. Can you feel the breath move through your body, through your nose and chest and into the soft rise of the belly? Same goes for sounds—for anything. How fine-grained can you make your sensing?

Any kind of noticing is clarity. A couple of things can help. One: stillness. The stiller you are, the clearer the signal. Two: an interest in how sensations move and change from moment to moment. Can you notice things with that level of detail? As usual, if you become aware of other stuff—distractions, thoughts, tensions—see if you can let all that recede into the background.

This is part of our next skill: equanimity. Equanimity is

lack of interference and uptightness. It's the delicate art of letting everything be what it is, even as you express a light preference via the direction of your focus. Let go of judgments. Let go of any bracing or rigidity. Let go of all the ways you may be subtly trying to control the experience. Let the sensations and sounds come to you, expressing themselves and moving on. What does it feel like to be receptive in this way? Some people say it feels like lightness, like openness, like maturity. What does equanimity feel like for you? The more you notice the taste of equanimity, the deeper it becomes—in practice, and in life. Equanimity is the profound art of accepting the moment.

Our last skills are friendliness and enjoyment. Sometimes our meditations can have a stern or serious quality. Notice if that is there and see if you can lighten up a bit. Can you have a slight sense of humor about the experience of breathing or feeling or listening? Where do you feel this subtle friendliness? A trace of a smile at the lips can help. And what about enjoyment—can you explore this possibility? Noticing the softest part of a sensation, letting it caress you. Finding something enjoyable in the way you sit.

Nothing else to do. Just breathing, just listening. Enjoying your own company.

Moment by moment, recommit to the breath. Feel it as fully as you can. You are building up your mental muscles in an atmosphere of simplicity and easygoingness. Training how you want to exist.

When you're almost done, keep your eyes closed and take a few minutes to coast and do nothing. Rest. Then open your eyes.

CHEAT SHEET

1. Choose an anchor for your attention—breath, belly, bum, hands—something on which you already know you can get concentrated. Let yourself get settled and focused. This will be your main meditation object throughout the sit.

2. After a few minutes, notice any subtle feelings of absorption, of being "into" the breath or sounds. How *into it* can you get? This *into it* feeling is the taste of concentration. If your sustained concentration is weak, you can still notice momentary pulses of being more focused.

3. Get curious about the details of what you're concentrating on. Get as still and stable as you can, and try to notice the edges, the center, the individual pixels of the sensation and the way it changes. This pop-out discernment is the taste of clarity.

4. Try to be easygoing about distractions, letting them play out in the background. How open can you be? Smooth, no friction, letting all sensations be there without resistance. This is the taste of equanimity.

5. Finally, see if you can find something enjoyable and even slightly amusing about this whole exercise, smile tugging at your lips. Good-natured about everything, including the breath. These are the tastes of friendliness and enjoyment.

6. When you're ready, let all that go and take a minute or two to just drift. Then open your eyes.

By the time we wrapped up our shoot with the officers in Tempe, all of them seemed to be on board with meditation—

even Raj. He said presenting the practice as a training made sense, because "cops are very good at taking information and retaining information, and putting it in a tool bag." We had watched him go from worrying that meditation might dangerously shave down his edge to vowing that he was going to give it a shot.

8

"_____ Is My Meditation"

It was the morning of day ten, the penultimate day of the tour, which would also be our last one on board the bus. We were en route from Tempe to Los Angeles, where we would get around by car instead of our unwieldy orange leviathan.

The remaining hours of the trip took on a sweetly elegiac vibe for me. I was genuinely going to miss this experience. The feeling persisted even when, as I was scavenging through the kitchen area for some breakfast, I discovered a hidden stash of cookies, a whole cabinet filled with all kinds of treats. Literally everyone else on the bus knew about it and had been hiding it from me for more than a week. Fuckers.

Other images from these final hours come back to me now like sequences from a cheesy movie montage.

Like when we stopped in Palm Springs and found a deserted side road, and Eddie pulled out a drone fitted with a camera. We used it to capture some deeply absurd video of me and Jeff striding purposefully down the pavement, the bus following behind us. I was picturing a movie trailer with a voice-over artist intoning, "In a world . . ." We were unable to keep straight faces, however, especially when Jeff deliberately walked into me and pushed me out of the shot.

Then, once we arrived in L.A., there was the scene that unfolded at a tony pedestrian mall where we set up the meditation booth one last time. Jeff sensed that I was feeling tight and self-conscious about talking to strangers, so he proposed we do a "no-fear practice." That, he explained, is where you decide to adopt the mindset of being utterly unencumbered by any fear or embarrassment. Jeff said he sometimes did this when he went out dancing—an activity that had been in my day planner approximately zero times in the last several decades.

In order to show me how it was done, Jeff began hollering, "Free meditation lessons! Not crazy!" Then he turned to me and said, "Now it's you."

I let rip. "Free meditation lessons!" It wasn't as bad as I thought it would be.

"Woohoo," exclaimed Jeff. "Right here! Dan Harris. ABC News. Nice guy!"

People were still ignoring us, but Jeff was undaunted.

"Free meditation! Totally free. Charming fellows. Not a cult!" Then a pause. "Maybe a cult!"

At this point, I was laughing too hard to participate.

But the truly standout moment came the next morning, on day eleven, when Jeff and I were stuck in L.A. traffic in the backseat of a taxi. We were having yet another of our long, rangy talks about life, career, and meditation when he put his hand on my shoulder and gave me a slightly goofy, utterly earnest look that only Jeff could pull off without being treacly. "I love you, man," he said. Shucks. I told him that I loved him right back, and that I couldn't have imagined a more perfect partner for this trip. And then I tried to figure out whether I was Paul Rudd or Jason Segel in this movie.

Throughout these dwindling hours of our road trip, I was able to muster a heightened awareness of my enjoyment of our figurative and literal journey. Occasionally my mind would go into fast-forward or rewind mode, but I was catching it pretty quickly. I was inhabiting a more gerundial way of being, mindful of the impermanence of it all. I could see clearly how meditation practice enabled this approach, and how the experience itself was a sort of meditation. These are the good old days indeed.

For me, all of this naturally leads to the following question: is it possible to milk this kind of enjoyment out of life without meditation?

There's a refrain I hear from meditation skeptics quite frequently: "I don't need to meditate; running [or gardening, or fill in the blank] is my meditation." Jeff and I encountered this sentiment repeatedly throughout our road trip, in fact. A woman in Las Cruces told us that her daily sunrise walk was her meditation. Josh Groban said performing onstage was meditative for him.

My answer whenever anyone asks me whether the aforementioned activities constitute mindfulness meditation is: maybe. It depends on how you do it. For instance, if you go running the way I do—spending most of the time rehearsing elaborate speeches you'd like to hurl at your boss, or listening to music and pretending you're the drummer—it is definitely not mindfulness meditation. If, on the other hand, you're deliberately paying attention to the sensations of your footfalls, the wind on your face, and the movement of your muscles, and then every time you get distracted, you start again—well then, that, to me, is legit.

This is not to say that running, gardening, or petting your dog can't be massively beneficial activities. Exercise, for example, not only is good for the body but also has well-demonstrated antidepressant effects. Bottom line, though: it's not mindfulness meditation unless you are knowingly paying attention to whatever you're doing, and then, when you inevitably get lost, beginning again and again and again.

Jeff and I are aware that it is unwise to get overly dogmatic about any one approach to happiness. There are certainly other ways to generate the skills that are honed in meditation. As Jeff says, being open-minded and ecumenical is "essential" for people in our position—"it's what prevents you from getting into the weird salesman thing." Or, as the psychologist Abraham Maslow once said, if the only tool you have is a hammer, you treat everything as if it were a nail.

This is a lesson we learned in rather dramatic fashion on the afternoon of the final day. We basically got schooled by a group of formerly incarcerated youth.

We had come to InsideOUT Writers (IOW), a nonprofit organization that connects Hollywood professionals with minors who have been caught up in the criminal justice system. IOW works with young people both behind bars and after their release, teaching them writing skills as a way to explore and manage their feelings. Jeff and I were hoping to see whether meditation might be of use as well.

We were seated in a circle of folding chairs with eleven alumni of the program, all now in their twenties or thirties. The IOW offices are on the second floor of a nondescript building in East Hollywood. The place has a lived-in feel, with brown carpets and lima-bean-green walls, one of which bears the organization's name in spray paint. The alumni, who had been out of prison for varying lengths of time, some of them for serious crimes such as kidnapping and assault with a firearm, use the space as a kind of clubhouse. They come here not only for weekly writing sessions but also for career advice and social time.

The vibe was companionable as the IOWers made get-to-know-you small talk with us. But when Jeff said he was going to lead a Concentration 101 meditation, there was a little bit of apprehension. "So we're going to sit quiet for fifteen minutes?" one of them said incredulously.

They gamely went along, though. And when it was over and we all blinked our way back into the room, they were clearly enthusiastic. In fact, some of them revealed that the practice Jeff had just taught was similar to mental strategies they had invented on their own. One young man, Omar Castaneda, who had served fifteen years for carjacking, said, "When I was in prison, I would wait until the night until everything gets shut down, everything gets turned off, my cellmate's asleep, and I would meditate because that would be the only time that I would be able to escape."

Things got even more interesting when we began putting pen to paper. At every session at IOW, the group is given a writing prompt. This time, the assignment, inspired by *10% Happier,* was to spend twenty minutes describing what they were worried about and whether that worrying was useful.

When the time was up, we went around the circle and gave everyone a chance to read what they had written. One of the most moving entries came from Mylrell Miner, whose hulking torso was offset by his incongruously doe-like eyes and soft voice. He had grown up in poverty and spent most of his teens and twenties in and out of prison for a series of crimes, including armed robbery. Now he was hoping to build a career as a screenwriter.

"This is called 'The Short List,'" he said, explaining that he would have written down more of his worries, but "I do not have enough paper for *War and Peace.*" Then he began his litany, which read, in part:

Friends of mine got killed. Family of mine killed themselves.

Bills are due; my baby is due, too.

My mechanic had to give me a ride here, and I do not have enough money to get back.

My sister's rent is due with two kids, and her husband is in
a coma.

My dad's on his deathbed. My mom's a cancer survivor.

Eating healthy is not cheap, so I count penny bank coins,
not calories.

I am worried that I might let everyone down.

I am worried that *down* might not let me *up*.

But too many paths have led me here, to this room. So
maybe I have worried enough.

Despite the staggering unfairness of his life circumstances,
Mylrell had a lightness, an incandescence about him. The dad
in me wanted to wrap the guy up in my arms. (Although, given
that he's about three times my size, that would have presented
some logistical challenges.)

Mylrell explained that he had, by sheer coincidence, recently seen me doing an interview in a documentary film on
Netflix called *Minimalism*. As he told the group, "He was like,
'Worrying only gets you so far. Once you worry too much, then
it becomes unhealthy.' And that really struck me. So through
all that stuff, all I was going through, my car breaking down—
our mechanic really gave us a ride here—all this dying, rent,
bills, parole . . . it was like, I'm only going to take it so far, and
then I'm going to just have to let it go. So that's really been
helping me get through." And then he added, looking around
in disbelief, "After I seen it, I'm sitting in a room with you, it's
crazy."

"Well, it's humbling for me to sit in a room with you," I replied, "because when I listen to you talk, I am reminded that
the things I'm worried about are ridiculous."

This impression was only further reinforced when it came
time to hear from Candice Price, who was wearing a hoodie

and bandanna and had a searing story to tell. She had been born as a crack baby to a mother with crippling mental illness. She was raised by her grandmother, whose boyfriend sexually abused her.

"One of the things that I'm worried about is the fact that my dad just got out of jail after doing twenty-five years and I don't know how to love him," she said, her voice cracking and eyes welling up. "It's like, 'Candice, what are you going to do? Don't treat him like that, he's just trying to love you.' But this is all I know: 'Fuck you, everybody else left me.'"

She went on to say that she now had many more family members getting out of jail with nowhere to go. "So I feel like it's up to me to figure out what to do," she said. "And I'm so tempted to go on the streets and get some dope and sell it, but then at the same time I gotta realize that that ain't me. I'm not the person that I used to be, and I'm here for a change."

Her reading also included a reference to her roughly twelve suicide attempts—"like a box of Dunkin' Donuts"—and concluded with this: "This shit gets deep. But I want to thank the man above that I was never found in a creek."

Candice was greeted by a round of applause from her peers, and then a seemingly effortless outpouring of compassion. They put their arms around her and held forth with words of encouragement and support. Omar told her, "Stop making it your problem. It's *our* problem." He added: "And as far as your dad and the love goes, just . . . You don't gotta do nothing. Don't feel nothing. Just be. You feel what I'm saying? Just be. Be you, and it's going to come."

Mylrell chimed in: "You've gotta love yourself in order to love your dad."

I found it incredibly moving to watch Candice take this leap and be caught so lovingly by her friends in this circle. It was also instructive for me as someone endeavoring to spread the word about mindfulness because these young people were demonstrating so many of the qualities that can be cultivated through meditation: listening closely, confronting emotions head-on, and living with compassion. They didn't need us; they were doing it already.

That is not to say that adding a meditation practice couldn't be beneficial, but clearly the process of writing—which allowed them to view their feelings with some distance—and group discussion, which was really a form of group therapy, was taking them a long way. Their talks were like our bus confabs, only closer to the marrow.

So while it may not be meditation per se, what these young people were doing through writing and mutual support was most certainly a practice—a deliberate cultivation of mental habits. Per Jeff, a practice is "something that you dedicate yourself to and it spills out into the rest of your life in a beneficial way." Playing in a band or on a sports team can teach focus and collaboration. Walking in nature can teach calm and connectivity. Being of service—as my physician father, the non-meditator, has done for decades—can teach compassion. As Jeff said of my father, "That's literally called a medical practice."

What exactly constitutes a practice? How can the skills of meditation complement and support our current practices? And what's the overlap between meditation, yoga, and prayer? I asked Jeff.

FAQ: *Practice*

I love meditation, but my real passion is understanding what makes people fulfilled. When I meet people who seem present and grounded and content, I'm always curious: how did they get that way? Maybe that's a question only someone who was so *not* that way for so long would ask. I know some of it is about genes, and some of it is about the early stuff that happens when we're kids. But I also know that practice—the various ways we commit ourselves in the time allotted to us—can play a big part. Sometimes these practices are explicit (prayer, helping, martial arts, etc.), but just as often, I think, they are *implicit* in the way we choose to live. Because that's what humans do, at least the wise ones. They learn. They pay attention. They make adjustments. They make *life* their practice.

What's so cool to me is that many of the skills people figure out at the macro level of their lives are actually the same ones that meditation teaches us at the micro level of the moment. So you see *concentration*, the ability to hold a direction, despite setbacks; *equanimity*, the skill of letting go and trusting, of not fighting with everything, of listening to life instead of only our own fixations; *compassion*, the practice of caring for ourselves and others, and being skillful about how to act on that caring; and finally *clarity* and *mindfulness*, the practice of looking with discernment at our own responses and habits, and ultimately of finding more perspective.

Meditation is like life skills for dummies. I am a supreme dummy. The big picture overwhelms me. It makes me race around like a headless chicken spewing out explanations and trying to think my way to a neat "conclusion," at which point everything will be fine, forever. This isn't a bad working definition of insanity. The genius of meditation is that it basically says: *"Hey, relax, bud, all you need to worry about is this moment. Can you find some focus? Some friendliness? A bit of perspective?"* Yes I can, meditation, thank you. And guess what? String together enough moments, you get a life. Go figure.

Okay, let's talk about the moment-to-moment training then. When people say "running is my meditation," how can they run in a way that makes this even more true?

Well, it's already a practice in terms of its intention and commitment: to improve health, to connect to the body, nature, and whatever else might be there. You can turbo-boost it by deliberately adding some of our meditation skills. How?

Start by setting an intention for how long you want to practice the meditation piece. Maybe it's five minutes, maybe it's the whole run. Consider opting out of music or podcasts while you do. Music is obviously fun and can make the run pass more quickly, but the whole point here is *not* to do this, not to "lose yourself," as Eminem raps in what's obviously the world's most epic running anthem. Rather, you want to try to be fully present with the whole sensory experience.

Once you start running, deliberately choose a sensation to focus on. You can choose to stay with one kind of sensation, or you can move your attention around. I do the latter. I start by noticing the feeling of air on my skin. Noting helps—*coolness* or *warmth*—at a pace that works for you. How sensitively can you feel as you move? When your mind wanders, bring it back. Then, a few minutes in, I go inside. I notice the breath in my body—*breathing*—or the sensations of my feet contacting the ground—*touching*—or any feelings of streaming energy and exertion through my core—*feeling*. At a certain point I shift to notice my whole body moving in space—*moving*—a giddy, almost vertiginous feeling of being in my center even as the landscape tracks by. I notice the ambient surround—*hearing*—as I move inside my bubble of sound—*moving*—back and forth between outside—*hearing*—and inside—*moving*. You get the idea. All this may seem like thinking, and it's true that the noting *is* thinking. But it's minimal, and in the service of the meditation. I actually don't strategize as much as I've suggested here; generally I let my attention go where it goes spontaneously. I notice and follow along, trying to get as deep into the feeling and the hearing as I can, even as my thoughts percolate (or settle) in the background.

So that's the mindfulness and the concentration and the clarity. There's also an equanimity piece, where you do your best to maintain a loose and relaxed state in the body as you move. You can be stiff and uncomfortable and still practice equanimity, but the looseness definitely makes a big difference; it's amazing how much unnecessary tension we bring to exercise, locomoting like robots, like we're fighting the air around us. The potent combination of equanimity, relaxation, and concentration—combined, no doubt, with a solid dose of euphoria-inducing endorphins—can create an experience in which all the physical sensations through the core and limbs—*breathing, feeling, touching, moving*—start to integrate and flow together: *flowing*. This is an awesome sensation to meditate on, whether you're swimming, running, biking, or doing any endurance sport.

Athletes say this quality can extend into our relationship with the world around us. We can enter a kind of flow state, or "zone," where, if we're focused and quiet enough on the inside, we find we're able to respond more effortlessly to changing circumstances on the outside. The experience is exquisite, even mystical, and actually what Eminem is probably pointing to in his song. One sports psychologist told me you can't really teach this kind of high-level flow, "you can only prepare the conditions for it to happen." We do this both by being well trained in our sport and by cultivating exactly the mindfulness skill set described above.

What about other practices like yoga and tai chi that many feel are inherently meditative? I get lots of questions about these.

Yoga is a rich and comprehensive system of practice, as are the many schools of Taoism, from which tai chi emerged. Both contain meditation techniques outside the postures, and both have figured out ways of integrating meditative principles *into* the postures. To focus just on the physical side, both practices center around the insight that a vital, open, and well-aligned body helps create the conditions for a vital, open, and well-aligned mind. Practitioners yoke their attention to the breath and to the physical sensations of energy and movement, and in so doing, they find that everything starts to move more easily.

You can apply mindfulness and the other skills to either of these practices, in exactly the way I've described in the running section. In fact, mindfulness is implicit in the way both are often taught, which is about tracking what is happening in the body and generally increasing interoceptive awareness.

The equanimity piece is particularly clear. In both tai chi and yoga, practitioners are encouraged to move smoothly and fluidly, to be on the lookout for ways in which the body may be subtly fighting with itself. In yoga, you notice where in your body you are blocked or holding tension, and then you breathe into those sensations, deliberately and systematically relaxing the areas around them. You try to find composure in the posture, even as you shake with exertion. The idea is that if you can find equanimity and balance under these strained and artificial circumstances, then you can find it in the office, or at home, or on the street, when you're not twisted around like a reef knot. So the skills naturally radiate out into life.

How about the connection between prayer and meditation?

This is a huge question that depends on the kind of meditation and the kind of prayer. The heart of prayer is humility and equanimity: it's not pretending your limited perspective is capable of figuring it all out. It involves the belief that sometimes the right move is to trust and surrender to both the flow and the source of life. This emerges naturally in meditation. Additionally, many people get very concentrated in prayer; they get still and quiet, and this allows them to reset. And of course, in all the Abrahamic traditions, you have a huge emphasis on compassion and service, the living practice of this. So many of the skills are there. The main difference is probably the feeling of being in *relationship*— folks who pray aren't sitting alone with their stuff, but sharing it with a wise and loving other whom they can ask for guidance.

Mindfulness can be a helpful adjunct to prayer—it can help improve people's focus, so they are less likely to get lost in discursive thought, for one. It also helps generate insight into how we are, into our various patterns and blind spots and biases.

Does meditation conflict with faith?

I'm not sure how it would, especially the secular approaches to mindfulness, which present all this very much as mental and emotional skills that anyone can benefit from, regardless of the nature of their existential belief wrappers. Personally I think it can enhance the beautiful qualities of faith I've already described—the humility, the joy, the love—and it might temper some of the more shadowy aspects that can emerge around doctrinal rigidity and intolerance. Although these are human challenges that go far beyond the faith-based religions.

I'll shift gears now and look at something many people consider "meditative"—walking—and show you how to inject a big dose of mindfulness into the activity. Actually, this is a twofer. I show you how to turn any walk into a meditation, and also how to do a more formal version. Formal walking meditation is a great alternative to seated practice and a big part of both my meditation life and Dan's. Sometimes it's the only practice you want to do—sitting feels too agitating, or you don't feel like meditatively working with your emotions. A walking practice at these times can be a huge relief, both grounding and refreshing.

WALKING MEDITATION
Option 1—Formal
5 minutes or more

Choose your field of operation—a small inside space cleared of obstacles or a circumscribed outside area. Decide: shoes on or off? Get curious about how completely you can stay with the physical sensation of moving, and how unhurried and deliberate you can make each step. The classic meditative focus points are the two feet. Take your first slow step and note: *lift* as the foot lifts, aware of the release; *move* as it glides forward, aware of the slightly unstable swing through space; *step* as it lands, aware of the miniature recalibrations of balance and pressure. And then do the same with the next foot. And so it goes, one foot after the other, a frankly weird and ungainly bipedal spectacle whose automaticity you are doing your best to undo. What *is* walking? What is this new tingling walking feeling situation?

Have a good time. Recruit your imagination. You're allowed to do this in meditation. Walk on the earth like you're Neil Armstrong walking on the moon, testing the gravity, pretending you don't know what's coming. Can you notice the little differences in each step? Can you be *that* clear and focused?

Slow it down—no rush. Here for the act of it, each step landing in the here and now. *Lift, move, step.* If your feet are bare, try sampling the textures beneath you, the bent grass or smooth floor, the bumps and depressions, each foot probing and feeling, like a long "downturned hand," to quote my pal the eco-philosopher David Abram. If emotions and thoughts intrude—as they will—just redirect to physical sensations, scooping out the body with your mindfulness.

If you're outside, from time to time look up and check out the size of life—the trees, the buildings, sky sky sky. Listen to the birdy-birds go chirp-chirp-chirp. Feel the breeze. Lick a random forest mushroom (no, don't do that). Life is all around, and you are aware and alive and walking in peace.

Option 2—Informal
30 seconds to ultra-marathon length

Our inner world of thoughts and feelings can exert a powerful gravity. This practice is a way to balance this, by shifting attention to the body and the world's *actual* gravitational pull. Start by noticing the feeling of your legs moving and your muscles working as you walk. Notice your swinging arms but also your core, this center line that moves with you, the world reorganizing itself in your peripheral vision, space parting in front and closing behind. Notice the air on your skin, the weather on your face, the solidity of the land against the soles of your feet. Choose how wide or narrow you want your focus, and whether you want to stay with one type of sensation or move your attention around. Both options are fine. See how totally you can commit to feeling your body move this way.

Some people like to walk slowly. I like to walk *fast*. I like to lope forward in long strides, the ground reaching up to catch each foot like I'm a giant striding across a continuously forming island volcano chain.

Experiment. Practice walking playfully, joyfully—set this as your experimental intention. What is it like to walk joyfully? Well, I don't believe I know. Let me attempt this unusual exercise. And so you do, newborn in your new skin in this newfound moment. How does it change the feeling, the action? Can you walk as an *offering* to Zeus, to the city's surveillance cameras, to our would-be extraterrestrial conquistadors? Show reality what it's like to be a happy human turning the planet with your measured stride.

Or slow it down and keep it simple. As you walk home from work, as you cut across the park, the formal practice remembers itself: *lift, move, step, lift, move, step.* Just this moment, uncoupled from lists and schedules. *Lift, move, step, lift, move, step.* Grateful to be here.

Intimate or expansive, make this meditation your own.

CHEAT SHEET
Option 1—Formal

1. Choose, inside or out, some circumscribed area you can move comfortably in, shoes on or off. Set the intention to move slowly and deliberately.

2. Bring your attention to your two feet. Take your first step and note *lift* as the foot lifts, *move* as it glides forward, *step* as it lands. Then repeat with the next foot.

3. Enjoy the simplicity. Be curious and clear and wonderstruck by the weirdness of it all. If emotions and thoughts intrude, redirect to physical sensations. Finish when you finish.

Option 2—Informal

1. Wherever you are, notice your body as you walk. See how totally you can commit to the feeling of your body moving.

2. Experiment. Practice walking *joyfully*—set this as your intention. How does it change the feeling, the action? Or slow it down and keep it simple.

In sum, any practice in which you are currently engaged can be infused with greater degrees of intentionality and mindfulness, to say nothing of the other skills we've been exploring.

One essential and challenging aspect to any practice, though, is consistency. That is the final obstacle we will tackle.

9

"I Can't Keep It Going"

In many ways, Wanderlust Hollywood embodies everything I've made it my business to mock. It's a giant, slick yoga studio and community center near Sunset Boulevard that serves Ayurvedic stewed mung beans in its café and offers classes with names like Soul Revival, Energetic Alignment, and Yin, Breathe, Chillax.

But the company—which also produces yoga festivals across the world and creates instructional content—operates in a refreshingly cool and unpretentious manner. Furthermore, I had gotten to know and like the CEO, Jeff Krasno, a wry, sharp businessman who gave us insightful advice about our 10% Happier start-up. So when the folks at Wanderlust offered to host the final event of our road trip in their giant yoga hall, which they modestly refer to as "The Greatest Place," how could we refuse?

I had been worrying, as is my wont, that no one would show up, but we got several hundred people to come out on a Wednesday night and join us in the cavernous room. Eddie had spent the previous twenty-four hours scrambling to edit together a series of highlights from our road trip, which we played to the audience. As I watched some of the best clips with Paula Faris, Josh Groban, and Sergeant Raj Johnson projected onto the hall's big screen, I was already nostalgic. I was also relieved when I spotted the elusive Moby slipping into the room and taking a seat in the back row, waiting to be called to the stage.

Unlike some of the people we had met over the course of our journey, the crowd in L.A. did not have much ambivalence about mindfulness. They lived in a city teeming with vegan restaurants, Pilates studios, and grown men and women who are paid millions of dollars to pretend to be superheroes in movies. Comparatively, meditation did not seem so weird. Here, a different concern emerged: how to keep the practice going.

A woman in the back raised her hand to say that she had gone on several streaks of daily meditation but had been unable to establish a regular habit. "How can I anchor into something consistent that doesn't end after seven days?" she asked.

Since we're about to release you into the wild as a fledgling meditator, let's go back into life-hack mode, with nine more pro tips that might help you commit to a regular practice.

PRO TIP: *Cut Yourself Some Slack*

The first thing I told the woman in the back of the hall was that the consistency issue is incredibly common, and the most important step is to "give yourself a break."

Jeff echoed this sentiment, pointing out that there will inevitably be times when "you fall off the wagon," and that the key is to realize that this is a "pattern that lots of people are in."

When people falter at meditation—or at any new habit—they tend to blame their lack of willpower. They tell themselves a story about how hopelessly undisciplined they are, which only makes them less likely to try again. As we've discussed, the maddeningly ephemeral inner resource of willpower may be one of the most insidious fallacies in behavior change.

In the face of a setback, instead of engaging in self-laceration, the vastly superior option is our sappy old friend, self-compassion. Studies suggest that, rather than making you smug, self-compassion can help you withstand daily indignities such as failure, rejection, and embarrassment. People with this attribute have a greater willingness to learn from and correct their perceived weaknesses or mistakes, which boosts resiliency, making them better able to get back into the fray.

PRO TIP: *Just Begin Again*

No matter how long it has been since you last meditated, no matter how mindlessly you have behaved in the interim, nothing has been lost; you can always just start over. It's just like when you get distracted during meditation itself—the game is to good-naturedly begin again, ad infinitum.

The best way to approach establishing a meditation habit—or, again, any habit—is with a spirit of experimentation. Don't expect to install a meditation practice into your life like a piece of software and never look back. You should view failure as an inevitable and even healthy part of the process. When you tumble off the wagon, just reevaluate the plan and come up with a new one. As Thomas Edison—himself no stranger to laboratory experimentation—is reputed to have said, "I have not failed. I've just found ten thousand ways that won't work."

Remember: different tactics work for different people at different times. You should feel free to explore, to tinker with ways to let the benefits of meditation hook you, rather than attempting to gut it out through sheer willpower.

PRO TIP: *Set Realistic, Achievable Goals*

A young woman in the front row at Wanderlust told us that she was balancing her full-time job, a three-hour commute, and three little kids at home. For a while she had managed to fit in twenty minutes of meditation a day on top of all that, but eventually, she said, "I just stopped, because I couldn't do it."

Then a friend recommended she try sitting for just five minutes per day. "And I have found that, out of the last thirty-five days, I think I've sat thirty-two. And I feel amazing on just five minutes."

Bingo. "You don't need to have such ambitious goals," I replied, "if the math just doesn't work out."

As you test ways to boot up a regular practice, it is best to set sustainable targets. My friend Richie Davidson, one of the leading neuroscientists studying the impact of meditation on human health and behavior, poses an interesting question when enrolling new subjects for his studies. He asks, "How much time do you think you can actually practice—and do it every day?" Some people choose just sixty seconds (which Richie says is good enough to gain enrollment). Personally, I have seen so many friends get excited about meditation and declare their intention to sit for significant periods of time every day, only to hit the rocky shoals of disappointment and self-recrimination.

True, lowering your sights can be frustrating if you feel your contemplative ambitions are being stifled. However, while meditation almost certainly confers more benefits the more you do it, there is no point in setting goals you can't achieve. As Jeff told the woman in the front row at Wanderlust, we have to accept that "we go through periods of our life where we're just not gonna have a lot of time to practice." The move, he said, is simply to acknowledge that "this is your life right now."

He added an important point, though: if you are only able to practice for a few minutes, there are ways to amplify your practice by injecting micro-hits of mindfulness throughout your day, as Jeff suggested in Chapter 3. This kind of free-range meditation can absolutely help get the habit more deeply ingrained in your life and boost the odds of consistency over time.

Our first guest of the evening had an interesting take on the dosage question. We invited to the stage Bill Duane, the "superintendent of well-being" at Google. Bill's job is to develop and run programs that help employees advance happiness and effectiveness in the workplace. He's a jolly guy who, with his long, graying beard and earlobe discs, looks like a fourth, rave-inflected member of ZZ Top.

An engineer and an atheist, Bill had come to meditation warily. "My methods of dealing with stress were along the ancient wisdom traditions of bourbon and cheeseburgers," he told the crowd. But the stresses of his work life, compounded by the death of his father, threw him into a tailspin. That's when he happened to attend a lecture at Google about the neuroscience of emotion, in which he learned that you can change your brain through meditation. He took a deep dive, attending more than a dozen long, silent retreats, which, he believed, drastically improved his life.

When he began promoting the practice at Google, his initial inclination was to recommend that people engage in significant amounts of formal daily sitting. His colleagues ultimately pushed back, telling him there needed to be a slower build-up. So now, to help people get over the hump, he instructs them to meditate in manageable five- to ten-minute segments, and sometimes even smaller. Like us, Bill had come to the conclusion that one minute counts. "Google is full of high achievers, and if we set our minds to do something and then we don't do it, we have a tendency to meet that with a fair amount of self-criticism," he said. "Imagine if someone gave you a device and they said, 'If you use this device, you will be happier and more effective and more compassionate.' And then the first thing you do is you start hitting yourself over the head with the device."

PRO TIP: *Continually Re-up Your Motivation*

When you're doing it all by yourself, meditation can start to feel a little stale. It's easy to lose touch with why you're putting yourself through it in the first place. Both Jeff and I have found that merely glancing at a few pages of a good book on meditation can have an enlivening effect (we make suggestions in the Appendix). My bedside table and bookshelves are stacked with dog-eared, note-filled volumes. I try to read a few pages every single day. It makes me realize why so many Christians have well-worn Bibles around the house. As Jeff has said, one definition of the word "mindfulness" is "remembering." Every time you glance at a good book, it helps you recollect and reconnect.

Additionally, most teachers also have online videos, podcast interviews, and guided meditations that you can check out.

PRO TIP: *Don't Overcomplicate Things*

One potential pitfall to the sort of intellectual exploration we're encouraging is that you may be tempted to try all sorts of different practices. This book is focused on mindfulness meditation, but there are scores of other flavors—from Zen to Tibetan to Vedic and beyond. At least at the beginning, our advice is to pick one path and stick with it. "If you're doing multiple practices at the same time, how are you going to know what works for you?" said Jeff.

Bill Duane agrees. "I would caution against getting too crazy with the mix-and-match," he told the crowd at Wanderlust. He believes it's best to fully explore one tradition before branching out too widely.

Here's Jeff's advice on how to combine the practices described in this book in order to create an abiding habit.

A PRACTICE BUILT TO LAST

The foundational meditation in this book is Chapter 2's Concentration 101. It's nice to have a home base practice—with a home base focus that you don't have to think about, you just do. My advice is that you make Concentration 101 your go-to, with some relatively consistent sensation that you like working with: breath, belly, heart, sound, body. As you do this, you are clear that you are building your basic skills and you know what those skills are: mindfulness, concentration, clarity, equanimity, friendliness, and enjoyment as a sexy bonus. You do your best to be relaxed and easygoing and curious about your experience. This, too, is part of the training. And, since you are human like everyone else, some days it will be easy, and some days it will be hard. Mind wanders, bring it back. Every moment is a new beginning. It's a new beginning because *it is not about building up to some special experience.* All experiences come and go. It is about the training underneath all this, our growing ability to notice and be with whatever is happening. This is literally all you need to do and to know; time and nature will do the rest.

If you want to thread in some investigatory insight work, then anytime you get pulled into a distraction, be curious about that distraction, as per Chapters 4 and 6. Name it, note it, spend a couple of minutes exploring its location and form and contour and triggers. The more curious you can get about these strangely familiar patterns, the less you will be fated to repeat them. Explore, and then go back to your main object. If doing this throws you hopelessly off course, then don't do it. Stick to the breath. Just this will still build up the basic qualities of attention.

I like to finish my sit with a compassion or loving-kindness practice, to build this muscle explicitly. I also do a version of what some call the "Dedication of Merit," in which I imagine the good generated by the practice, and then I imagine giving it away to various rich celebrities and CEOs. Just kidding. I imagine giving it to whoever needs it. Then I sit for a bit and do nothing, resting, letting everything integrate.

Right there is a solid sequence that you can use as your default. It can easily last you a lifetime and give you plenty of insight and peace. But you also have these other tools that you may want to check in with as opportunity and interest arise. So if you are cruising around town, there are many endlessly customizable free-range options for listening, looking, feeling, and touching (Chapter 3), to say nothing of running (Chapter 8) and walking (Chapter 8). If you feel ruinously ass-kicked by life and want a break, then crash out on the floor and do a Taking Back Lazy (Chapter 5) or a self-compassion practice (Chapter 5). If someone is standing in front of you in pain, then implement a Smart Compassion practice (Chapter 5), which is as much about steady presence as it is about warmth and concern. And finally, if you find yourself inside some emotional challenge, then one option is to decide to face and explore your feelings, always with desire not to change them, but to know and understand and honor them (Chapter 6).

Through all of these practices, through life itself, there is one constant to always come back to: mindfulness. What's actually happening right now? Thinking, feeling, seeing, hearing. I *know* these things are happening. This is the ultimate habit to build, the ultimate training, one that you can come back to every moment of the day. The more you do this—the more you deliberately *live* inside this awareness—the more that awareness expands. Awareness itself gets more open, more roomy.

PRO TIP: *"Just Put Your Body There"*

Even on days when you really don't feel like meditating, try to see if you can wrangle yourself onto your cushion or chair or wherever you sit, even if only for a few seconds. Often just being in the posture will lead to a few minutes of practice. As the brilliant meditation teacher Sharon Salzberg was advised by one of her teachers during the rocky early days of her practice, "Just put your body there." Don't think about what is going to happen or how long it's going to last. Just get yourself there.

Per Jeff, one thing that can make this process easier is having a regular spot in your home to meditate. "All the associations with meditation pile up," he says. "As soon as you sit down, the various contextual cues help the habit take over."

PRO TIP: *Use Meditation as a Prophylactic*

Back at our event at Newton South High School, we heard from a woman named Rebecca who explained that she was prone to depression and anxiety, both of which were inflamed when she encountered difficult life events such as a "sick parent, or a medical issue, or a job that sucks." Of late, she said, her circumstances had been quite smooth, which had prompted her to cut back on her practice. "It's like, 'I'm calm, I feel good. I don't need to meditate.'"

If you're only meditating to deal with acute situations, you are setting yourself up for streakiness. I approach meditation the way I approach working out. "I don't just exercise when I'm feeling overweight. I do it to prevent feeling overweight," I said to Rebecca. "The vicissitudes of life are always going to reemerge. You should be prepared to handle them as best as possible." Meditation, in my experience, is best used as a prophylactic, rather than as first aid.

PRO TIP: *Take It Easy with the "Practice Assessment Tapes"*

At Wanderlust, we heard from an older gentleman with salt-and-pepper hair who told us that, after decades of flirting with meditation, he had finally established a daily habit. For the past year, he said, he had been sitting twenty minutes a day. Now, however, he was encountering new issues: doubt and disappointment in his meditative abilities. He said he was still getting distracted frequently. "I'm disappointed in myself that, after a year, I don't feel like I've progressed."

My kind of guy. I have spent an inordinate amount of time gnashing my teeth over what an awful meditator I am. There's one thing I've learned as a result of all this angst: it is a gigantic waste of time.

"Expectations," I said to my new friend, "are the most noxious ingredient you can add to the meditation stew." Straight back to the time of the Buddha, desire has been considered to be a hindrance; maddeningly and paradoxically, it blocks you from the very concentration and mindfulness you're hoping to achieve. This is why meditation is such a counterintuitive pursuit for type-A Westerners. Ambition and striving—the assets that often help us so much in the rest of our lives—can work against us on the cushion.

The following quote from scientist–cum–meditation teacher Jon Kabat-Zinn is one of the most valuable things I've heard anyone say about the practice: "Meditation is not about feeling a certain way. It's about feeling the way you feel."

If you're expecting meditation to be a bubble bath or a blissful, laser-focused escape from your relentless inner news crawl, you're likely setting yourself up for disappointment. The goal is to be open to whatever comes up, and to approach it all with mindfulness, friendliness, and interest. If you find yourself encountering a murderer's row of boredom, restlessness, and physical discomfort, so be it. Your only job is to try to see it all clearly—and then, when you get caught up, to start again.

In fact, a "bad" sit can often be where you grow the most—like a particularly vigorous workout—because you are learning how to relate to difficulty. After all, equanimity, as Jeff has told us over and over, is one of the key mental muscles you're trying to build here. It helps to have faith—or, if you prefer, confidence—that even when you feel like you're totally wasting your time, you're not. As Bob Roth, a prominent teacher of Transcendental Meditation, has said, "Even in a shallow dive we get wet."

There are two little tricks that I have found useful when I find myself playing and replaying what my teacher Joseph Goldstein calls "the practice assessment tapes."

First, when you catch yourself worrying about the state of your contemplative career, try making a soft mental note of *doubt*. For me, that often unties the knot—at least temporarily: "Oh yeah, all this crazy thinking is just the mental state of doubt."

The second hack is called an "attitude check." Every once in a while, during meditation, ask yourself, "What's the attitude in my mind right now?" Am I wanting something to be different? This can smoke out subconscious striving or aversion, which then often dissipates.

I'm not arguing that you should never inquire about the state of your practice. This is where talking to a teacher can be especially helpful, because that person can point out if you're stuck in some sort of rut. But obsessing about it all the time is almost certainly not constructive. For myself, I've found that, slowly but surely, my ability to concentrate has improved over time. However, progress is uneven, and backsliding—perceived or real—happens frequently.

Even though I still endure frequent bouts of doubt, I have generated a certain level of trust that this meditation thing really does work. All you have to do is look at the MRI scans of longtime meditators—their brains are different. The trick is to just do the practice and then, as Jeff likes to say, let time and nature do their thing. Joseph Goldstein tells the story of how, when he was a kid, his parents helped him plant a garden. But Joseph, impatient, kept pulling up the carrots to see how they were growing. Time and nature.

One additional note on the practice assessment tapes: the best measure of your meditation skills is not the quality of your last sit but, instead, the quality of your actual life. How are your relationships? Are you a better listener? Are you losing your temper less frequently? In short, are you less of a jerk? As Sharon Salzberg has said, "We don't meditate to get better at meditating; we meditate to get better at life."

Obviously, the practice won't erase your fallibility or flaws. I hope Jeff and I have amply illustrated how illusory the notion of perfection is. Don't write yourself off as a failure if you are still popping off in anger once in a while. I still get captured by my emotions—but I find that I catch myself earlier, and apologize more speedily.

Also, pay attention to what my friend Sam Harris (no relation), a writer and neuroscientist, has called "the half-life of anger." For me, I've found that my anger is much shorter-lived (and also less intense) these days. As Sam says, the difference between the amount of damage you can do in two minutes of anger and what you can do in two hours is incalculable.

And that leads to the final piece of advice.

PRO TIP: *Tune In to the Benefits*

In many ways, we are all like rats in a maze, constantly pressing the levers that deliver food pellets to us. Behavior change science strongly suggests that the best way to ensure a consistent meditation habit is to identify where and how the practice is giving you pellets. Just like rats, we are much more likely to keep doing something if it feels good and we get something out of it.

There are at least two levels to this.

The first level, as we've previously discussed, is to pay attention to how the act of meditating, in itself, can be pleasurable. As Jeff told the man at Wanderlust who was worried about the progress of his practice, it's nice to have goals, but also, "you want to be enjoying yourself in the practice." Notice how good it feels to step out of the traffic and get quiet, said Jeff; tune in to your "juicy animal body." (That last Jeff-ism made me wince a little, but hey, we were in L.A., and it was the last night of the tour.)

The other level is to notice the benefits as they arise in the rest of your life, in terms of both inner weather and outer comportment. Bill Duane told the crowd that a year after taking an in-house meditation course, Google employees reported a 23 percent decrease in emotional reactivity and a 19 percent increase in the ability to manage workplace stress.

One of the best ways to see the benefit of meditation is to feel its absence when you fall off the wagon. We heard this from many people throughout the road trip. For instance, Elvis Duran, the radio host, said when he neglected meditation, "the days are usually more stressful." Personally, I notice that when I've been forced by circumstances to reduce my meditation quotient, my inner toxicity skyrockets.

And here's a rich irony: while focusing on the pellets you get from meditation can help create consistency, the more you do the practice, the less driven you may be by pellet-seeking generally. You might find a new kind of happiness.

While humans have been bred over millennia to chase the pleasant, run from the unpleasant, and zone out in the face of neutral stimuli, meditation, as we've discussed, provides an alternative: the ability to engage with it all fully. This skill allows you, however briefly, to step off the treadmill of getting and doing. Many of us assume that we will finally be happy and complete when all of our wishes are fulfilled—when we hit the lottery, master the Stanky Leg, or get more likes on our Instagram posts. It's the primordial lie we are constantly telling and retelling ourselves. But this is to confuse happiness with excitement.

All of which inexorably leads to another question: what is happiness, anyway? For years I asked tons of smart people about this and never got a truly satisfying answer. Then one night over dinner, I put the question to my friend Dr. Mark Epstein, a psychiatrist, author, and meditator. He said, "More of the good stuff and less of the bad." Initially, I was unmoved.

Over time, though, I began to see the wisdom of this modest assertion.

Allow me to draw upon my vast experience as a Newton South mathlete and put it in geometrical terms:

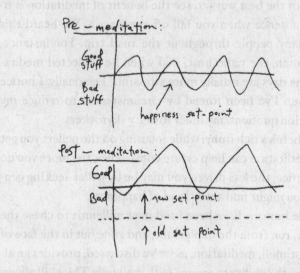

Psychologists have a concept called the "happiness set point." That's the *x*-axis in the above graphs. When "good" things happen, our happiness level spikes. When "bad" things happen, it dives. Eventually we tend to revert to our set point.

After years of meditation, I've found that the top of my graph has gotten taller and more sustained, because I am spending more time enjoying the positive developments in my life, rather than rushing on to the next thing. The bottom of the graph has become shorter and shallower, because I am not getting as lost in useless rumination over my perceived misfortune. Meanwhile, the happiness set point has gone up. This is what I mean when I say that the 10 percent compounds annually.

I'm pulling this out of my behind, obviously—but it's basically true, in my experience.

The cool part is that, unlike physical exercise, this kind of mental training is not limited by the laws of physics. If you can get 10 percent happier, what is the ceiling?

We've thrown a ton of tips at you. Don't let the sheer volume allow you to fall into the biggest and most common trap of all: not getting started. Here's a quick, brass-tacks summary.

· Approach the establishing of a meditation habit as an experiment. You're not making a lifetime commitment.
· Be willing to fail. Know that it's part of the process.
· Start small. Don't take on too much too soon. One minute counts!
· Try attaching meditation to a pre-existing habit. (For example, "After I shower [or run, or have my morning coffee], I meditate for a minute.")
· Stay on the lookout for the life benefits. Let them pull you forward.

Good luck out there.

Back at Wanderlust, as we entered the final hour of our final event of the road trip, we called Moby up to the stage.

I explained that I had known Moby off and on for more than a decade, back from when we were both younger, more social guys in New York City. He looked pretty much the same after all these years, wearing a khaki military jacket with a hoodie underneath. He had a trim, graying beard and was lean from his vegan diet and alcohol-free lifestyle. Even after the platinum records and world tours, he still carried himself with the outsider intensity of a kid who grew up poor in a wealthy town in Connecticut.

Despite knowing Moby for some time, I had just recently learned that not only was he a meditator but he was also, in his words, a "secret" meditation teacher. He had first practiced as a little kid because his single mom, "a spiritual dilettante," would have him do it. As a grown-up, he learned Transcendental Meditation from fellow celebrity David Lynch, and then later explored various forms of Buddhist meditation.

Moby is a famously shy person, but he was in fine form on this night, dropping f-bombs alongside some real wisdom as he spoke from personal experience about the often illusory links between success and happiness.

"The people who've had the most material success, I grew up with these people. They're so unhappy," he said. "We assume that it's going to create some happiness that's not available to us right now. I thought, 'If I have the right career, the right girlfriend, the right other girlfriend, the right other-other girlfriend, the right combination of alcohol, drugs, fame, public notoriety, money, et cetera, et cetera, then I'll be happy.' But then the universe gave all that to me and I was miserable."

In response to all the people in the crowd who had voiced doubts about their own meditation, Moby argued that we shouldn't fall prey to similar assumptions. "Don't use meditation as an opportunity to be critical of yourself, because no one is doing it better than you are." He said he had tortured himself in this way for years. "It's like, I'm convinced I'm not doing it right, and I'm not doing it enough, and if only I did the right meditation practice . . . then I'll finally find enlightenment."

He said he had come to the conclusion that enlightenment is not some magical transcendence. "Enlightenment, I believe, is right where you are, right now. It's just having a different relationship to it that's based on kindness and acceptance."

I have spent an enormous amount of time trying to figure out whether I believe in enlightenment, but if there is indeed such a thing, Moby's definition sounds about right to me.

Then it was time to meditate. After weeks of to-ing and fro-ing over email about whether Moby was going to lead a musical meditation, and despite actually bringing a music track with him, he decided on the spot to ditch it and go in an entirely different direction.

"For the first part," he announced, "we're going to do some very simple chanting."

Oh dear Lord, I thought. *Please, no no no.*

It turned out to be fine. Better than fine, even—poetic. After eleven days of trying to tamp down on the weirdness factor, here I was, in a situation beyond my control, chanting in Sanskrit with Moby and a few hundred strangers. Jeff was kicking my leg and trying to stifle his laughter.

The only regret I had was that this situation was maybe a little unfair to my man Jeff. After all the time spent relentlessly hazing him into repressing his tendency toward esoterica, here was Moby closing out our road trip with a long and lusty round of chanting. So, now that we are nearing the end of the book, I think Jeff deserves his shot to get as mystical as he wants about what meditation can do for us.

Okay, my friend, go for it.

Let's talk about where meditation and mindfulness practice lead. Imagine, if you will, one of those thirteenth-century Scottish fight scenes with Mel Gibson. The untrained and distracted mind is a melee of broadswords, hideous grimaces, war cries, people's heads flying off. As we practice returning to the breath, we slowly build up the necessary stability in awareness to notice this battle that we've been waging with ourselves. We recognize, we accept. We remember. Very slowly, the internal thugs get disarmed. Eventually they're gathered in a circle, drinking mead and hiccupping and singing weepy Gaelic ballads. A great calm descends upon the land. So that's one part of it. The other is we start to notice and appreciate the gorgeous green highland scenery that these idiots have been standing in front of the whole time.

So practice leads to a keener awareness of what has always been there.

Kind of like what Moby said. It's being right where you are, only now you're noticing it in a new way. But for this to happen, it does help to take care of the Mel Gibson problem.

None of that seems particularly far out. It seems like common sense.

The mystical piece has to do with that open landscape. Because it isn't just that you have a new capacity to notice and appreciate the sights and sounds and smells of the world (although this part is more than enough reward for your efforts). It's also that the world itself gets increasingly permeated with . . . something. . . .

Something else, something more. An extra sparkle and mystery that you start to realize has always been there.

Let's try to represent this visually. Here's a version of your graph, Dan . . .

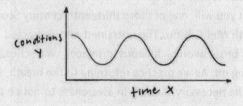

I've relabeled the y-axis so it says "Conditions" instead of "Happiness." For many of us, the two are glued together. When conditions are right, we're happy. When they're not right, we're unhappy.

So, for long-term practitioners, life still has its ups and downs. They get sick, they lose their jobs and loved ones, and they deal with hardship like everyone else. But many also report something else: just like you report in your own sketch, their baseline level of happiness or fulfillment increases. What's actually happening is that their baseline is now no longer entirely determined by those ups and downs. It's as though a third dimension has entered into experience. To show this, we need to move from a two-dimensional grid to more of a three-dimensional box.

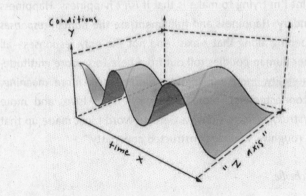

We have the same curvy line moving along the x-axis, which is "Time." But now we also have a third axis—the z-axis—which represents "Depth," both on the graph and in life. It spreads like a widening ribbon out from both our high points *and* our low points equally. You could say this ribbon is like a shadow that extends out beyond our life circumstances and conditions, a kind of invisible breadth and volume.

What *is* that line?

That's the mystery! I can't really say. It doesn't seem to be particularly amenable to concepts. Over the years, mystics and meditators have struggled to come up with language to describe the ineffable. So we get jargon-y spiritual terms like "Being," or "oneness," or "awareness," or "God," or "the moment," or even "emptiness." And actually, my diagram is misleading; this thing/ non-thing that I'm trying rather futilely to describe has always been there, in exactly the same "quantity." It doesn't change. What changes—what gets wider—is how much we notice and *live* from this place.

But is this just another way to talk about happiness?

The point I'm trying to make is that it *isn't* happiness. Happiness is secondary. Happiness and fulfillment are the human *responses* to deepening along that z-axis. And not the only responses—all the other human goodies roll out from here too: more gratitude, more humility, more equanimity, more peace, more meaning, more connectedness, more poignancy, more love, and more *Wunderstrukfladen*, to quote a German word I just made up that means, roughly, "miracle constructed cow patty."

Holy *Scheiße*.

These qualities tend to increase, but they also come and go, as all effects and experiences come and go. The z-axis is more about the space these qualities can spread into. It stabilizes people, gives them purchase in more and more of life. And as contemplatives have said again and again, it has more to do with how we are than what we do.

And that's what our last meditation is about. The pure practice of—yes—enjoying your beingness. Dan's mockery ends here! This shift is hard to describe, and yet nothing is more important. We all exist, so we may as well notice and enjoy it. In this sense, it's the ultimate training.

Call it a "do nothing" meditation. The idea is to try not to control things in any way. To sit like a samurai inside your experience with the attitude that nothing needs to be any different, the moment is complete. So you don't need to intentionally notice the breath, or get concentrated, or deliberately pay attention to anything. You just sit and try to be okay with that.

I struggled with this during the "Taking Back Lazy" meditation. When you tell me to do nothing, it stresses me out. I like to have a clear technique.

That's fine. It's normal, especially for type-A people. We're in a panic to do, to get shit done, to check items off our existential to-do lists. This practice is about seeing if we can reverse that momentum a bit. Actually and truly relax. Which is extremely hard to do when all you know is go.

I'll try.

If this particular meditation doesn't ultimately appeal, no big deal. But it's definitely worth exploring at least once, particularly since some people *love it*. They're grateful for the opportunity to not have to do anything for once.

So let's see what happens. We'll start with a basic concentration practice, and then we'll move into the do-nothing piece, for contrast. The reader can just go through this and try it after. I'll give you the two-word cheat sheet summary now: "Do nothing."

DO NOTHING MEDITATION

5 minutes or longer

Start in the usual way. Close your eyes if that's your go-to, taking a few deep breaths, and settle on the exhale. Set your attitude of openness and easygoingness: just exploring, nothing to get uptight about. We're sitting with our eyes closed, getting ready to do nothing. It's hard to imagine the stakes being any lower.

Like I said, it can be nice to get a bit of a contrast, so for the first few minutes of this meditation, start by seeing how deliberately concentrated you can get. This is not yet doing nothing—we're doing something, working up to nothing. Choose an object—breath, belly, hands, bum, sounds—and try as best you can to hold that direction. See if you can find a little enjoyment in the opportunity to do just one thing: to feel, to breathe, to listen. Nothing else you need to do. So it is definitely simplifying. You can note *in* and *out*, or *feel*, or *sound*, or whatever helps you get focused. Mind wanders, bring it back.

As you get into the meditation, your breathing may start to slow naturally. See how still you can be—the stiller you are, the subtler and deeper you may go. The process is very delicate. How smoothly can you experience this sensation, this sound? Can you feel it as a single continuous and *enjoyable* thing? The idea is to get as concentrated as you can here, but, as always, to enjoy the process.

Okay, now we make our big shift. For the remainder of the meditation, drop all noting, drop all attempts to deliberately focus on anything, and just do nothing. Let go. The idea is to stop trying to control your experience in any way and to let your attention just spontaneously be pulled where it gets pulled, settling where it settles. It may feel weird at first, but try to surrender to it. You are saying yes to everything. See what happens.

> Okay, so I have a report. I got concentrated on my breath like you instructed, and then I moved into the do nothing. And almost immediately it was like my mind got thrown into a blender of neurotic thinking. And of course, when I notice I'm thinking, I want to revert back to what you taught us earlier in the book and note *thinking*. But then I remember that I'm not supposed to do anything. I want to grab you by the metaphorical lapels and beg you for an actual instruction!

The instruction is to do nothing. Let the thinking happen. Either it will play itself out or it won't. Both are fine. Noting is also fine if it happens automatically. I know it's a bit confusing, but *you don't actually have to prevent your mind from implementing any habitual meditation technique.* If it's really a habit, then by definition it is not in your control, and trying to stop it would be a "doing." The instruction is to let whatever happens happen, without striving or adding anything. Just completely back off and let the whole ball of yarn unspool all on its own. If that means you get all spaced out, or end up helplessly replaying the stupidest conversation you ever had with yourself, then so be it.

> It's incredibly frustrating.

That's because it's all you know, bro. It's okay. In a really gentle way we're working to unclench the part of your brain that thinks it needs to endlessly negotiate with reality, to make all these adjustments, to prove yourself and improve yourself. To earn your keep. To get it "right." But you don't have to get anything right here, or prove anything to anyone. It's okay. You are right where you need to be, and you are 100 percent allowed to be here. Forgive yourself for not being perfect at this, and see what happens.

Okay.

(bird chirping, sound of wind in the trees)
You okay?

Yeah. Actually, something sort of clicked when you said that. I stopped caring that thinking was happening, and things started to get peaceful and drifty. Every time I noticed I was distracted, instead of getting pissed at myself, I realized I wasn't breaking any rules. I went from feeling angry at you for refusing to give me something to do . . . to feeling a lot of gratitude.

Good. Keep going. When we loosen up, we make room for new things to make their visit. This is about trusting we'll be okay.
(sound of a heartbeat, breath soft)
This is the end of effort. No more striving, no more work. You can rest here.
(something opening)
No longer meditating at all. Let nature meditate you.
(something falling away)
When you're ready, open your eyes.
(Dan's hands gather; he bows to the still point—the center—where nothing needs to happen)
Oy, Daniel.

EPILOGUE

There was a nice little afterglow before everything went pear-shaped.

In the first few weeks after I got home from the road trip, I embraced with increasing robustness some of Jeff's primary teachings, including moves I had previously written off as too embarrassing to even consider.

I was beginning every sit with a commitment to not being uptight; I was attempting to enjoy my "juicy animal body"; and, of course, I was continuously endeavoring to up my "welcome to the party" game. It was becoming ever more clear to me—not intellectually but experientially—that when I extended hospitality to my distractions and obsessions rather than fighting with them, it conserved a lot of otherwise wasted energy and helped my meditation to flow more smoothly.

I even caved and started naming my various inner voices. When Jeff initially told me how he gave his competing neurotic programs friendly nicknames such as "El Grandioso," I thought it was amusing but too cute for me to pull off personally. However, the more I welcomed all of my mental *meshugas* to the proverbial party, the more playful my attitude became toward the internal dramatis personae. Plus, as Jeff often said, no one else is there to see what you're doing in the privacy of your own mind during meditation, so why bother getting self-conscious?

The easiest voice to identify was, unsurprisingly, Robert Johnson. Whenever I felt a surge of anger, resentment, or paranoia, I would give him a cordial greeting: *Bobby J., you old so-and-so, welcome to the party.*

Then there was the inner hustler, constantly plotting, scheming, and worrying about my career. I decided to name him Sammy, after the backstabbing, rabidly ambitious Hollywood climber from the novel *What Makes Sammy Run?* I would salute him with a big blast of cheesy air horn like a DJ at a bad nightclub in New Jersey.

I made up names for my anxious inner planner (Julie the Cruise Director) and also for the voice that was always working on writing this book (Arthur—which, for some reason, I decided was easier to mentally pronounce than Author).

Finally, I had to come up with a name for the voice that was always popping up to spout nonsense. I opted for Randy, short for "random," and also, serendipitously, the name of the obnoxious comic played by Aziz Ansari in the movie *Funny People.*

In

Out

Want to hear some of my favorite tag lines?

From the trailer for the 1980s B-movie Hardbodies: *"If you see only one movie this summer, see this one also."*

From a pamphlet spotted in the Colby College health center in 1993: "Chlamydia Is Not a Flower."

Okay, Randy, welcome to the party.

In

Out

Reminder: Ask the ABC News polling people to investigate my theory that there is a statistical correlation between people who like cats and people who prefer vanilla ice cream—and likewise for dogs and chocolate.

Remember that store that used to be on Main Street in Waterville, Maine, called Strictly Pets and Birds? Were they trying to say that birds aren't pets? And if so, how could it have been "strictly" pets? Are you fucking kiddingggg . . . I mean, welcome to the party, Randy!

It was not uncommon for the welcoming words to be unaccompanied by the intended sentiment. As I delved more deeply into this practice, I saw that there was often an underlying attitude in my mind that these "interruptions" should not be happening. When I could sense the misty black tendrils of Johnsonian fury curling around the edges of the good cheer I was attempting to extend, I would make a double note: *Randy with a side dish of RJ.*

I persevered, though, keeping in mind Jeff's helpful advice that you could "fake it until you make it." Sure enough, gradually but steadily, I began genuinely generating increasing amounts of goodwill for my inner Greek chorus. I could acknowledge what Jeff had pointed out on the bus lo these many weeks ago: that many of these voices—the anger-monger, the logistician, the strategist—were actually trying to help me, even if they were a little overzealous.

When I would notice myself getting carried away by one of these characters, I would invite him or her in, and investigate with the help of the RAIN tool that Jeff taught us earlier. Where does worry show up in the body? Is my jaw tight, my stomach roiled? More often than not, that openness and interest would defang the visitor, even if he or she reemerged nanoseconds later.

It wasn't foolproof, but the overall effect was unmistakable. The punitive vibe was improving. Sometimes I would catch myself actually smiling when I noticed that one of my inner rascals had come along and commandeered my mindfulness. If this wasn't an example of Jeff's concept of friendliness, what was? At other times, I was able to muster unaffected self-compassion. One day when I had a cold and kept falling asleep during meditation, instead of greeting the bouts of fatigue with self-recrimination, I found myself saying, "You're sick, dude; no worries." Another day, I noticed that I had spent the first few minutes of the sit preoccupied by concern over some health issues my dad was having. After an initial lurch toward criticizing myself for being distracted, I realized that the worrying about my father was a voice I had not perceived very clearly before: Nice Dan. I got the warm and fuzzies for him. That guy deserves more airtime.

It was humbling to realize that it had taken eight years of meditating to start following my own advice about seeing the moment of waking up from distraction as a victory, but at least it was nice to be less of a hypocrite.

This interior liberality allowed me to relax somewhat in the face of a gigantic challenge: writing this book on an absurdly tight deadline. We finished the road trip in February and the manuscript was due in early June. That set up a punishing schedule.

We divided the labor. While I worked on a chapter, Carlye (aka Rage Fairy—although, for the record, I have never seen her in anything other than a sunny mood) would comb through the hours and hours of transcripts from our many shoots, creating an outline for me to use for the next chapter. Jeff, meanwhile, was busy writing and inserting all the meditation instructions. As soon as one of us finished our work, we would share it on Google Docs, and everyone would jump in and make their notes, which would show up along the digital margins of the page. The commentary was filled with cheerleading, brainstorming, and spirited debate.

Generally speaking, I have a love/hate relationship with writing, and it's about 98 percent hate. It took me four years to write my first book, and the process was characterized by rampant self-doubt, frustration, and fear. As the old cliché goes, "No one likes writing; they like having written." However, the writing experience this time was markedly different, in part because of the camaraderie; it was fun to be involved in a group effort with such smart partners, which was similar to the way we work in TV news. The process was also ameliorated by the fact that I was employing techniques I'd learned from Jeff. When I would find myself spinning off into hand-wringing over how I was going to get all of my work done, and whether it was all going to stink in the end, I would try to reconnect to my core intention, which was to further our collective aim of helping people meditate. Motivation, in my view, runs along a spectrum. It's natural to have financial and self-promotional goals, but when you can mindfully tune in to the desire to benefit others, it can make the whole endeavor more buoyant.

Mindfulness was also useful during the writing process when I would bump up against the racking pain of a seemingly insoluble stylistic or structural problem. Instead of getting all tight and constricted, I would remember what I had learned about the science of creativity: work hard, study your material diligently, and then let it go; the answer may come later, when you're relaxed. (This is why people talk about having epiphanies in the shower.) This time when I hit a roadblock, instead of trying to bulldoze my way through it, I would meditate— just sitting with the discomfort of unknowing. Often these meditations would produce geysers of ideas, even if they weren't necessarily the ideas I was looking for.

On one of our group Skype video chats (me in my apartment, Carlye at home in exurbia, and Jeff streaming in from

Costa Rica, where he was teaching meditation as part of some boondoggle, the details of which remain opaque to me), I told Jeff that I was using meditation to boost my creativity, and he lit up with excitement and encouragement. He called the discomfort that often accompanies an apparently uncrackable obstacle "the bloom of unknowing," and said that learning how to relax into the agony of uncertainty could be carried over to so many aspects of our lives—from career to health to parenting—where circumstances are out of our control. Watching his beaming face on my computer, I thought about the Buddhist term *mudita*, which means "sympathetic joy." I describe it as the opposite of schadenfreude. Jeff is a *mudita* samurai.

The good vibes did not last, though.

After about a month and a half of maintaining an insane work tempo, the sheer wear and tear started to catch up with me. Having to write a chapter a week, on top of a day job and a family, was an immense strain. I was falling asleep on the couch every night with pages from various chapters in my hand, which would lead inexorably into macabre stress nightmares. Meanwhile, I entered a particularly hectic stretch at ABC News and was finding less and less time to rest or hang out with Bianca and Alexander. I was withering.

Jeff was not helping. Under many conditions—say, sitting on a bus driving across the country—Jeff's idiosyncrasies, such as his penchant for lofty notions, labyrinthine reasoning, and wildly enthusiastic overthinking, can be endlessly charming. However, as I was laboring in the fields of composition, hobbled by stress and exhaustion, I was starting to lose my sense of humor. Things came to a head when he sent me a seventeen-page memo describing, often in rather abstruse terms, how he envisioned the flow of the meditation instructions through the book. If I had read it under normal circumstances, the document, which was well crafted and deeply thoughtful, would have been fascinating. But in my diminished state, it was instead massively anxiety-producing. As my eyes washed over the seemingly endless verbiage, I was toggling between barbed-wire *prapañca* and defensive dissociation.

Jeff: "The various 'absolute' qualities or facets—i.e., things that somehow feel more *fundamental* (meaning, peace, equanimity, intimacy . . .)"

Jeff wants to turn this book into a turbid, turgid exegesis on gnosis →
People are going to think his elevator doesn't go to the top floor →
Jazzercise

Jeff: ". . . insight into the subtle 'like/don't like' layer (*vedana*), which is part of grokking equanimity . . ."

Clowder of cats. Colony of bats. Rafter of turkeys. Richness of ravens . . .

Jeff: "Insight *is* perspective!"

. . . Parliament of owls. Paddling of ducks. Tidings of magpies. Murder of crows.

We hopped on another Skype chat, and I gave Jeff a lengthy cri de coeur about how, given my limited bandwidth and diminishing inner resources, I really, really, really needed him to simplify things. I begged him to channel the version of Jeff that had shown up in Jackson Square in New Orleans and was able to talk to rank amateurs about basic meditation. I wanted the beery, buccaneering Jeff, not the guy who seemed like he wanted to anoint your head with oil. He reacted with a characteristic—but no less impressive—empathy and lack of defensiveness, promising he understood my dilemma and wanted to help out.

Just days later, though, he fired off an email with more grand editorial and pedagogical plans that ranged over "grounding and containment," "natural awareness," and "Buddha nature." It sent waves of peevish juices sluicing through my brain. Intellectually, I knew that this was not personal; Jeff was just excited about the project and this was his way of working. Viscerally, though, I was tumescing with righteous, Robert Johnson anger. Carlye may occasionally be overtaken by the Rage Fairy; I temporarily became the Rage Ferret, a small and otherwise harmless varmint who happened to have rabies. I was so mad at Jeff that out of sheer, self-destructive cussedness, I refused to do "welcome to the party" anymore. My comments in the marginalia started to take on a rather acidic tone. (A sample: "For the love of God . . . please no more mention of *kleshas*!") Jeff seemed mystified and taken aback. The goodwill from the road trip was in acute danger of evaporating.

My mood soured even further as we began the process of reaching out to the people we had met on the road trip to see if we had been able to help them start meditating. We had sent many of them recordings of personalized meditations from Jeff, which we hoped would provide real incentive.

The initial results were decidedly mixed.

Three months after our session on day one of the road trip, I sent my co-anchors from weekend *Good Morning America* an email with the subject line "Moment of truth." Sara Haines replied that she had not been able to get over her consistency problem. Ron Claiborne said he had never even started. Rob Marciano refused to give me a straight answer of any kind.

Via text, Josh Groban said that he had meditated pretty

steadily for a few weeks but then had fallen off, although he fully intended to restart at some point. (One positive side note: after having spoken candidly in our interview about his career anxieties, he had been honored with a nomination for a Tony Award.)

I reached out to Danielle Monaro from Elvis Duran's show, for whom we had also created a special meditation. She replied with an email that read:

Lol! sooooo I could not open the file! I kept meaning to email you and then always forgot. Sorry. Is there a way to send in another format?

Sorryyyyyyy

These responses were, to say the least, disheartening. If we couldn't even help people we had personally met and for whom we had tailored meditations, what did that say about the thesis of our entire book? I felt like Dan Quixote.

Then things started to turn around. Paula Faris got back to say that she had meditated for a few weeks, stopped, but then started strong again and was currently doing it daily. "You sold me!" she wrote. She found doing the practice on a nearly-every-day basis had given her the shot of equanimity she so deeply craved in her supremely busy life.

Bethany Watson, also from the Elvis Duran show, wrote to say that she was "doing short sessions a few times a week, usually before bed, and it's helping me deal with stress in a much more positive way."

Our friends at Virginia Military Institute had taken a minor PR hit when we posted the audio of our interview with the meditating professors on my podcast. The cadets at a rival school, The Citadel, posted the following online: "First coloring books and now meditation? About time to change the name to Virginia Military Commune." But we heard from Professor Holly Jo Richardson, who said that, in fact, "we have had very positive press within the VMI community after your visit." And Anthony Wilson, the cadet who was on track to join the army special forces, sent an email saying that he was meditating with his roommates for ten minutes nearly every day, and also employing the RAIN technique. "As someone with a quicker temper and a tendency to be a grump," he said, "this structured mindfulness helps me the most in dealing with relationships, and avoiding needless arguments."

To my delight, we received an encouraging update from Sergeant Raj Johnson, the Tempe officer who initially told us he feared that meditation would erode his edge. He reported that he had been meditating after workouts and also after stressful calls, which had helped both his focus and his sleep. Since our meeting, he reported, meditation was something he was growing into.

Mylrell Miner from the InsideOUT Writers program called to say that he, too, was meditating. He still had bills to pay and his car was still giving him problems, but he said meditating helped him not overdo it on the worrying. Also, he and his girlfriend recently had a baby girl. They named her Serenity.

Candice Price, Mylrell's friend from IOW, not only was meditating but also had cajoled her father, who had recently gotten out of prison, into doing it with her. She said it made him "more relaxed, more at ease." As for what the practice was doing for her, she said, "It helps me forgive, and to be accepted, to be forgiven."

The update I was most worried about seeking was Bianca's. After years of studiously avoiding lecturing her about meditation, I feared that merely asking her whether she was doing it would result in either spooking her or landing me in the dog-house. I seriously considered asking Carlye to do it for me.

I sucked it up, though, and broached the topic on my own. On a sunny weekday morning, after our son had gone to pre-school, we sat at the dining room table in our apartment. Ever the diligent student (she hates when I mention this, but the woman graduated at the top of her class in medical school), she pulled up a whole litany of notes she had made in a file on her phone.

"Just so you know," I said, hoping to minimize the pressure from the outset, "I have no expectation that you did it. I only want the truth."

"Well, I only want to give you the truth," she replied, "but I *have* been doing it, so I would like some credit."

That provoked a big belly laugh of relief from me.

"I don't want to ruin your shtick as me being your anti-mascot," she said. "But . . . too bad!"

I was ecstatic. Not only because I had won over my tough-est mark, but because I knew this practice could be incredibly useful and healing for her.

Mind you, Bianca didn't give me any of the credit. She rightly praised Jeff for cleverly reframing the practice from a chore into an act of indulgence and also self-care. She was par-ticularly moved by the meditation he made for her, in which he told her she could escape from "Dan's gulag."

"When I first listened to it," she said, "I cried. Because I couldn't believe somebody who didn't know me that well would put so much thought into something special for me. It was so nice that I was almost ashamed that I couldn't be that nice to myself."

Every night, when putting the kid to bed, she had been meditating while snuggling with Alexander as he drifted off to sleep. She would be mindful of her breath, his breath, random noises, passing emotional squalls—whatever came up. And when she got distracted, she just started over. She described it as a "fun, roll-with-it kind of experience." Additionally, she was doing the occasional body scan whenever she had a spare moment, or even just stopping to take a few deep, mindful breaths while at work or sitting on a bench in Central Park.

She said she had learned two major lessons from her experiences thus far. "It's made me feel how important it is to take care of yourself in order to take care of other people. Which has been 100 percent the opposite of my mantra my entire life: take care of other people, don't take care of yourself. You can do that for a time, but then inevitably it catches up to you."

Also, being connected with her body—which, interestingly, given that she's a physician, she said she'd never been good at—had helped her get out of her head and act less mindlessly. When anxiety or anger arose, she was allowing herself to fully experience it, instead of acting impulsively. "It's not haphazard," she said of her practice. "Doesn't mean I don't feel it. Doesn't mean I don't want to go there. But I can see it very, very, very quickly."

All of which had left her better equipped to manage perhaps the most challenging person in her life: her husband. "I'm very attuned to your mood. I want to make sure you're okay. A lot. And when I can't tell, my go-to is: I must have done something wrong. Even though I also know you and know that's kinda just your face sometimes. But it's still a reflex for me to assume it's me." Of late, though, when she sensed I was burning over something, "either I would probe gently, or I'd leave it alone. And it's very survivable and quite empowering and healthy, I hope."

In fact, I had been pretty damn moody of late. Not just

moody—clearly fried. It had gotten so bad that Bianca, on one particular morning, had felt compelled to take me aside for an intervention. She pointed out that I had been working literally every moment of every day since the end of the road trip. When I wasn't engaged in my day job, I was writing this book. I had taken zero downtime. No rest. Exacerbating matters, I would reward myself with sugar bonanzas a few nights a week, which only further degraded my sleep. Bianca convinced me that I needed to slow down or I was going to crash and burn.

I was struck by the thunderously obvious fact that I had been neglecting my own self-care, to my detriment and that of everyone around me. I had been running myself ragged, which was making me exhausted and irritable. I agreed to take more downtime and, perhaps more challenging, to cut out sugar, at least until the book was done.

Ironically, given that I was annoyed with him, I drew yet again upon the Wisdom of Jeff. To make my meditations more restful, I started doing entire sessions while lying down. (By and large, they did not, as I had feared, turn into inadvertent naps. Although, when they did, so be it.) I also began using Jeff's notion of friendliness to deal with my sugar cravings. Desire is the apex predator of my mental jungle. During my previous attempted sugar fasts, I had white-knuckled my way through my usual post-dinner bouts of howling want. *Just one cookie! Are you really going to deprive yourself? Don't be a slave to conventional dietary concerns cooked up by the food police. Why punish yourself when you know it won't last anyway?* Instead of fearing or, worse, believing the samizdat circulated by my ego, I started to welcome it the way I'd welcome my son when he wanted to wrestle: *bring it on*. It was vastly more effective than anything I had previously tried.

Pretty soon I started to sleep and feel better. I became more rational, less quick to anger. My comments in the margins of the Google Docs were decreasingly antagonistic.

I called up Jeff and we talked it all out. I explained my frustrations about the fact that I often felt like he was trying to turn a book designed for skeptics into a modern version of the *Bhagavad Gita*. He apologized, while also pointing out that it could be rather unpleasant to be on the receiving end of my exterior Robert Johnson (for which I, in turn, apologized). It was a case of conflict resolution every bit as successful as our confab on the bus with Eddie and Ben. As can sometimes happen when you have a thorough airing of grievances with a friend, the result was that I felt even closer to Jeff.

It also gave me a deeper understanding of the centrality of ADD to his psychology. Yes, I had heard him discuss his condition at length when we were out on the road. But during the writing process, I truly experienced it firsthand—with all those compulsive digressions into deep-end meditative theory. In our call, he explained that his habit of getting carried away was a source of shame for him. "The honest truth here," he said, "is that when I get super activated in a nerdy idea-explainer way, I can lose mindfulness. I feel like a fraud when it happens. It is embarrassing."

What a story, I thought: a meditation teacher with impostor syndrome.

The good news is that over the course of the road trip and the subsequent writing process, I have watched Jeff come into his own. Days after our heart-to-heart, he was banging out some of the most hilarious and useful instructions I have ever seen anywhere. (That *Braveheart* metaphor in the last chapter? Come on!) He has also begun to own his challenges in a whole new way. He started off our road trip dealing with nagging self-consciousness, "because I felt like I wasn't some teacher with perfect mental hygiene." Now he has truly internalized the idea that his flaws actually make him a better teacher. "I have learned how to be comfortable in my own public skin. I feel like I am finally ready to do this—and the book and road trip experience helped cement that."

I love the poetry and symmetry of it all. Just as Jeff taught me to not be so uptight and striving in my meditation practice, our experience working on this book together has played a role in making him more comfortable furthering his teaching and writing career—although, in typical fashion, Jeff primarily embraces the idea of professional advancement because he feels it will enable him to help more people. Whatever the motivator, it's been incredibly gratifying to watch my friend finally feel ready to step out and let other people see that he is as talented as I know him to be (even if he isn't always aware of it himself).

Oh, and . . . one last update. Jeff no longer lives with roommates. He and Sarah got married—and got their own place—shortly before we finished the book. Below is a wedding picture. She's wearing a dress she bought during a visit to her

mother in Arizona. By complete coincidence, our big orange bus happened to be traveling through the state at the same time. We decided to pick her up so she could come with us on the last few days of our journey. I have a vivid memory of her climbing on board carrying the garment bag that contained that dress. She and Jeff were beaming.

The reason I relate all of the ups and downs of the post-road-trip period is to make an important point: just because you've started meditating—or even if you've written a whole book on the subject—your life is not going to become a non-stop parade of rainbows and unicorns. The whole 10% Happier thing is simultaneously flippant and the most accurate description I can muster of the benefits of meditation. You will, as I do, get caught up in the mindless momentum of doing and getting, of being stingy or distracted. We're all like schnauzers who soil the rug and need to have our snouts shoved into it. (For the record, Jeff doesn't like the schnauzer analogy. He says it's aggressive, like the lion tamer. But this is my part of the book.) The game—and you truly can't hear this enough—is just to start over, again and again. "On the cushion," this means noticing when you're lost in thought, and then escorting your attention back to the breath. In the rest of your life, this means seeing when you have messed up, engaging in a little bit of what the Buddhists call "wise remorse" (as opposed to unconstructive spirals of self-flagellation), picking yourself up, and getting back into the mix.

It ain't easy, but you almost certainly will get better over time. Remember: you are trying to hack millennia of evolution. We are bred for threat detection and self-centeredness. The lessons learned through meditation run so counter to our instincts—to let the voice in our head run wild, to chase pleasure blindly, to grasp at things that won't last—that we need constant reminders, and constant permission to fail and begin again. I find this notion hugely comforting, and so should anyone who tells themselves they're not cut out for meditation. In the end, we're all shitting on the rug.

Meditation, per Jeff, is a kind of disembedding from the various trances—of, say, insufficiency or unworthiness—in which we live our lives. The more mindful you are, says Jeff, the more you see that you are, in fact, ensnared in "dozens of nested trances." But it is possible to burst your own bubble of self-absorption, to break the chains of emotional peonage and psychological serfdom. When you clear away the cuckoo, what comes forward is greater attunement to other people (and animals), and also closer connection to life's fundamental mysteries. You shift from being stuck in the content of your thoughts to being amazed that you are thinking in the first place. This is what Jeff had in mind when he said on the bus that the most important thing in the world "is to understand the sacred fact that you're alive."

At the heart of the meditative act is a deeply empowering notion: as I stated at the beginning of this book, happiness is a *skill*, one you can train, just as you can train your body in the gym. Desirable qualities such as calm and compassion can be cultivated. Human beings can change. Old schnauzers can learn new tricks.

Speaking of which . . . I should point out that Robert Johnson—the real person, not the voice in my head—underwent something of a personal revolution later in life. He started being reasonably nice. In his eighties, he discovered email and Twitter as a way to keep in touch with his grandkids. He would bang out—via the hunt-and-peck method—trenchant analyses of current events, and even, on occasion, words of grandfatherly encouragement. He became a pleasant presence at holiday parties. In fact, Bianca, who met him after the transformation, only remembers him as a courtly older gentleman. I'm not sure how or why he effected this change. As far as I know, meditation was not involved. Maybe dotage mellowed him? Maybe he just got tired of being an asshole? He ultimately died of a stroke at age ninety, reportedly flirting with a nurse on the medevac flight. My wife and I gave our son the middle name Robert as a nod to the potential for human transformation. (And also in honor of my dad, whose middle name is Robert, and who, for the record, has never been an asshole.)

While Robert Johnson changed without the aid of meditation, I do not advise you to leave your own happiness to chance. As Jeff and I have tried to make clear, we do not believe meditation is the only route to personal fulfillment, but it is a pretty damn good tool to have in your kit. An insightful bit of philosophy can give you temporary doses of perspective. Somebody smart can point out to you that you live in an infinite universe and that you are just a speck, subject to the whims of health and love and economics and weather, and maybe that leaves you inspired or more spacious for a day. But does it survive first contact with a traffic jam? Or a toddler tantrum? What the practice of meditation does is help actualize this wisdom into your everyday life, drilling it into your neurons. It's like the difference between watching sports and working out.

So come on, join the next big public health revolution. Help create a saner world. Do it for yourself. Do it for everyone in your orbit. Get off your ass and then . . . uh, get back on it and meditate.

Welcome to the party.

APPENDIX:
RESOURCES TO HELP YOU
KEEP MEDITATING

If Jeff and I have done our job correctly, this book should leave you wanting to dive more deeply into meditation. What follows are some practical ways to do so.

THE 10% HAPPIER PODCAST

From the Dalai Lama to RuPaul, every week I interview a fascinating person about his or her meditation practice. (And if the person doesn't have a practice, we teach them—live.) Writers, teachers, scholars, athletes, military officials, politicians, celebrities—we welcome all sorts. Hearing personal stories—and varying perspectives on practice—can provide motivational rocket fuel. Available on Apple Podcasts, Google Play, or wherever you get your podcasts.

THE 10% HAPPIER APP

While a guided audio version of every meditation in this book is available to you for free on the app, we also have much more on offer. My teammates and I have brought together some of the best teachers in the world, who provide lessons about how meditation can help with stress, eating habits, relationships, sleep, and more. We believe that what sets us apart is our mix of both video and audio content as well as our insistence upon approaching the meditative endeavor with a sense of humor. Plus, if you sign up, you will get a coach—a real person, not a robot—who can answer your questions and help you stay on track.

Once again, here's the link to download the app and unlock the content: **10percenthappier.com/access**.

THE CONSCIOUSNESS EXPLORERS CLUB

The CEC is a registered not-for-profit dedicated to exploring meditation and personal growth practices "in a playful, social, pluralistic way." The website features free guided meditations, short articles, and various course and retreat offerings. Jeff says he hopes the CEC can become a resource for "community practice around the world," so all ideas and support are welcome. To sign up for the CEC's newsletter and get involved, go to **cecmeditate.com**.

DAN, JEFF, AND 10% HAPPIER ONLINE

Facebook.com/DanHarrisABC
Twitter: @danbharris
Instagram: @danharris
jeffwarren.org
Facebook.com/10percenthappier
Twitter: @10percent

BOOKS WE LOVE

You'll notice that many of the titles listed below contain the word "Buddhism," which may—at first blush—seem out of place in a reading list designed for skeptics. However, Buddhism is practically tailor-made for freethinkers. The Buddha did not claim to be a god or a prophet. And to the extent that he espoused ideas such as karma and rebirth, he explicitly told his followers to take them or leave them. He didn't even envision something called Buddhism; he was simply teaching people to meditate and behave ethically. It is true that in many parts of the world people do practice Buddhism as a religion, complete with elaborate metaphysical claims. But you are under no obligation to accept these. I was raised by secular scientists in the People's Republic of Massachusetts. (As I like to joke, I did have a bar mitzvah—but only for the money.) I've spent my career as a proud skeptic. My favorite part of being a journalist is the right—the obligation, really—to examine everything and everyone with a healthy amount of doubt. Nevertheless, I call myself a Buddhist. That doesn't mean I believe in anything I can't prove. I'm not sure the Buddhists are right about reincarnation or enlightenment. But I am convinced that they're correct about the ego, about the inevitability of death, and about the superiority of compassion over unbridled selfishness. The books below approach Buddhism (and related contemplative traditions) with both clear eyes and open minds.

FROM DAN

Why Buddhism Is True by Robert Wright

Waking Up by Sam Harris

Buddhism Without Beliefs and *Confession of a Buddhist Atheist* by Stephen Batchelor

Real Happiness and *Real Love* by Sharon Salzberg

When Things Fall Apart by Pema Chödrön

Altered Traits by Daniel Goleman and Richard J. Davidson

The Trauma of Everyday Life and *Advice Not Given* by Mark Epstein

One Dharma and *Mindfulness* by Joseph Goldstein

On Having No Head by Douglas E. Harding
Evolving Dharma by Jay Michaelson

FROM JEFF

The Varieties of Religious Experience by William James
Coming Home by Lex Hixon
A Path with Heart and *After the Ecstasy, the Laundry* by Jack
    Kornfield
The Science of Enlightenment by Shinzen Young
Cutting Through Spiritual Materialism by Chögyam Trungpa
The Making of Buddhist Modernism by David L. McMahan
The Progress of Insight by Mahasi Sayadaw
Mastering the Core Teachings of the Buddha by Daniel M. Ingram
Be as You Are: The Teachings of Sri Ramana Maharshi, edited by
    David Godman
Waking the Tiger by Peter A. Levine
Destructive Emotions: A Scientific Dialogue with the Dalai Lama,
    narrated by Daniel Goleman
Waking, Dreaming, Being by Evan Thompson
Radical Dharma by Angel Kyodo Williams, Lama Rod Owens,
    and Jasmine Syedullah
The Mind Illuminated by Culadasa (John Yates)
Nonduality by David Loy
Mysticism by Evelyn Underhill
For the Time Being by Annie Dillard

This is by no means an exhaustive list. We will continue to update and expand it at **10percenthappier.com/reading**.

RETREATS

For many reasonable people, the idea of going away to a retreat
center and sitting silently with a bunch of strangers is irremedi-

ably abhorrent. I get it. That's the way I used to feel. I have four pieces of good news for you. First, doing a retreat is by no means mandatory. I did one for the first time in part because I was working on a book and needed some stuff to write about. However, if what you're looking to do is establish an abiding, daily-ish habit, you can do so successfully without attending retreats. No shame in that game. Second, the other reason I attended (or, to use a term of art, "sat") my first retreat was curiosity. I had an inkling that meditation was both useful and meaningful, and I wanted to see what would happen if I dramatically upped the dosage. I certainly got results—although not always the ones I wanted. For the first few days, I was thoroughly miserable. But then I had a breakthrough of sorts where, for about a day and a half, I experienced a dramatic diminution of mental chatter and, as a consequence, a kind of happiness I had never tasted before. Then I went straight back to being miserable. I have gone on to do many more retreats, and hope to continue for the rest of my life. They are a fantastic way to train the skills that Jeff describes in this book: concentration, clarity, equanimity, friendliness, and enjoyment. Speaking of Jeff, here's his take.

I love retreats. First of all, it's nice just to switch gears and get out of the daily grind. Retreats give us perspective on our lives. They also lead to insights and breakthroughs: suddenly we _really_ understand this thing we may have heard a hundred times before. Whatever it is—acceptance, being in the moment, impermanence, some pattern of thinking or behavior—the teachings now make sense on a whole new level. These insights ripple out into our lives and boost our motivation to continue with practice.

Third piece of good news: if you can't stomach a full seven- or ten-day meditation-a-palooza, there are plenty of options for daylong workshops or weekend retreats. (Although, in my experience, there is a real benefit to doing the longer retreats because it can take a few days for the mind to settle.) Fourth and final positive tidbit: at the two spots listed below, the physical settings are beautiful and the food is surprisingly delicious.

Insight Meditation Society: Founded by Sharon Salzberg, Joseph Goldstein, and Jack Kornfield in the 1970s. Located in sylvan central Massachusetts. Offers everything from weekend retreats to—for real—a three-month course. People actually do that!

Spirit Rock: The West Coast sister center, founded by Jack Kornfield, is located on a gorgeous patch of land north of San Francisco.

For a full list of retreat centers, check out **1openhappier .com/retreats**.

Whether you opt for the retreat option or not, there is practically infinite potential for expansion in your meditation practice. As my teacher Joseph Goldstein says about our inner world, "This whole thing is vast." As Jeff puts it, "The insights go on and on. What begins as a technique to manage stress can become an inquiry into who and how we are. We find things are not quite as they seem. Life is broader than we once imagined it to be—and so, it seems, are we."

In sum, keep it going. In the words of the Vietnamese Zen master Thich Nhat Hanh, "Happiness is available. Please help yourself to it."

ACKNOWLEDGMENTS

Jeff Warren was the perfect fit for this crazy little project. He brought to the table an enormous amount of affability, creativity, and straight-up wisdom. On top of being a superlative collaborator, Jeff has become a real friend. Yes, we occasionally wanted to kill each other during the writing of this book, but like those mead-swilling, ballad-singing Scottish soldiers Jeff invokes in Chapter 9, it didn't take long until we woke up and noticed how lucky we were to be on this adventure together. The Buddha said having good friends is 100 percent of the meditation path, and in Jeff, I have hit the jackpot: a hilarious fellow traveler as well as a brilliant teacher who has had a massively beneficial impact on my practice. I can't believe I'm doing this, but . . . I send you an un-ironic namaste.

Next to Carlye Adler. Throughout this often arduous process, she was a beacon of intelligence, calm, and unshakable good cheer. (Again, that whole Rage Fairy thing remains a myth, at least in my experience.) Carlye bravely agreed to ride along on a bus filled with eleven complete strangers, even though she had deep reluctance about being away from her daughter for that long—never mind sharing a bathroom with a bunch of dudes. Once we hit the road, though, she played an invaluable role, not only providing editorial input but also engaging in behind-the-scenes peacemaking.

Thanks to Ben Rubin, for his steadfast leadership of the 10% Happier company, and for talking me into doing this book, which I tried hard to get out of.

To Eddie Boyce, for his outstanding creative contributions to the

10% enterprise, and for handling with aplomb the impossible situation in which we put him while out on the road. He is a walking example of the benefits of meditation.

Also: director of photography and on-site comedian Nick Lopez; audio tech, musician, and Tinder maestro Dennis Haggerty; production manager Jamie Proctor Boyce, who kept everything rolling from afar with some mind-blowing logistical skills; ABC News producer Lauren Effron, who honchos the 10% Happier podcast and who also played a clutch role in the field, such as getting us in to see the folks at Virginia Military Institute; ABC News live producer David Merrell, who oversaw innumerable livestreams from the road; 10% Happier course producer Susa Talan, who was always willing to provide a sympathetic ear to many of us on the bus who needed it; 10% Happier associate producer Mack Woodruff, who organized meals, operated cameras, and made us look cooler than we deserved; and driver Eddie Norton, who kept us safe over thousands of miles.

Can't forget honorary bus rider Sarah Barmak, Jeff's then-fiancée and now wife. Very grateful to her for enduring the fact that Jeff worked like a demon on writing the meditation instructions straight up to their wedding date and was then on call during their honeymoon.

Big thanks to the many folks we met along the way, who coordinated our visits in advance, warmly welcomed us, and found parking for that giant bus: Dave Vago, Jeff Krasno, Josh Groban, Luke Burland, Samantha Stavros, Samantha Coppolino, Steven Levine, Nate Marino, Elvis Duran, Bethany Watson, Danielle Monaro, Ed Hauben, Ursula Steele, Congressman Tim Ryan, Colonel Stewart MacInnis, Linda Manning, Ariane Nalty, Caroline Zamora, Abel Covarrubias, Josie Montenegro, Darren Martinez, Chief Sylvia Moir, Jorie Aldrich, Jimmy Wu, Todd Rubenstein, Zev Borow, Cary Dobkin, Sarah Moritz, Moby, Bill Duane, Fabian Alsutany, Nicole Franco, and Suze Yalof Schwartz.

A shout-out to the staffers, coaches, investors, and advisors involved with the 10% Happier company: Jason Pavel, Samuel Johns, Jeff Lopes, Mike Rong, Matt Graves, Kelly Anne Graves, Jill Shepherd, Rae Houseman, Emily Carpenter, Devon Hase, Joshua Berkowitz, Phoenix Soleil, Evan Frank, Gus Tai, Anjula Acharia, Sarrah Hallock, Eric Paley, Lee Hauer, Irene Au, and Derek Haswell (who, along with Ben and me, is the third co-founder of the company). Derek played a foundational role in this book: he was the one who first introduced the concept of the "secret fears," and his encyclopedic knowledge of behavior change science proved invaluable during the writing process.

To my ABC News family: Ben Sherwood, James Goldston, Tom Cibrowski, Barbara Fedida, Kerry Smith, Roxanna Sherwood, Steve Baker, Jenna Millman, Ben Newman, Geoff Martz, Karin Weinberg, Kevin Rochford, Hana Karar, Mike Milhaven, Michael Corn, Simone Swink, John Ferracane, Almin Karamehmedovic, Miguel Sancho, David Peterkin, Steve Jones, Eric Johnson, Laura Coburn, Josh Cohan, Juju Chang, Byron Pitts, George Stephanopoulos, Robin Roberts, Michael Strahan, David Muir, Diane Sawyer, and, of course, my weekend *GMA* littermates Paula Faris, Ron Claiborne, Rob Marciano, Adrienne Bankert, Diane Macedo, and Sara Haines. While I'm on the TV tip, big thanks as well to my television agent, Jay Sures.

Our editor, Julie Grau, deserves an enormous amount of credit for pushing us to go beyond a dry meditation manual, for skillfully guiding us toward an improved manuscript, and for maintaining her patience when some of us (me) got a little uppity at times. Thanks as well to the rest of the team at Spiegel & Grau, including Mengfei Chen, Greg Mollica, Thomas Perry, Dennis Ambrose, Steve Messina, and Natalie Riera.

My literary agent, Luke Janklow, must get the credit—or blame, maybe?—for coming up with the idea of renting a rock star bus for our road trip. Luke has become an integral part of the 10% universe, advising us on strategy and making sure we stay true to the original vision. (Worth noting that Luke would be utterly helpless without the steadfast support of Claire Dippel. Thanks, Claire!)

Some close friends generously agreed to take time out of their busy schedules to read the manuscript and provide important feedback: Susan Mercandetti, Gretchen Rubin, Karen Avrich, Liz Levin, Annaka Harris, Dr. Mark Epstein, and my brother, Matt Harris, who, aside from my wife, is my most trusted advisor and favorite adult human on the planet. (While I'm at it, sending love to Matt's wife, Jess, and kids, Tess, Eliot, Alice, Solomon, and Benjamin.)

Hat tip to some of my contemplative co-conspirators, including Sam Harris (from whom I appropriated the joke about the voice in the head being the most boring person alive), Cory Muscara (who helped sharpen my thinking about the value of one-minute meditations), and Sharon Salzberg (whose excellent book *Real Happiness* was a source of inspiration for Jeff and me). And finally, to Joseph Goldstein, who generously volunteered to be my personal teacher several years ago, and who has probably been regretting it ever since. JG, your teaching and friendship have improved my life immeasurably.

Thank you to my parents, Drs. Nancy Lee and Jay Harris, for being two of the smartest and coolest people I know, for being extraordinarily loving grandparents, and for weathering my adolescence. Sorry about that.

Oceanic gratitude to my wife, Bianca, for supporting me in all of my off-the-wall endeavors, providing a priceless sounding board, gently but firmly pointing out when my ideas are dumb, and putting up with me when I got all strung out and unpleasant toward the end of the writing process. You are an incredible doctor, wife, and mother. You're my best friend and most valued consigliere. I love you.

And finally to Alexander, the best thing that has ever happened to me. Merely gazing at you makes me 1,000 percent happier—except when you're chasing the cats or drawing on the wall. Maybe in a future book, we'll get you to start meditating? First, though, potty training.

JEFF'S ACKNOWLEDGMENTS

The voice of Dan Harris officially joined my internal chorus on August 3, 2017, thirty thousand feet above sea level. I was on a flight from Chicago to Toronto, feverishly writing an *extremely* important and highly technical caveat about consciousness for this book, when I heard, quite distinctly, the voice of my friend: "Dude."

I looked up.

"Look at these people."

I surveyed the cabin. A businessman reading a newspaper, a strained-looking couple struggling to calm a crying baby, two middle-aged women—they seemed like old friends—chatting over the aisle.

"Start here," Dan's voice said. As he himself had tried to say—patiently, humorously, sometimes exasperatingly—a dozen times before. His guidance finally sunk in. I looked down at my laptop, laughed, and started deleting.

Sometimes a friend can do what no amount of meditation can. Dan helped me understand that when I get heady and obsessed, I'm not actually writing for my readers; I'm writing for myself. Instead of opening a door, I'm putting up a wall. Real accessibility means starting where people actually are. It emerges from a disciplined combination of caring and paying attention.

Despite his many self-deprecating protests to the contrary, Dan is among the most discerning and caring people I've met. He refuses to leave anyone behind. He'll expose the most vulnerable parts of himself if he thinks his honesty will help people. He keeps it moving and he keeps it real. I've learned a lot about being a teacher and writer and leader from him. Thank you, brother. At least one of the voices in my head isn't an asshole.

It turns out Dan is ringmaster to a dazzling troop of media professionals. Carlye Adler for one, the book's puppet master. To use a terrible metaphor, she hovered like a kindly superego over Dan's ego and my id (sorry, Freud), encouraging and suggesting and generally making everything better. She is considerate, wise, and wonderfully upbeat—a joy to spend time with.

Thank you Ben Rubin, 10% Happier's CEO and someone who's become another pal. Everything Dan says about him is true: a man of great intelligence and practicality who seems to have been born with a total lack of comic timing. His copilot, Derek Haswell, is pretty awesome too. Of course, Eddie Boyce, one of my besties—generous, smart, and bawling with happiness at the drop of a hat like some punch-drunk mystic saint. Ed embodies the best of this practice, plus a few bonus crazy moves they don't teach you in books. His wife, Jamie Proctor Boyce, is another friend; she organized our entire road trip from a laptop in Halifax and misses nothing. Also Susa Talan, fellow teacher and somatic experiencer, whose patient and often delighted voice I will never tire of hearing through my studio earphones.

Thanks to Nick and Dennis and Mack and Lauren and David and driver Eddie. Thanks to the casually brilliant Luke Janklow; to our patient and seemingly all-seeing editor, Julie Grau; and to my fabulous agent and friend, Shaun Bradley. Thanks to David Vago, my favorite contemplative scientist, a deep and original thinker with a cutting-edge research lab.

We met many amazing people en route, doing the real work of integrating meditation and mindfulness into their lives and jobs. Most of these folks don't care about the theory and the Pali translations and the academic controversies; they want to know how to apply the practices, right now, in serious caregiving situations with serious consequences. Whatever insanity may be happening in the world, this felt like a movement of sanity—of people pausing to take responsibility for themselves, so that they might help others do the same. What an honor to be a student of—and to—this larger movement of innovators and educators.

Thanks to my primary teacher, Shinzen Young, who disambiguated so much of this path for me. Shinzen's students ("Shinheads") will recognize his influence in these pages—his is another good voice in my head. And thanks to the many other teachers, healers, scientists, thinkers, and meditator friends whom I've had the privilege of practicing next to and/or corresponding with and/or reading and/or consciousness-expanding alongside over the years.

My teacher friends at the Consciousness Explorers Club get their own paragraph, especially the excellently confusing James Maskalyk (Google James Maskalyk + girlfriend), whose unwavering friendship I am eternally grateful for, and the tender Erin Oke, who fits six lifetimes' worth of feeling into each of her meditation sits and still manages to hold it down for every shy newcomer hiding in the back of the room.

All magic: Caitlin Colson, Jude Star, Stephanie De Bou, Alexandra Shimo, Laurie Arron, Katrina Miller, Andrea Cohen-B. "Being human takes practice"—we do it every week, live and in community. Special mentions to Avi Craimer—who read over all my meditation instructions and made helpful comments—and Kevin Lacroix, the actual illustrator of the fabulous graphs in Chapter 9. Thank you both.

Thanks to Susan and Ted Warren, my loving and supportive parents, who don't meditate, don't plan to, and—truth be told—probably don't need to (well, maybe a little). Ditto for my neuroscientist brother, Chris, who makes me smarter every time I talk to him, and my equally brainy sister, Jane, who actually does meditate these days—she texts me every morning with her latest report ("that one sucked, thanks for introducing me to this ridiculous habit, I love you, byyeeee").

And finally, thanks to my wife, Sarah Barmak, about whom I could wax on for ten more pages and test the patience of even the most generous Acknowledgments readers. Suffice to say she gives my life meaning and coherence. Falling in love with her put meat on the bones of all these Hallmark-sounding contemplative ideas. The deeper our commitment, the truer our love becomes. "Wanderer, there is no road, the road is made by walking." Because of her I'm a better thinker and person, and for that, I . . . will write ten more pages of embarrassing poetry in private, which she will then read and patiently correct for grammar.

CARLYE'S ACKNOWLEDGMENTS

I am grateful to the many people already mentioned above who made this book possible and who also made it better. A sincere thank-you to everyone we met along the way for your warm welcome and for allowing us to share your stories.

I am forever thankful to Dan Harris for inviting me to collaborate with him. You really get to know someone when you live together in a small space on wheels and write a book under an impossible deadline. Dan's as intelligent and witty as you see on TV, and his hair is perfect even when there are no cameras around. More important, there is no one with more integrity, who works harder, or who is more generous, more understanding, more thoughtful, or fiercely funnier.

This book would never be *this* book without the unmatched genius, creativity, and million ideas a minute of Jeff Warren. He's not only the MacGyver of meditation but the MacGyver of book making, figuring out new ways to create something wild and wonderful out of prose and pages that no one has done before. Thank you for teaching me to meditate and for motivating me to seek a more meditative life.

I'm thankful to many mentors whose support and wisdom led me here: Carin Smilk, for giving me my first opportunity in a newsroom; Lynn Langway, for helping me get my first big article way back when, and ultimately an incredible job; Hank Gilman, for taking a bet on me early and always; Jeff Garigliano, for truly teaching me how to write; Marc Benioff, for knowing I could write a book before I knew I could; Maynard Webb, for showing me the value of soul food and sharing it with me; Ray Javdan and Nina Graybill, for your wise counsel and for helping me grow my business.

I'm lucky to have an incredible home team: my parents, Alan and Karen Adler, with my mom being my number one fan (she's probably writing an Amazon review right now); Matthew, Emily, Oliver, Jack, and Charlotte Adler, for their love always.

Finally, to my husband, best friend, and love of my life, the very smart and very fun Frank Nussbaum. Thank you for holding down the fort, not questioning (too hard) why I would leave my family to go on a bus across the country with ten guys, and for supporting every crazy thing I want to do—always. And to my greatest project, my daughter, Mia Fieldman, who's always up for adventure, forever inspiring, and always enlightening. I love you more than I could ever put into words.

ABOUT THE AUTHORS

DAN HARRIS is an Emmy Award–winning journalist and the co-anchor of ABC's *Nightline* and the weekend editions of *Good Morning America.* He is the author of *10% Happier,* a *#1 New York Times* bestseller. He went on to launch the 10% Happier podcast and an app called 10% Happier: Meditation for Fidgety Skeptics. He lives in New York City with his wife, Bianca, their son, Alexander, and three ASPCA cats.

JEFF WARREN is a writer, a meditation instructor, and the founder of the Consciousness Explorers Club, a meditation adventure group in Toronto. He is a former radio producer for the Canadian Broadcasting Corporation and author of *The Head Trip,* an acclaimed travel guide to sleeping, dreaming, and waking.

CARLYE ADLER is an award-winning journalist and co-author of many books, including three *New York Times* bestsellers. Her writing has been published in *Business Week, Fast Company, Fortune, Forbes, Newsweek, Time,* and *Wired.* She lives in Connecticut with her husband, daughter, and skateboarding bulldog.

Facebook.com/DanHarrisABC
Twitter: @danbharris
Instagram: @danharris

ABOUT THE TYPE

This book was set in Hoefler Text, a typeface designed in 1991 by Jonathan Hoefler (b. 1970). One of the earlier typefaces created at the beginning of the digital age specifically for use on computers, it was among the first to offer features previously found only in the finest typography, such as dedicated old-style figures and small caps. Thus it offers modern style based on the classic tradition.

You may also enjoy reading *10% Happier*
by Dan Harris:

Paperback ISBN 9781444799057
Ebook ISBN 9781444799064
Audio ISBN 9781473685314

yellow
kite

books to help you live a good life

Join the conversation and tell
us how you live a #goodlife

🐦 @yellowkitebooks
📘 YellowKiteBooks
📌 Yellow Kite Books
📷 YellowKiteBooks